Dear General
Eisenhower's Wartime Letters to Marshall

Dear General

Eisenhower's Wartime Letters to Marshall

JOSEPH PATRICK HOBBS

THE JOHNS HOPKINS PRESS

Baltimore and London

345653

The Johns Hopkins Press, Baltimore, Maryland 21218
The Johns Hopkins Press Ltd., London

Library of Congress Catalog Card Number 72-123573

International Standard Book Number 0-8018-1205-4

Table of Contents

Preface

In MAY, 1966, Professor Alfred D. Chandler, Jr. asked me to join the staff of the Eisenhower Project, which was then collecting the correspondence of Dwight David Eisenhower for the period of World War II. As editor, Professor Chandler would have to select the most meaningful from among the many thousands of documents which involved General Eisenhower during World War II. He would then have to annotate these records to furnish the context and clarification the documents themselves could not provide. He wanted me to help in this task. *Dear General* represents an attempt to use my training in selection and annotation of documents to show that an analysis and evaluation of Eisenhower's wartime career can be made by focusing on a single set of what I consider to be the most significant documents of the period—the letters that Eisenhower sent to George C. Marshall. All the letters appear in *The Papers of Dwight David Eisenhower: The War Years*, edited by Alfred D. Chandler, Jr., *et al.* The occasional deletions in the letters as they appear both here and in the *Eisenhower Papers* were nearly all unfavorable evaluations of subordinate officers.

I have placed the documents into four groups, after the appropriate section of my analysis, and have limited footnotes to the function of identifying persons and terms. Only 75 of the 108 documents, those that seemed the most representative, were retained. In nearly all cases, this meant eliminating the shorter ones. Occasionally, in my analysis, I cite letters not reprinted here (see Appendix for list); these too appear in *The Papers of Dwight David Eisenhower: The War Years*. I have also usually not included every comment from the letters in my analysis, attempting to be representative here as well.

It would, of course, be ludicrously inadequate for me to attempt to credit properly Professor Chandler for his role, so I will only thank him for trying to show me the way to accomplish what he considers the most important aspect of all these endeavors—asking the right questions. I find it equally impossible to express adequately my gratitude to the associate editor of the project, Professor Stephen E. Ambrose. My respect for his work on Eisenhower is as deep as my gratitude for his advice and friendship. I must also thank Doctor Forrest C. Pogue, not only for his magnificent work on Marshall, but for giving me valuable personal counsel as well. Further, I wish to thank Miss Joyce Daidakis, who was forced to type from illegible copy, for her invaluable assistance in checking on myriad items. Mrs. Carol Zimmerman as copy editor then made the manuscript twice as readable. Finally, but not the least, I wish to thank my wife Faye, who had the most difficult task of all—putting up with me.

Dear General
Eisenhower's Wartime Letters to Marshall

CHAPTER 1

Training for Command

On June 26, 1942, two days after he had arrived in England, General Dwight David Eisenhower, commanding general of the European Theater of Operations, U.S. Army, sent a personal letter to General George Catlett Marshall, Chief of Staff of the U.S. Army. By the end of the war in Europe Eisenhower had sent 108 such letters to Marshall. Because Eisenhower himself wrote these letters and intended them for Marshall alone, this unique correspondence traces not only the growth of the relationship between the two men but also Eisenhower's response to the problems he faced as the commander of the largest and most complex military organization in history. A clear theme emerges—the education and growth of Eisenhower as Commander in Chief. In addition, by describing Eisenhower's response to various challenges, these letters provide an inside view of the problems of high command in modern war.

Eisenhower and Marshall were opposites in personality—Marshall was cool and aloof, Eisenhower open and gregarious. They were ten years apart in age and from dissimilar backgrounds.[1] Eisenhower had spoken only briefly to Marshall on three occasions before Marshall selected him for a key position in the War Plans Division. After Eisenhower left for England six months later, they, of course, saw each other infrequently. Marshall was Eisenhower's teacher and chief supporter, yet he kept the relationship professional. Marshall maintained an iron grip on his emotions toward everyone. He wrote only a few personal letters to Eisenhower and

---

[1] Forrest C. Pogue, *George C. Marshall*, 2 vols. (New York, 1963–66), vol. I, *Education of a General, 1880–1939*, is the definitive and highly readable biography of Marshall's early career. Kenneth S. Davis, *Soldier of Democracy* (New York, 1945), has an excellent account of Eisenhower's early life.

called him "Eisenhower" not "Ike."[2] To Eisenhower, Marshall was "General Marshall."

Yet the similarities are important. The pre-World War II careers of the two men show that each spent the greater part of his career in staff as opposed to command assignments. They came into contact with individuals whose judgment concerning people and military tactics they respected. Later they claimed common heroes. Marshall's wife, writing immediately after the war, said that the general most admired Benjamin Franklin—for his common sense and ability to get people to work together—and Robert E. Lee, for his military talent and character.[3] Twenty years later Eisenhower listed these two figures along with Washington and Lincoln as the historical figures he most admired.[4]

It was this bond of professional training, experience, and performance which attracted Marshall's eye to Eisenhower. Marshall selected him to come to the War Plans Division in December, 1941, sent him to London in June, 1942, chose him to command various Mediterranean operations of 1942 and 1943, and saw him chosen by the President to command the cross-Channel invasion of June 6, 1944, which was to lead to German surrender on May 7, 1945.

In these assignments, Eisenhower's life became intertwined with that of Marshall. Eisenhower decided to send these letters to keep him informed of his progress in the command of a coalition army, in part because he was so close to Marshall. He wrote primarily about building an organization, planning and carrying out strategy and tactics (and the allocating of resources involved), and somewhat less on personal cares, diplomatic matters, and visits to troops.

An effective leader of any large organization must set his priority of concerns. In his letters Eisenhower discussed the problems involved in creating a command organization. Marshall and Eisenhower fully realized that the head of a huge army simply does not have the mental or physical capability for handling the details involved in the planning and execution of operations. Above all else he must establish clear lines of authority in order to receive the information needed to make major decisions and in order to have the means to carry out those decisions.

Eisenhower knew that he had to be the Supreme Commander with no equals, especially since the vast scale of modern warfare makes it imperative that subordinate commanders in a military theater of operations enjoy

---

[2] Marshall slipped once and called Eisenhower "Ike" but to make up for it, he used "Eisenhower" five times in the next two sentences. Pogue, *Marshall*, Vol. II, *Ordeal and Hope, 1939–1942*, p. 476.

[3] Katherine Tupper Marshall, *Together: Annals of an Army Wife* (New York, 1946), p. 135.

[4] Richard L. Tobin, "Dwight D. Eisenhower: What I Have Learned," *Saturday Review*, September 10, 1966, p. 31.

a great degree of latitude. There is not enough time to obtain the agreement of a committee composed of the heads of three different services from two different countries, each with its own practices and ideas. So above all, Eisenhower believed, the Supreme Commander must insist upon unity of command.

Setting up an efficient organization is of no value unless proper personnel are selected to staff it. The commander's most important continuing responsibility is to recognize and act on achievement and failure in his subordinates. If a senior commander or executive builds a smooth-running organization he will have the time, data, and power to make and execute the most crucial decisions. Eisenhower wanted to be certain that he could concentrate on grand strategy—the broad decisions as to where operations would be undertaken—and tactical planning—setting of basic objectives and allotment of necessary resources. Rather than draw up detailed tactical plans, he preferred to choose between alternate ones prepared by subordinates. In active operations he would make the necessary shifts of men and material as the combat situation warranted.

Eisenhower had been made aware of these matters most forcefully by Marshall himself. As he carried out his job, his greatest support came from Marshall. Marshall sent him Omar Nelson Bradley and Walter Bedell Smith, who quickly became his most valued subordinates. He sent him as many men and as much material as he could. He told the War Department not to bother Eisenhower, and defended him to the President, to England's Prime Minister, and to other key figures. The nature of the dispute might change—command, tactics, troublesome commanders, diplomatic entanglements—but Marshall's support never wavered. Marshall did not write many letters, but did visit Eisenhower several times. Throughout, he told him not to worry or to let any of the opinions he offered unduly influence Eisenhower's own judgment.[5]

Because of this support and his own experience, Eisenhower displayed a growing confidence as he learned his trade. His personal comments to Marshall shifted from a tendency toward fulsomeness to a more balanced relationship. The letters do not, of course, simply speak for themselves. The introductions to the letters, therefore, are an attempt to explain and analyze these raw materials of history and thus to provide an insight into the challenges and education of General Eisenhower as Commander in Chief of a large modern army.

Before discussing the period covered by Eisenhower's letters—June, 1942, through May, 1945—it is useful to give a brief prewar biographical sketch of the two men, followed by an account of their relationship from Decem-

[5] Forrest C. Pogue, *The Supreme Command*, U.S. Army in World War II, ed. Kent Roberts Greenfield (Washington, 1954), p. 35.

ber, 1941, to June, 1942, the period when Eisenhower worked directly with Marshall in Washington.

The younger man, Eisenhower, was born in Denison, Texas on October 14, 1890. In 1892, when Dwight was two years old, the family moved back to Abilene, Kansas. After graduating from high school in 1909 with no definite career plans or money for college, he worked in a creamery and at other odd jobs. A friend told him of the opportunities for a college education at the service academies. He finished first in the Annapolis and second in the West Point competitive examinations. Too old for Annapolis, he entered West Point on July 1, 1911, because the top applicant was unable to accept the appointment. At the Academy he won letters in baseball and football before a knee injury cut short his athletic career. When he graduated in 1915, sixty-first in a class of 164, his record included a healthy collection of demerits.

The new second lieutenant did not go overseas in World War I but was given routine infantry assignments in the United States. Nonetheless, he performed well enough to earn a Distinguished Service Medal and gained entrance to the Infantry Tank School at Fort Meade. The school was part of the new program of advanced training which General John J. Pershing had implemented after World War I. Next came duty under Major General Fox Conner in the Canal Zone and a short tour in Colorado. It was through the efforts of Conner, by then Deputy Chief of Staff, that Eisenhower was sent to the Command and General Staff School at Fort Leavenworth. He graduated first in a class of 275 in 1926, and after a short field assignment, served for a time with the American Battle Monuments Commission under General Pershing. Following graduation from the Army War College in 1928, he was assigned to another tour with Pershing. It was then that he first met Marshall (in 1930). Eisenhower served as executive assistant to the Assistant Secretary of War, graduated from the Army Industrial College, became a staff assistant to Chief of Staff General Douglas MacArthur, and went to the Philippines for four years as MacArthur's military assistant. After the outbreak of war in Europe he returned to the United States for duty with the 15th Infantry Regiment, with the 3d Division as Chief of Staff, with the IX Corps, and then with Lieutenant General Walter Krueger's Third Army. In the fall of 1941, Colonel Eisenhower's skill as Krueger's right arm during the Louisiana maneuvers impressed, among others, George Marshall.

Marshall was born at Uniontown, Pennsylvania, on December 31, 1880, the son of an operator of coal and coke enterprises in southwestern Pennsylvania. When he graduated from the Virginia Military Institute in 1901 as first captain of the Corps of Cadets, his first assignment was in the Philippines. In 1907 he was senior honor graduate of the Infantry-Cavalry School at Fort Leavenworth. After graduation from the Army

Staff College in 1908, he remained for two years as an instructor. From 1913 to 1916 he again served in the Philippines, spending the last year as aide-de-camp to General Hunter Liggett. Following completion of various duties in the United States, including the post of aide-de-camp to General James Bell, he was assigned to the General Staff in July, 1917, and sailed for Europe with the first convoy of the 1st Division. In July, 1918, he was detailed to General Headquarters and then First Army to draft the plans for the St. Mihiel operation. He became Chief of Operations of First Army in October, then Chief of Staff of the VIII Army Corps. In the spring of 1919, he returned to General Headquarters (where Fox Conner was operations officer) for work in connection with the proposed advance further into Germany. He had been promoted to lieutenant colonel in 1918, only a few months before Eisenhower received the same rank. After field promotion to colonel, he, along with Eisenhower, reverted to the permanent rank of captain in 1920; they were both then immediately promoted to major. Marshall's promotion to lieutenant colonel, however, came in three years, while Eisenhower had to wait six years. During much of that time, when Eisenhower was attending the advanced schools, Marshall was teaching at some of these schools and turning out men whom he could call upon later with confidence. Subsequent to a five-year tour as aide-de-camp to General Pershing, he served as a National Guard inspector. Then, in July, 1938, he became head of the War Plans Division; in October, Deputy Chief of Staff; and in July, 1939, Brigadier General Marshall assumed the duties of Chief of Staff, with the rank of general.

Marshall's official inauguration as Chief of Staff in September coincided with the outbreak of war in Europe. His first two years were spent in formulating war plans and in trying to expand and train the army. With the Japanese attack on Pearl Harbor on December 7, 1941, and the attack on the Philippines, Marshall faced a new crisis. War plans had to be completely revised, especially those for the Pacific. For this task he needed Brigadier General Eisenhower.

The reason for his selection, Eisenhower later reflected, was reasonably clear—he had just completed a long tour of the Philippines as MacArthur's chief assistant.[6] Colonel Harvey Bundy, who had been scheduled to become Major General Leonard Gerow's successor at Operations Division (OPD), died in early December, creating a vacancy. In addition, as Marshall's biographer Forrest Pogue notes, "As was his habit, General Marshall had been gathering information on his new commander for many years. Fox Conner thought well of him; he had worked with Pershing on the American Battle Monuments Commission."[7]

[6] Dwight D. Eisenhower, *Crusade in Europe* (New York, 1948), p. 14.
[7] Pogue, *Ordeal and Hope*, p. 337.

Eisenhower's association with Conner and especially that with Pershing was indeed critical in Marshall's decision. The Chief of Staff's affection for Pershing and respect for his judgment knew no bounds. Often in his comments about tactics or personalities, he would cite Pershing's opinion, and, whenever possible, while Chief of Staff, Marshall went to Walter Reed Hospital on Sundays to see Pershing.[8] Service under Conner was also important. Eisenhower himself has pointed out his own great affection for Conner and Conner's high regard of Marshall as a "genius," especially in the technique of arranging Allied commands.[9]

Thus, Marshall's selection of Eisenhower was based on the evaluation of Eisenhower by those whom Marshall respected, Marshall's own impressions gained during the Louisiana maneuvers, and Eisenhower's knowledge of the Philippines. Obviously, Marshall did not know much about Eisenhower's conception of and approach to problems. He would soon find out.

In his first talk with Eisenhower, Marshall outlined the critical situation in the Pacific and then abruptly asked, "What should be our general line of action?" Eisenhower responded, "Give me a few hours."[10] This was a big job and a big test. Eisenhower had little to guide him except his knowledge that official overall strategy called for the major offensive to take place in Europe and a holding action to be in the Pacific. Yet it was also already apparent that the Philippines could not be held.[11] Eisenhower felt that American morale as well as popular opinion in the Far East dictated against simply abandoning the garrison. Therefore, he outlined immediate practical steps to aid the Philippines, with Australia as the critical area: "Our base must be Australia, and we must start at once to expand it and to secure our communications to it. In this last we dare not fail."[12]

When Eisenhower finished his presentation Marshall replied, "I agree with you." Eisenhower realized that he had met the challenge.[13] Marshall later commented, "If he hadn't delivered he wouldn't have moved up."[14] In mid-February Eisenhower did move up to become head of the Operations Division when Gerow left to take a field command for which he had already been scheduled. During the next few months Eisenhower and

---

[8] Marshall, *Together*, p. 76.

[9] Eisenhower, *Crusade in Europe*, p. 18.

[10] *Ibid.*

[11] Louis Morton, *The Fall of the Philippines*, U.S. Army in World War II, ed. Kent Roberts Greenfield (Washington, 1953), is the definitive account of the Japanese success in the Philippines.

[12] Eisenhower, *Crusade in Europe*, pp. 21–22.

[13] *Ibid.*, p. 22.

[14] Pogue, *Ordeal and Hope*, p. 338.

Marshall worked closely together on critical immediate problems and long-range strategic plans.

Eisenhower had an opportunity to learn from Marshall. He already knew that Marshall's most persistent concern was the need for unity of command. This concept had arisen among the Americans during World War I, and Marshall and Fox Conner had both come to hold a passionate belief in it. They felt that the forces would have been used more effectively under a single commander. In its simplest terms, the idea was that one commander should be in command of all forces within a given theater of operations. Few military officers accepted this doctrine; for example, in 1941, the British used the committee system, with the commander of each branch serving as a member of a council of equals. The various American services were less than enthusiastic about being commanded by officers outside their own sphere. Each had its own practices and ideas as a result of different technologies employed, and each was jealous of its own prerogatives. But Marshall knew that the most effective way of conducting a major military operation was to give one man clear authority and responsibility. He pressed his case at the ARCADIA meetings with the British in December and had Eisenhower draw up the directive for the first Supreme Allied Commander, General Archibald Wavell.[15] The directive was necessarily most circumspect in granting powers to Wavell, but it was a beginning—the British had finally accepted it. From this moment on, attention to organizational problems occupied Eisenhower most. Although the intensity of his reaction and the precise nature of his concern necessarily varied with the particular situation, Eisenhower's first reaction to a change of situation throughout the war was to seek assurance of proper lines of authority, and in such critical moments he always had Marshall's support.

Eisenhower also became even more aware of Marshall's strategic commitment to an amphibious invasion of Germany from England. Because Marshall felt that Germany represented the greatest threat, he favored building up a reserve in Britain at the expense of sending forces to the Pacific. Only in this way would the squandering of American troops in operations around the world be prevented. Marshall also realized that the attack against Germany was the only operation Americans would place before an offensive against Japan. This plan clashed directly with the British strategy of "tightening the ring"—fatally weakening Germany through attack of her periphery, and then a final plunge through direct invasion. This difference of opinion would dominate Anglo-American

[15] Eisenhower to Marshall (hereafter cited as E. to M.), December 26, 1941, in *The Papers of Dwight David Eisenhower: The War Years* (hereafter cited as *EP*), edited by Alfred D. Chandler, Jr., *et al.*, 5 vols. (Baltimore, 1970), vol. I, pp. 28–31.

strategy talks for the next two years.[16] Eisenhower set his own recommendations in this context of the grand design of the war, especially since he was now not only the spokesman for the Pacific but the Chief of the Operations Division as well. He did this most clearly in the memo of February 28 in which he differentiated between operations "necessary to the ultimate defeat of the Axis Power" and those which "are merely *desirable*." The three priorities were to maintain the United Kingdom, keep Russia in the war, and prevent an Axis junction in the India–Middle East Theater. Eisenhower urged that the minimum should be diverted to *desirable* objectives and the maximum to *primary* operations. His recommendation presented a reasonable alternative to those who urged pulling back to Hawaii and those who advocated priority for the operations in the Pacific, but he did urge that the main effort be directed at Germany through a cross-Channel invasion.[17] Also in the February 28 memo, Eisenhower formulated the "Strategic Responsibility of the United Kingdom and the United States" proposal, stating that in those areas in which the two nations operated together the Combined Chiefs of Staff would be in charge; in the independent areas the Chiefs of Staff of the concerned government would exercise jurisdiction.[18]

Eisenhower was also involved in drafting early plans for the cross-Channel invasion itself. He knew that

> the basis [of the plan] was the conviction that through an overpowering air force, numbering its combat strength in thousands rather than in hundreds, the German defenses could be beaten down or neutralized, his communications so badly impaired as to make counterconcentration difficult, his air force swept from the skies, and that our ground armies would have an ever-present asset of incalculable power.[19]

In dealing with both these long-range problems and more immediate ones such as rushing supplies and troops to critical areas, Eisenhower did not show brilliant flashes of insight—that was not his job. Even when writing memos on strategic responsibilities he was essentially working within a framework laid down by Marshall. But his work of detailed implementation gave him a keen awareness of the limitations imposed by logistics. His deep involvement in the setting up of an Allied command prepared him for his own later practical application of it.

---

[16] Pogue, *Ordeal and Hope*, pp. 305, 315–16; Maurice Matloff and Edwin M. Snell, *Strategic Planning for Coalition Warfare, 1941–1942*, U.S. Army in World War II, ed. Kent Roberts Greenfield (Washington, 1953), p. 177; Louis Morton, *Strategy and Command: The First Two Years*, U.S. Army in World War II, ed. Stetson Conn (Washington, 1962), pp. 308–11, 376–86.

[17] E. to M., February 28, 1942, *EP*, pp. 149–55.

[18] E. to U.S. Chiefs of Staff, March 8, 1942, *EP*, pp. 174–76.

[19] Eisenhower, *Crusade in Europe*, p. 47.

Eisenhower was learning other things as well. He often heard Marshall remark that "he could get a thousand men to do detailed work but too many were useless in responsible posts because they left to him the necessity of making every decision."[20] Marshall ". . . insisted that his principal assistants should think and act on their own conclusions in their own spheres of responsibility, a doctrine emphasized in our Army schools but too little practiced in peacetime."[21] By the same token, Marshall had nothing but scorn for the man who attempted to do everything himself. He disliked the truculent personality, the man who too avidly sought the limelight, and the pessimist. He warned that a commander had to beware of any action that might be construed as a sign of discouragement, and recalled that a tired gesture by General Pershing during World War I had been so interpreted.[22] Above all, Marshall insisted upon dedication and selflessness, a demand which led to the following incident. Lecturing Eisenhower on promotion, the Chief of Staff said: "Take your case. I know that you were recommended by one general for division command and by another for corps command. That's all very well. I'm glad they have that opinion of you, but you are going to stay right here and fill your position, and that's that!" To make the point more emphatic, he added, "While this may seem a sacrifice to you, that's the way it must be."[23] This calling down, which Eisenhower rightly considered both unnecessary and unjustified, triggered an appropriate response from Eisenhower, "General, I'm interested in what you say, but I want you to know that I don't give a damn about your promotion plans as far as I'm concerned. I came into this office from the field and I am trying to do my duty. I expect to do so as long as you want me here. If that locks me to a desk for the rest of the war, so be it."[24] Eisenhower then moved to hasten out of the office, but, as always when he lost control of his mercurial temper, he quickly regained composure. He turned back with a sheepish grin, only to see Marshall with a wisp of a smile on his own face. Eisenhower had apparently passed yet another test. All of these trials, all of these admonitions, were to serve Eisenhower well, for each of them drove home the message: build a good organization and select capable subordinates.

Eisenhower's most decisive and perhaps his final test occurred in early May and, not surprisingly, involved the question of the command structure in England. Deputy Chief of Staff General Joseph McNarney had submitted an organizational proposal entitled "U.S. Setup for Administrative Purposes." The U.S. organization was to be headed by the command-

[20] *Ibid.*, p. 35.

[21] *Ibid.*

[22] Marshall, *Together*, p. 110.

[23] Dwight D. Eisenhower, *At Ease: Stories I Tell to Friends* (New York, 1967), p. 249.

[24] Eisenhower, *At Ease*, p. 249. See also Pogue, *Ordeal and Hope*, p. 338.

ing general, with the heads of the U.S. ground forces, air forces, Service of Supply (SOS), and naval forces directly under him. The overall command of the buildup in the United Kingdom (BOLERO) was to be exercised by the task force commander, probably British (at this time the British would have to supply the bulk of forces), who would report to the Combined Chiefs of Staff.[25]

In his comments to Marshall on McNarney's proposal, Eisenhower agreed with the basic organization, although he feared that the use of the word "administrative" might dilute the authority of the overall leader. But Eisenhower, as always, recognized the limitations of reality. Considering the British wariness of a single commander, he conceded that this was all that could be achieved at the time.

Eisenhower did feel, however, that the U.S. should press the British by emphasizing the powers rather than the limitations of the American commander's authority. Thus he questioned the use of the word "administrative" in describing the U.S. organization. The American commander must be "a Theater Commander in every sense of the word."[26] To aid in this, he wanted the top American to be called "Commander."

Eisenhower then commented at length on the type of officer needed to fill this position. The first necessity was that he have Marshall's full confidence and be in complete agreement with basic ideas of the latter. He had to be able to command: all U.S. activity "must be cleared through him; otherwise his position will be intolerable." He had to be flexible, able to play any of several different roles, as well as be able to fit into the final organizational pattern, whatever it might be. This flexibility of roles was necessary because BOLERO might take any of several forms—Europe might even become a less important theater. If Europe did in fact become the major area of operations, however, the commanding general would probably serve as Marshall's deputy in the likely event that the President named Marshall to head the operation. Finally, the officer must be set to work at once.[27]

Eisenhower was obviously describing himself. Who better than Eisenhower had most recently shown himself as committed to Marshall's ideas on command organization and strategy; who better than Eisenhower had demonstrated absolute loyalty; who more than Eisenhower enjoyed the confidence of the Chief; who more skillfully than Eisenhower had changed his view from that of champion of the Pacific to a more global one; who more than the optimistic, likable Eisenhower could make a coalition command work?

But Marshall did not make his final decision immediately. Instead,

[25] E. to M., May 11, 1942, *EP*, pp. 292–94.
[26] *Ibid.*, p. 292.
[27] *Ibid.*, pp. 292–94.

he sent Eisenhower to England to look into the lack of coordination between the command in London and the War Department in Washington, and to get Eisenhower's reactions to being on the ground.[28] Eisenhower returned more convinced than ever that a new commander ought to be selected at once to mobilize the American buildup. He dispatched a memo to Marshall on June 3 recommending that Clark be sent over immediately as U.S. ground commander and that McNarney be named to the overall U.S. command.[29] On the 6th Eisenhower again advanced McNarney, stressing his patience. He concluded, "Patience is highly necessary because of the complications in British procedure," a complaint that he would echo in England.[30]

In a note of May 12, Eisenhower maintained that the theater should encompass all areas in the British Isles from which forces might emanate. It was necessary that "absolute unity of command should be exercised by the Theater Commander."[31] He restated his belief that the officer had to be able to organize and command the combined forces in the BOLERO plan, and also be able to be Chief of Staff to the ROUNDUP commander (presumably Marshall).

Eisenhower then brought Marshall a final directive for the commander of ETO on June 8. This stressed the principle of unity of command and charged the commanding general "with the strategical, tactical, territorial, and administrative duties of a theater commander." It required that "the forces of the United States are to be maintained as a separate and distinct component of the combined forces."[32] When Eisenhower asked Marshall to read the document carefully because it was likely to become quite important, Marshall responded, "I certainly do want to read it. You may be the man who excutes it. If that's the case, when can you leave?"[33]

In this way Marshall set Eisenhower on the path to the greatest military command of all time—although certainly neither could have suspected that Eisenhower would lead the Allied forces to total victory over Germany. Ability, circumstance, and even luck would all play a part. For the moment, Eisenhower was to fulfill the role that he himself had envisioned for the U.S. commander—organizing Marshall's army.

Directive in hand, he flew to London.

---

[28] Pogue, *Ordeal and Hope*, p. 339, says that the trip constituted another test by Marshall, who also wanted to get the reaction of the British to Eisenhower.
[29] E. to M., June 2, 1942, *EP*, pp. 327–28.
[30] E. to M., June 6, 1942, *EP*, p. 331–32.
[31] E. to M., May 12, 1942, *EP*, p. 295–96.
[32] E. to M., June 8, 1942, *EP*, pp. 334–35.
[33] Pogue, *Ordeal and Hope*, p. 339.

CHAPTER 2

Planning for Invasion, June–November, 1942

ISENHOWER ARRIVED IN LONDON with no previous experience in the command of large units, having served in staff positions through most of his career. Yet he had learned from masters, especially the head of the entire United States Army, Marshall. Could Eisenhower now put his lessons into practice? Initially, he was charged only with the implementation and organization of the European invasion which Marshall would probably lead. But he very quickly became commander of an invasion army in his own right when the Allies decided to prepare an assault on North Africa in 1942.

Eisenhower's eighteen letters to Marshall during this period show primarily a concern with organization and the allocation of resources. In writing of these and other matters, Eisenhower at times displayed an uncertainty quite natural in a man so rapidly elevated to command the first American offensive of the war. He also exhibited knowledge of a Supreme Commander's essential concerns and a willingness to learn the practical responsibilities of command.

COMMAND ORGANIZATION

Eisenhower's first letter to Marshall on June 26 revealed his awareness of the central problem of rule by coalition. He complained about the British reluctance to accept unity of command, as reflected by the failure of General Sir Bernard Paget, commander of the British Home Forces, to designate a single officer with headquarters responsible for the actual cross-Channel assault training. In his next letter, he noted, "The job of overall organization is a very complicated one. . . ." He furnished a clue to his way of solving the problem, however: "I am quite sure that the organization finally adopted will follow no particular book nor be molded exactly on any organization of the past, but we are going to make one that will work effectively." Eisenhower assured Marshall that the U.S. naval commander in England, Admiral Harold Stark, would cooperate fully.[1]

But he soon faced leadership problems other than those evolving from his role as commander of the American forces in England. As a result of the July decision to plan an invasion of North Africa (TORCH) for 1942, Eisenhower came to occupy three positions simultaneously: commanding general of the European Theater of Operations (ETO); Deputy Supreme Commander (it was assumed Marshall would be Supreme Commander) over the entire buildup in England (BOLERO) and the planned landing in France (ROUNDUP); and Supreme Commander of TORCH if that operation should actually be staged. If the North African assault did take place, then Marshall would appoint a new deputy commander of ROUNDUP. A temporary confusion in command arrangements was caused by Marshall's refusal to acknowledge the decision for TORCH as final.[2] Nevertheless, Eisenhower proceeded with plans for the several contingencies. He wrote Marshall on July 29 that one problem Marshall would face as ROUNDUP Supreme Commander was "the development of a proper staff to plan the over-all operation." He proposed that overall assault planning be delegated to Vice Admiral Louis Mountbatten and his Combined Operations, charged with the planning and execution of British amphibious missions. "Details will be planned and executed by Force Commanders, but the Supreme Commander's staff must draw up a comprehensive scheme for this critical part of the job." Eisenhower stressed the importance of naming the principal commanders at once and added, "Whoever is selected C.G. [commanding general] should come over here as soon as firm decisions and Supreme Commander are announced."

Firm decisions were not long in coming—Eisenhower was officially named TORCH commander on August 6 and shortly thereafter Major General Mark Clark was named deputy in charge of the planning.[3] Eisenhower also indicated in several letters his need to retain command of ETO during his stay in North Africa.[4] Ultimately there were to be three separate amphibious assaults on North Africa—at Casablanca, Oran, and Algiers— and Eisenhower had to insure that he had clear control over the disparate

---

[1] Eisenhower had written Arnold on June 26 about air force organization problems. E. to Arnold, June 26, 1942, *EP*, pp. 362–63.

[2] Pogue, *Ordeal and Hope*, p. 400, notes, "The Chief of Staff told members of his staff as late as August 19 that the operation in North Africa was still subject to the vicissitudes of war."

[3] Eisenhower, *Crusade in Europe*, p. 76.

[4] See Richard M. Leighton and Robert W. Coakley, *Global Logistics and Strategy, 1940–1943*, U.S. Army in World War II, ed. Kent Roberts Greenfield (Washington, 1955), pp. 480–87, for the impact of the TORCH decision on BOLERO.

forces involved. It was through Eisenhower's urging in a letter of August 9 that a separate U.S. air force for the TORCH operation was created.[5] Both this American Twelfth Air Force (led by Brigadier General James Doolittle) and the British air force for TORCH, the Eastern Air Command, reported directly to Eisenhower. Although he preferred and would later have a single air commander, the complexities of particular situations and the variety of tasks given the air force precluded his having clear-cut command at this time.

The assurance of clear command procedures was not easy. Eisenhower oversaw naval activities through Admiral Andrew Cunningham, but his directives to the American naval task force commander and the British naval task force commander left their exact relationships to each other undefined. As usual, Eisenhower determined to make the best of an imperfect situation and act as if these relationships were clearly defined—a device he was to use throughout the war. On October 3 he wrote, "So far as Cunningham and myself are concerned, we are prepared to accept anything that is workable and go to it."

Eisenhower had to confront more directly a problem involving the British ground commander, General Kenneth Anderson. The British directive to Anderson, which seemed to grant Eisenhower no more authority than Marshal Ferdinand Foch had in 1918, alarmed Eisenhower greatly. In the earlier war the Allied Commander in Chief was empowered to coordinate the action of the various armies but had no final control over the tactical conduct of the armies or their commanders.[6] The British modified the directive at Eisenhower's request, and on October 20 he ended an account of the episode to Marshall: "From the day I came over here, I have dinned into the British the fact that you consider unity of command to exist only when the Commander of an Allied Force had the authority— so far as it was legal to confer it upon him—with respect to all troops involved, as he had to those of his own nationality."

Eisenhower expressed his satisfaction over the command arrangements in a final letter to Marshall before the invasion: "We have established a pattern for Combined Staff operations that might well serve as a rough model when expeditions of this nature are undertaken in the future." He proceeded to enumerate the features contributing to the current status. The most important of these was "the fact that there was one responsible head." The other necessary feature in building a strong organization was

[5] Frank Wesley Craven and James Lea Cate, eds., *Europe: TORCH to POINTBLANK, August 1942–December 1943*, The Army Air Forces in World War II, vol. II (Chicago, 1949), pp. 50–60.

[6] Harry C. Butcher, *My Three Years With Eisenhower: The Personal Diary of Captain Harry C. Butcher, USNR* (New York, 1946), p. 137; George F. Howe, *Northwest Africa: Seizing the Initiative in the West*, U.S. Army in World War II, ed. Kent Roberts Greenfield (Washington, 1957), p. 36, reprints the final directive.

that "the officers detailed to the Staff and to command positions, were the ablest that could be found."

Awareness of the need to conserve the time of the Supreme Commander made Eisenhower realize that a commander had to delegate responsibility. He wrote Marshall on October 3 that for this reason he would have Clark act as his deputy in North Africa during the early weeks after the initial landings and before consolidation and reorganization occurred. On the 29th Eisenhower told Marshall that because he had to be available for the top-level discussions in England he had sent Clark in his place on the famous clandestine mission to the Vichy leaders in North Africa.[7]

The problems of proper use of staff and proper selection of subordinates occupied much of Eisenhower's time during this period. Eisenhower has written that "the teams and staffs through which the modern commander absorbs information and exercises his authority must be a beautifully interlocked, smooth-working mechanism."[8] He insisted that an air of optimism permeate his headquarters, that the staff be one happy family. He realized the value of promotion and decorations both as a morale factor and as a supportive one, having observed at first hand Marshall's careful attention to selection of subordinates.[9] He realized too that this was the leader of any large-scale organization's most important role. People, after all, determine whether the structure will work. A characteristic of Eisenhower's letters during this period—indeed, throughout the war—was the favorable mention of subordinates, usually American, by name, either by referring to their promotion status, or possible candidacy for decoration, or by noting that they were doing a good job. It is impossible to list all such references; only some representative ones are included. Of course he could and did show anger in the unfavorable mention of individuals, but since his general method of dealing with poor performance was to send the man home, incidences of this are much less frequent.

In his first letter of June 26, dealing at length with personnel, he absolved the individual members of the staff and commanders for the confusion and delays that had characterized the American buildup. Part of the problem had been "some conflict in instructions received here prior to the issue of your recent general directive. That document is now the Bible—it governs in everything." As his first request in organizing the staff, Eisenhower asked for Brigadier General Walter Bedell Smith as his Chief of Staff. Eisenhower felt he needed Smith for two reasons. Smith was a genius at running a headquarters—having served as Secre-

[7] Robert Murphy, *Diplomat Among Warriors* (New York, 1964), pp. 109–23; Mark W. Clark, *Calculated Risk* (New York, 1950), pp. 67–89.

[8] Eisenhower, *Crusade in Europe*, p. 79.

[9] *Ibid.*, pp. 34–35.

tary of the War Department General Staff and then as Secretary to the Combined Chiefs of Staff, he was brilliant at detail as well as larger issues. Moreover Smith combined toughness with absolute loyalty to his superior.[10] Marshall finally allowed Smith to join Eisenhower in September, and on October 3 Eisenhower wrote that the British respect for Smith was important in Eisenhower's creating a truly Allied staff with officers of each nation in key positions.

After his appointment as TORCH commander, Eisenhower immediately sent Marshall his recommendations for American heads of assault forces for TORCH and BOLERO, but left the choice to him. At the same time he urged filling all the senior command posts as quickly as possible. In letters of September 19 and October 3, Eisenhower discussed the selection of TORCH task force commanders, settling on Major General Lloyd Fredendall, Major General Charles Ryder, and Major General George Patton, Jr. Eisenhower did not know Fredendall, but Marshall did and Eisenhower accepted his judgment.

On the day before the North African invasion Eisenhower found time to write about promotions and remarked on "the calm atmosphere that has been maintained throughout the Allied Staff and among all Senior Commanders." Apparently he felt that he had succeeded in the task of properly staffing a command organization.

STRATEGY AND TACTICS

In addition to these problems of command organization, Eisenhower was deeply involved in the formulation of overall strategy and, to a much greater extent, in the implementation of agreed-upon strategy. His planning role during this period was essentially the same as it had been when he was in OPD. Moreover, because he was in constant contact with the British, he often served as conciliator. As a result, Eisenhower at times compromised on his personal views. He thought SLEDGEHAMMER (the plan for an emergency 1942 cross-Channel invasion) was hazardous but prepared defenses of it for Marshall anyway.[11] Likewise, he differed with Marshall over TORCH strategy but backed down. In his memoirs he made clear that he regretted this hedging.[12]

Even though the decision to invade Europe was far from a certainty, on his arrival in London Eisenhower immediately gave his attention to planning for it. He complained to Marshall in a letter of June 26 about

[10] Pogue, *Ordeal and Hope*, pp. 408–9.
[11] Memorandum, July 17, 1942, *EP*, pp. 388–92; E. to Butcher, July 22, 1942, *EP*, pp. 405–6; Eisenhower, *Crusade in Europe*, p. 70.
[12] Eisenhower, *Crusade in Europe*, p. 80.

the apparent British lack of commitment to the operation. In mid-July the President sent Marshall, Admiral Ernest King, and Harry Hopkins to London to thrash out plans for grand strategy.[13] The conference—due to British resistance to a 1942 invasion of Europe and Roosevelt's insistence on an offensive somewhere in 1942—decided to plan for an invasion of North Africa. Suddenly Eisenhower had weeks, not months, to mount an invasion. He had to confront a host of problems, the most immediate of which was to decide on the precise areas to attack.[14]

Eisenhower was both planner and intermediary in the debate that followed over the location of the landings. The British preferred the bold plan of landing as far to the east on the Mediterranean coast as possible. Besides avoiding the rough surf at Casablanca, this would insure the capture of Tunis from the French, a vital step in driving Rommel out of North Africa. With Tunis in German hands the enemy could pour in troops from Sicily and Italy. Eisenhower personally favored a landing as far east as possible for these reasons.[15]

The American planners in Washington were more cautious. Anxious to avoid defeat in the first U.S. action, they preferred to seize Casablanca, some 1,500 miles to the west of Tunis and situated on the Atlantic coast of Morocco. Then, after securing all approaches to Gibraltar to forestall a possible threat from the Spanish, they would move eastward into Algeria. Casablanca, the terminus of a single-track railroad line which wound through Oran and Algiers into Tunisia, would insure adequate supply lines.[16] The Americans feared that transporting four divisions through the Straits of Gilbraltar would eliminate the element of surprise and permit the Germans to bottle up the Allied forces inside the Mediterranean.[17] The primary American goal was simply to get the troops into action—this is why Roosevelt had agreed to TORCH in the first place. The U.S. Chiefs of Staff did not view the operation as other than that and did not want to become heavily involved in the Mediterranean.

Eisenhower was shaken by this first and "only instance in the war when any part of one of our proposed operational plans was changed by intervention of higher authority."[18] When Marshall reacted strongly and negatively to Eisenhower's original plan for the landings, one employing landings inside the Mediterranean, Eisenhower assured his Chief that the

---

[13] Pogue, *Ordeal and Hope*, pp. 343–49; Matloff and Snell, *Strategic Planning*, pp. 272–84; Robert E. Sherwood, *Roosevelt and Hopkins: An Intimate History* (New York, 1948), pp. 600–612, describes the trip and the issues.
[14] Eisenhower, *Crusade in Europe*, pp. 77–80; and Howe, *Northwest Africa*, pp. 25–31, cover the debate.
[15] Eisenhower, *Crusade in Europe*, p. 79.
[16] *Ibid.*
[17] Matloff and Snell, *Strategic Planning*, pp. 288–90.
[18] Eisenhower, *Crusade in Europe*, p. 80.

plan was only "tentative and temporary" and represented the views of the British planners.[19] Eisenhower then modified his plan for TORCH considerably and in a way typical of him by calling for landings inside *and* outside the Mediterranean. This plan—involving inside landings at Oran, Algiers, and Bône and outside landings at Casablanca—became known as the August 9 plan.[20] Eisenhower wrote a long letter defending the plan, pointing out that it represented the optimum compromise between scarce resources and desired goals and discussing each of the landings, including the logistic requirements of each.

The British argued that there were insufficient naval forces for all of these attacks, and Eisenhower told the War Department, "Assuming accuracy of naval statement this situation clearly calls for deferment of the Casablanca attack."[21] Informed of this, Marshall countered that without the Casablanca landings as protection from a Spanish attack, the chance for success seemed less than 50 percent. He pressed Eisenhower for his estimate of the probability of success[22] and Eisenhower replied that it was less than 50 percent.[23] Eisenhower's agreement on the risk factor hardened Marshall's resolve upon the landing at Casablanca.[24] But Eisenhower stopped short of recommending that TORCH be dropped— writing on August 17 that when he assumed command he had immediately told his subordinates "that the time for analyzing the wisdom of the original decision had passed."

After many more twists and turns, Roosevelt and Churchill agreed that assaults would be made at Casablanca, as desired by the Americans; at Algiers, as desired by the British; and at Oran, as desired by both.[25] The solution came about in part because Roosevelt had finally persuaded Admiral King that the American Navy did have sufficient shipping and escort vessels for all three landings.[26] But the decision had been made at the highest level—the theater commander was not yet the guardian of such trust and confidence. On September 19 Eisenhower wrote Marshall that he was sending Clark to Washington with "every detail of the plans," another indication of Eisenhower's lack of latitude and assurance.

With the dust from the TORCH dispute barely settled, Eisenhower dis-

---

[19] E. to M., August 1, 1942, *EP*, pp. 433–36.

[20] Matloff and Snell, *Strategic Planning*, pp. 290–93.

[21] E. to Handy, August 13, 1942, *EP*, p. 461.

[22] *Ibid.*, n. 7.

[23] E. to M., August 15, 1942, *EP*, pp. 469–71.

[24] Pogue, *Ordeal and Hope*, p. 403.

[25] Matloff and Snell, *Strategic Planning*, pp. 290–93; Winston S. Churchill, *The Second World War*, 6 vols. (Boston, 1948–53), vol. IV, *The Hinge of Fate*, pp. 538ff.; E. to M., August 9, 1942, *EP*, p. 455, n. 1; E. to M., September 3, 1942, *EP*, pp. 529–31; E. to Handy, September 5, 1942, *EP*, p. 541, n. 1.

[26] E. to Handy, September 5, 1942, *EP*, p. 541, n. 1; E. to M., September 3, 1942, *EP*, p. 530, n. 1.

cussed the implications for overall strategy raised by the decision to invade North Africa. On September 21 he reported to Marshall with astonishment and exasperation that Churchill had finally come to realize that, by mounting TORCH, a 1943 cross-Channel invasion of Germany was made impossible—a point he and Marshall had emphatically stressed in the July meetings.[27] Eisenhower again recommended to Marshall "in the interests of economy, the concentration of U.S. troops in the south of England rather than scattering them throughout the U.K."[28]

On October 7 Eisenhower once more raised the question of long-term grand strategy, pointing out, "I still believe that some day the ROUNDUP idea *must* be revived: We should plan and prepare deliberately." And in the midst of a detailed explanation of the immediate TORCH operations on October 12 Eisenhower reiterated, "As I have said several times, I thoroughly believe that the War Department should make superhuman efforts to build up U.S. strength in the United Kingdom after the TORCH requirements have been satisfied." His last letter from London, on October 29, dealt primarily with imminent TORCH plans and likely developments. Yet the Supreme Commander advised against exploiting TORCH success and pointed out that the argument for ROUNDUP would still prevail as long as Russia stayed in the field as a fighting power. "Consequently, the spring of '43 may see the ROUNDUP idea revived with the purpose of launching a decisive blow in the spring of '44."

Eisenhower's continuing attention to planning for the cross-Channel invasion shows a concern with placing the North African invasion into the broader scheme of grand strategy. But it also illustrates an uncertainty as to his own position and an almost abject loyalty to Marshall. He was facing a large-scale operation but, in effect, repeated that he would not forget that it was secondary to cross-Channel assault.

DIPLOMACY

Attention to command, strategy, and tactics dominated Eisenhower's letters, but he also kept Marshall informed on diplomatic developments. The diplomatic situation in TORCH was exceedingly complicated. The Allies were invading neutral countries governed by Vichy French collabora-

[27] Leighton and Coakley, *Global Logistics*, pp. 480–87; Matloff and Snell, *Strategic Planning*, pp. 307–27 and Howe, *Northwest Africa*, pp. 13–14, discuss the impact of the TORCH decision on overall strategic planning.

[28] The U.S. forces in 1944 attacked Europe on the right of the British forces. Churchill used as support for his advocacy of British occupation of the northwestern zone the fact that British troops were to the north of the Americans in Germany. Herbert Feis, *Churchill–Roosevelt–Stalin: The War They Waged and the Peace They Sought* (Princeton, 1957), pp. 338–43, 358–73; and Pogue, *Supreme Command,* pp. 347–58, discuss the division of Germany.

tors, but hoped they could convince certain key figures to defect to the Allied side. The alternative of working with Charles de Gaulle, leader of the Free French, was ruled out both because of Roosevelt's antipathy toward De Gaulle and because De Gaulle regarded the Vichy leaders in power as traitors. Obviously, the French military leaders in North Africa would not rally to him. The Allies therefore tried to arrange an accommodation with one or more Frenchmen whom the others might follow. This frustrating task involved them with several ranking figures, but the two principal hopes were General Henri Giraud and Admiral Jean Darlan, commander of the Vichy Armed Forces. Robert Murphy, the U.S. Ambassador to Vichy, was a key figure in the conception and execution of this policy, and in September he arrived in London to explain the plan to Eisenhower.[29] Eisenhower referred to the problems of dealing with the French officials in several letters of this time.

Eisenhower considered the problem of command posed by dealing with the French a difficult one. On October 29 he wrote, "Unquestionably, if Giraud comes over, he is going to argue that he should be given immediate Supreme Command of the whole effort." His premonitions were correct. On November 7, on the eve of TORCH, he added to a letter to Marshall: "I've had a 4 hour struggle with Kingpin [Giraud]. He—so far—says 'Either I'm Allied C-in-C or I won't play!' He threatens to withdraw his blessing and wash his hands of the affair." It had become clear that there was no simple means of reaching a settlement with the French.

VISITING TROOPS

Eisenhower's letters mention visits to the troops much less frequently than they do other matters. No doubt, this was because there were only a few stock phrases a commander could use concerning morale, discipline, and efficiency. Moreover, there were very few troops in the British Isles. Finally, Eisenhower's deep involvement in planning limited, for a time, the frequency of his trips.

In his first letter of June 26 he told Marshall of his intention to visit the U.S. flyers in the Eighth Air Force who would participate in "a secret operation"—the first air attack by Americans against the Germans, scheduled for July 4. He also intended to visit the troops in Ireland. Four days later he said that he was to see a special landing exercise in Scotland.

Eisenhower made no further references to visiting troops until October 7 when the debate on grand strategy and TORCH landings had been com-

---

[29] For accounts of the diplomatic maneuvering involved in TORCH, see Murphy, *Diplomat Among Warriors*, pp. 124–61; Howe, *Northwest Africa*, pp. 77–83, 249–73; and Eisenhower, *Crusade in Europe*, pp. 86–88, 99–114.

pleted. He then complained about the appearance and lack of discipline of many of them. His final comment came on the 20th when he wrote to Marshall the impressions gained from an amphibious exercise of the 1st Division in Scotland. He discovered that "their greatest weakness was uncertainty. Most of them did not know exactly what was expected of them." Although he might deny it, Eisenhower could well have applied the same comment to himself.

PERSONAL COMMENTS

Eisenhower's uncertainty was understandable. He had been pushed ahead of hundreds of seniors to command; the Allies were in disagreement; Marshall still opposed the TORCH operation; the British balked at giving him clear-cut command; and he undoubtedly saw himself as loyally conducting a holding operation for Marshall.

This lack of confidence reveals itself throughout this period in many ways. In the areas of strategy and planning, Eisenhower had essentially been Marshall's staff man during the July meetings. After the TORCH decision, he went along with Marshall's belief that perhaps it wasn't really going to happen. In the debate over the landing areas he had taken great pains to assuage Marshall's doubts about his own position. He had even argued for SLEDGEHAMMER possibilities after being named TORCH commander; he never ceased thinking of ROUNDUP. He had deferred to Marshall over key personnel, offering him Clark and accepting Marshall's recommendations on key TORCH commanders.

There are other indications. One example is Eisenhower's discussion of the British. In several letters he complained about the British lack of urgency, although in an August 17 communication he did single out for praise General Humfrey Gale. On September 21 he wrote a lengthy and caustically critical letter about Churchill's late awareness of the implications, in terms of delaying the attack on Germany, involved in the mounting of TORCH. He had commented rather frequently about his previous meetings with Churchill, but had been brief and noncommittal. On the 23d he wrote favorably about his British officers in general and commended Admiral Cunningham, no doubt with sincerity, but noting, "I strongly suspect that you may have lent a helping hand toward getting him into this job."

Then on October 3 Eisenhower wrote, "Incidentally, upon receipt of your letter discussing the necessity of avoiding friction between ourselves and the British, and between the Army and Navy, I have frequently emphasized your points in strong emphatic language—every man in this theater should know, certainly all of the seniors know—that any violation along this line will be cause for instant relief." From this point until the invasion a month later Eisenhower wrote no criticism of the British and his agreeable references increased sharply. On the eve of the invasion, in listing the principal reasons for the successful experiment in combined staff operation, he noted that "the British government made absolutely certain that commanders and staff officers, detailed to the expedition, had no mental reservations about their degree of responsibility to the Supreme Commander."

This shift of emphasis in Eisenhower's comments on the British was due to several factors. The British were not enthusiastic about his early assignment, BOLERO, or about serving in a unified command under an American officer. However, after TORCH was decided upon, relations were bound to improve. Yet the real change in Eisenhower's comments did not come until Marshall, finally convinced that TORCH was to proceed, wrote stressing the need for cooperation.[30] All of this, of course, is not to suggest that Eisenhower was ever really "anti-British." It does suggest a certain tendency to tell Marshall what he wanted to hear, and to follow closely his senior's wishes.

In order to be sure of Marshall's views, Eisenhower carefully maintained liaison with Washington, and his letters dealt with this on several occasions. But his concern later became more positive, as on October 7 he wrote at length about training, discipline, efficacy of daylight bombing, logistic needs, and grand strategy and noted, "This letter deals with a few subjects that I feel you may desire to have studied by some of the War Department sections." Here was a preview of the sort of communication he would occasionally send later, explaining lessons learned in combat. And in the final month before the landings, as he concentrated on his own operations, he referred back less frequently to the War Department.

Eisenhower also frequently made direct personal references to Marshall himself—professing loyalty, confidence, and gratitude, pledging his effort, and expressing guarded confidence. A few examples are illustrative. On June 26 he assured Marshall "I shall try to apply your dictum—'Persuade by accomplishment rather than by eloquence!'" In the midst of the debate over the TORCH landings he worried that Marshall might think him irresolute and went to extremes to prove otherwise. Eisenhower wrote on August 17, "It seems to me that the rougher the prospects, the more necessary it is that superior commanders allow no indication of doubt or criticism to discourage the efforts and dampen the morale of subordinates and of troop units." In assuring Marshall that although he thought the operation hazardous he would not hesitate to carry it out, he said that Clark and Patton wanted him to add to the gloomy forecast an affirmation of their

[30] E. to M., October 3, 1942, *EP*, p. 593, n. 5.

willingness to carry it out. "I declined to include this sentence on the grounds that you needed no reassurance of this particular kind; that unless you took these sentiments for granted you would not have named any of us to our present posts." And yet, later in the same letter he stated, "Whatever the other burdens and problems that rest upon you, I do hope you will be spared any concern as to the determination of the senior American officers involved in TORCH to carry out your instruction determinedly, enthusiastically and, to the best of their ability, efficiently." He pointed out, as he frequently did, that Marshall had realized implications—in this case, the effect of TORCH on shipping—that others had failed to understand. After the TORCH debate had been settled, he wrote, "I have the keenest appreciation of the tremendous burden placed upon you and General [Brehon Burke] Somervell [head of the Army Service Forces] in the task of solving this problem . . . I assure you that everyone here has given his whole energy to this enterprise."

In his last three letters before the landings, a new note of tension crept into Eisenhower's personal comments. On October 20, he confessed to Marshall, "I do not need to tell you that the past weeks have been a period of strain and anxiety. . . . To a certain extent, a man must merely believe in his luck and figure that a certain amount of good fortune will bless us when the critical day arrives." He continued in this vein at some length, but concluded, "Whenever I'm tempted to droop a bit over the burdens cast upon us here, I think of the infinitely greater ones you have to bear and express to myself a fervent wish that the Army may be fortunate enough to keep you at its head until the final victory is chalked up." On November 7 he wrote from Gibraltar, "Tonight we start ashore." He gave a briefing on the situation and cautioned against permitting failure through some unexpected factor to destroy all the lessons in Allied command that they had learned.[31]

Eisenhower had a right to be nervous, for he was now commanding an army in combat. Preliminary planning had been essential, but the most brilliantly devised plans were worthless without proper execution. Despite his commitment to delegation of authority, he felt agitated because he could not personally carry out each detail of the operation—at the moment, there was little he could do. But he had done as much as he could to assure success. He had played a key role in deciding the details of the TORCH allocation of resources; in later operations he would play a still larger one. He would have preferred more clearly defined lines of authority, but he felt that his organization was a viable one, for he had staffed it with superior people. He had helped to prevent the Americans and the

[31] Marshall's biographer notes that Eisenhower's statement "moved the man who made a virtual fetish out of interservice cooperation and unified allied command," Pogue, *Ordeal and Hope*, p. 418.

British from falling into a paralysis of disagreement. In doing so he had at times acted timidly, appeared to reverse himself, and displayed a perhaps excessive loyalty to Marshall. He had remained flexible, for he considered this the key to leadership.[32] Considering the nature of his position and the disagreement between the Allies, his apparent uncertainty was probably good for everyone involved. He was, after all, the commander of an operation that the U.S. military chiefs had only reluctantly approved.

Amidst all this discord, Eisenhower, by the force of his own personality and by attention to the proper concerns of command, accomplished the task with which Marshall charged him—the welding of an Allied army. The true test of his command was yet to come. As he told Marshall a few hours before the landings: "We are standing, of course, on the brink and must take the jump—whether the bottom contains a nice feather bed or a pile of brickbats!"

[32] Eisenhower, *Crusade in Europe*, pp. 74–75.

Dear General: This is the first of my informal reports to you, written exactly twenty-four hours after I landed here. It will be longer than those to follow, because I'd like to give you the high lights of the current picture.

One interesting thing I immediately encountered is the state of mind of Lord Louis Mountbatten.[1] He has been waging a rather serious even if friendly argument with General Paget[2] about a matter in which I think Lord Louis is quite correct, but in which we have no direct concern. It involves Paget's conception of training for the actual assault. Instead of designating a corps, with its commander and attached troops, to begin training and organizing *now* for this particular task, the British Army officials persist in viewing the cross-channel movement as merely another advance guard exercise. They therefore apparently propose to send in two or three corps abreast, expecting that the leading detachments of each corps will have received some special training before that time in landing from boats. This of course diffuses responsibility and is almost the exact antithesis of our idea, under which we have designated General Clark[3] as the assault corps commander to lead the American Army on its great venture. It seems to me that our method is so logical, simple and sound that I cannot perceive any reason for attempting to do the job otherwise. General Clark has already begun the job of planning for the receipt, special organization, training, and support of his command. In view of the British insistence that only through the immediate appointment of a single supreme commander can planning for this operation receive the necessary impetus, it is quite impossible to uncover the reasons why they do not see the same necessity in this particular case. I fear that some interservice jealousies or politics may be involved. At any rate, realizing that I am powerless to intervene, I hope to demonstrate such successful results from our own method that the British will adopt it speedily. For this reason I am more than ever determined to be as forward, in the matter of time, as is humanly possible.

I shall try to apply your dictum—"Persuade by accomplishment rather than by eloquence."

Thirty of our officers and men will take part soon in a secret operation. I deeply regret that my better judgment compels me to refrain from participating myself. I am going to see each of the thirty, individually, before D-day, and if it is humanly possible I am going to greet each one personally upon his return. I hope you will not be astonished if I deal out decorations rather generously on that occasion. I believe it will have a tremendous moral effect, particularly because the occasion will mark the first offensive action by Americans in this theater in this war. Immediately upon the conclusion of the operation I hope to send you a succinct narrative account.

Now that everyone here is at liberty to talk to me freely about our problems and what has been accomplished in the past, it becomes abundantly clear that some change was necessary. Delays and confusion that have existed cannot, however, be fairly attributed to any individual or to any lack of will to do the correct thing. It has been largely a matter of circumstances growing out of the mission with which this staff was originally charged (which was not fighting the war), to an excessive concern for minor regulations and rules, that have no application to the present problem, and to some conflict in instructions received here prior to the issue of your recent general directive. That document is now the Bible—it governs in everything. I am quite certain that this staff and all commanders now realize that we have a unique problem to solve, that we have full opportunity and freedom of action in solving them, and that no alibis or excuses will be acceptable to you.

I do not want to appear to be pushing you in the slightest degree in the matter of General Smith.[4] After my conference last Monday evening with the Prime Minister I asked General Smith to explain to you the reasons why I believed it highly desirable for him to come as soon as you could conveniently spare him. From here, that conclusion is a correct one, but I realize that your own weighty problems may dictate a considerable delay. I hope you will promote him; it will be most helpful in carrying on the planning with the British, which will give me greater freedom in visiting troops and field activities. In any event I have informed General Bolte[5] that the Ground Forces have requested him for division command and that he would be free to go back to the United States after he had had full opportunity to inform General Smith as to the many intricacies of this job. Incidentally I should like right here to put in a plug for General Bolte. There is no better type of officer. He will deliver for you in any task you assign him and in my opinion will keep on going *up* from there.

Within a short time I shall start carrying out the idea I expressed to you of sending back staff officers, periodically, in order to keep close familarity with War Department plans and purposes. Discussion with these officers, all of whom are of top-flight caliber, convinces me that this idea is not only a good one, but that it must be carried out if we are to be successful. Many individuals here are completely unaware, or at least only dimly aware, of the tremendous upsurge in activity, enthusiasm, and general progress that the United States has experienced in the past months.

I am calling on the British Chiefs of Staff immediately.[6] A member of the War Cabinet Secretariat has called on me to state that he will arrange for my duty call on the King, and I am getting all these chores out of the way as rapidly as possible. Early next week I go to visit the troops in Ireland and am taking along Spaatz, Clark and Lee,[7] so that I may have a conference with all Senior Commanders. All of them are working enthusiastically and all are agreed with me that this army must exemplify, in addition to professional efficiency, courtesy, smartness, law-abiding habits and morale, to a degree that has never been excelled in any service.

I find that great progress has been made in the matter of the mail service.

Everyone reports that it is now on a rather satisfactory basis but I am going to make a thorough inspection myself on this point, in which I have the greatest personal concern.

General Clark tells me that the promotion of his Chief of Staff, and his artillery officer has been approved by you in principle. There are two or three men on this staff whose promotions were temporarily held up by G–1,[8] pending my arrival here. I shall send the list in at once, with the request that the individuals be promoted as you can get a chance to work them in.

I have just returned from a call on the Ambassador,[9] to whom I gave your felicitations. He came in last night from Ireland where he was accompanying the King and Queen on an inspection of our troops. He reports that the King and Queen were tremendously impressed by what they saw, particularly with the appearance of men, messes, quarters, and so on.

With best wishes for your good health. *Very sincerely*

[1] Vice Admiral Lord Louis Francis Albert Victor Nicholas Mountbatten, as the British Chief of Combined Operations, had been engaged in a study of amphibious operations against the Continent.

[2] General Sir Bernard Charles Tolver Paget was commander of the British Home Forces.

[3] Major General Mark Clark (USMA 1917) had been named commander of II Corps. In August he became Eisenhower's deputy commander and took charge of planning for the North African invasion. In November he was promoted to lieutenant general and the next month assumed command of the United States Fifth Army, which would land at Salerno on September 9, 1943.

[4] Brigadier General Walter Bedell Smith was presently the United States Secretary to the Combined Chiefs of Staff. Smith came to London in September and remained Eisenhower's Chief of Staff throughout the war. He was promoted to major general on December 3, 1942.

[5] Brigadier General Charles L. Bolté was Chief of Staff of the U.S. forces in the British Isles. He had been in London since May, 1941, and left in August before Smith arrived.

[6] The British Chiefs of Staff (BCOS) were Alan F. Brooke, Charles F. A. Portal, Dudley Pound, and Hastings L. Ismay.

General Sir Alan Francis Brooke was Chief of the Imperial General Staff. Educated at Woolwich, he had served with distinction in World War I. In 1941 he became Chief of the Imperial General Staff (CIGS). His predecessor, Field Marshal Sir John Greer Dill, became head of the British Joint Staff Mission (JSM) in the United States and senior representative for the British Chiefs of Staff in Washington.

Marshal of the Royal Air Force Sir Charles Frederick Algernon Portal was Chief of the Air Staff (CAS). Portal had served since World War I and had worked closely with Lord Trenchard, the creator of the modern Royal Air Force. Admiral of the Fleet Sir Dudley Pound was First Sea Lord and Chief of Naval Staff. In 1935 he became Commander in Chief Mediterranean, and in 1939, First Sea Lord.

Lieutenant General Sir Hastings Lionel Ismay was Chief of Staff to the Minister of Defence (Churchill). Educated at Sandhurst, in 1938 he became the Secretary of the Committee of Imperial Defence (CID); in 1940, Churchill's Chief of Staff; and during the war, head of the Secretarial Staff of the War Cabinet and the British Chiefs of Staff.

The American Counterpart to the BCOS was the Joint Chiefs of Staff (JCS). Its members were Marshall, Ernest J. King, Henry H. Arnold, and William D. Leahy.

Admiral Ernest Joseph King (USNA 1901) had become Commander in Chief U.S.

Fleet on December 30, 1941. On March 12, 1942, this office was combined with the Chief of Naval Operations and Admiral King assumed that title.

Lieutenant General Henry Harley Arnold (USMA 1907) was a pioneer in the development of air techniques in the U.S. Army. In 1941 he became Chief, Army Air Forces; in 1942 his title was changed to Commanding General, Army Air Forces.

Admiral William D. Leahy (USNA 1897) had been U.S. Ambassador to Vichy. Roosevelt had designated him to be the fourth member of the JCS as the President's personal representative.

In order to effect coordination between the British and American Chiefs of Staff, a Combined Chiefs of Staff Committee (CCS) had been established in Washington, consisting of the American Chiefs and the British representatives led by Sir John Dill.

[7] Major General Carl Spaatz (USMA 1914) began his Air Corps career with the 1st Aero Squadron of the Mexican Punitive Expedition, 1916. In May, 1942, he had taken command of the Eighth Air Force.

Major General John Clifford Hodges Lee (USMA 1909) commanded Eisenhower's Service of Supply (SOS). The function of SOS was to supply the U.S. forces. In effect, Eisenhower used SOS as his administrative headquarters for U.S. theater affairs.

[8] Eisenhower's staff was organized along conventional army lines. Under Smith there were four principal sections: G–1 was the staff division in charge of matters affecting personnel; G–2 handled intelligence material; G–3, operations and plans; and G–4, supply.

[9] American Ambassador John Gilbert Winant came to London in 1941 and stayed at that post throughout the war.

2 LONDON   *June 30, 1942*

Dear General: During the weeks prior to my arrival here, a considerable amount of planning, most of it on the lower levels, was carried out on the basis of solving the tactical phases of a map problem. The most beneficial result has been the accumulation of considerable data on the German defensive arrangements and a rather accurate calculation as to possibilities in air cover. I can discover little if any real progress in the formulation of broad decisions affecting the operation as a whole. To force decisive action along this line is becoming my principal job; so far I have visited everyone except General Brooke who has been practically incommunicado since his return from Washington. I had a rather interesting discussion with General Paget. In reply to my direct question as to why such matters as the exact frontage of the attack had not yet been decided upon, he replied about as follows—"If we could only have the organization you have here, we could settle these matters in a morning. As it is we constantly go over the same ground and no real progress has been made." This, of course, was an off-the-record opinion but it is repeated to you confidentially.

There seems to be some confusion of thought as to the extent of the British commitment toward a 1942 operation. I have repeated to them emphatically your statement that we are ready to cooperate with everything available to us, and will do so by attaching our forces to appropriate commands of the British forces in order to get the job done. In this particular matter a decision must be quickly reached because of the length of time necessary to collect coastwise shipping and available landing craft.

General Ismay told me that, because of the Prime Minister's preoccupation this week in political matters, he would appreciate it if I would put off my formal call until Monday or Tuesday. This I was glad to agree to, not only because of the Prime Minister's convenience, but because I have a very busy week involving trips all over the United Kingdom.

Both the S.O.S. and the 8th Air Force are making progress in the preparation of facilities and organization, and General Clark has already gotten into full swing in his problem of establishing a headquarters and planning the initial stages of the assault. It becomes immediately apparent that there should be attached to Clark a small group of officers to carry on the "Army" phases of planning and preparation. Both General Clark and myself agree that, to set up an army headquarters now, even in skeleton form, would be a mistake. However, the integration of all the planning applying to the Assault Corps with the remainder of the Army, and the carrying on of a vast amount of logistical planning lying in the gap between front line divisions and the S.O.S., must begin without delay. Some of the officers for this job can be picked up here, particularly after the first and succeeding divisions come in, but we need a few from the States, and my first choice for the head of the committee is Brigadier General A. M. Gruenther.[1] I should like to have two or three assistants for him, say in the grade of major or lieutenant colonel, one of whom should be from the paratroop organization, and the other from the antitank. I will be most appreciative if you would have a radio sent me telling me whether we might count on getting General Gruenther and such assistants in the near future.

The job of overall organization is a very complicated one, but is made much easier by the very earnest desire of every officer concerned to cooperate toward the common end. My belief is that the senior commanders in this theater cannot be improved upon. I am quite sure that the organization finally adopted will follow no particular book, nor be modeled exactly on any organization of the past, but we are going to make one that will work effectively.

Tonight I will see a special landing exercise with Lord Louis, and tomorrow I am having a conference in Ireland with all senior commanders.

I have had several long talks with Admiral Stark[2] and he has expressed every desire to cooperate with us to the fullest extent. He is quite sure that the purpose of establishing unity of command here, involving all naval forces actually assigned to the operation, is eminently correct.

With best wishes for your continued health, *Very sincerely*

---

[1] Brigadier General Alfred Maximilian Gruenther (USMA 1918) took charge of Eisenhower's planning staff in August, 1942, and on August 11 became Deputy Chief of Staff for Allied Forces Headquarters (AFHQ), Eisenhower's organization for operations in the Mediterranean.

[2] Admiral Harold Raynsford Stark (USNA 1903) had been Chief of Naval Operations until March 12, 1942, when he became Commander of United States Naval Forces in Europe.

Dear General: General Clark and I have been trying to devise a proper staff organization for the Supreme Commander, based upon the conversation I had with you just before you left for Chequers last Saturday. We've come to the conclusion that it is practically impossible for Clark to command a Corps in the TORCH[1] operation if we are to assure, to you, a satisfactory set-up if and when TORCH operations begin, and if Clark is to carry forward all the work for which he should naturally be responsible. Naturally it is a wrench for me to think of giving up Clark—but that is my recommendation. He and I see it about as follows:

You will, for the present, act largely through your deputy in order to prepare for:

    a.–TORCH.
    b.–SLEDGEHAMMER[2] (possibly).
    c.–ROUND UP[3] (as long as there remains any prospect of its execution).

Clark commands the American Corps that would participate in SLEDGEHAMMER. This is the same corps that would *lead* the American attack in ROUND UP. The two operations are closely related—at least geographically—so Clark is the natural person to plan them, so far, at least, as American forces are concerned. He will also supervise training of 1st Division for either TORCH or ROUNDUP. ROUND UP would involve an American Army, so Clark (through a special committee headed by Brigadier General Gruenther) would develop also the complete Army plan. In this way he will necessarily be in constant touch with all phases of theater activity and in position to be of the greatest use to you in any capacity in which you may want to use him.

If the above is accepted then the next problem for the ROUND UP Supreme Commander will be the development of a proper staff to plan the over-all operation. The attack will be in two phases, one the assault, next the advance by land. My own idea—which is expressed only as suggestion to you—is that here is where Lord Louis fits in. I should like to see him assigned, with the bulk of his staff, as the *assault Chief of Staff*. Details will be planned and executed by Force Commanders, but the Supreme Commander's staff must draw up a comprehensive scheme for this critical part of the job. Under Lord Louis should be a deputy to carry forward plans for early land operations, and Lord Louis would be relieved from his post as Chief of Staff as soon as the assault phase was completed. All planning would be generally supervised by the Supreme Commander and closely by the Deputy Supreme Commander.

I think there is little need to point out the several advantages of the scheme—and I know that Mountbatten and his staff can do this work without detriment to the execution of raids this summer, fall and winter. No other trained land-sea-air staff exists, and already there is good

American representation on it. Moreover the individuals in the group are *friends*, and work in a single building of their own (no small item). Most important of all, that staff is intimately acquainted with the French Coast.

The TORCH job would be somewhat similarly set up, except that the Joint Staff will have to be built up from scratch. Under our plans Smith will eventually head that staff—in the meantime he should have a good deputy to carry the detailed burden for him. Dahlquist[4] will be his deputy for running the Theater, and will provide the necessary continuity when Smith goes to TORCH. Smith should pick out his TORCH assistant now—and select at least two or three good men to serve on that staff—including a fine air man.

I wonder who you will select to command the American part of TORCH? It is an appointment in which I'll take keen interest but, needless to say, anyone you name to important commands in that force will be completely acceptable to me. Assuming, for the moment, that we would put in an infantry and an armored corps, the following names might be considered:

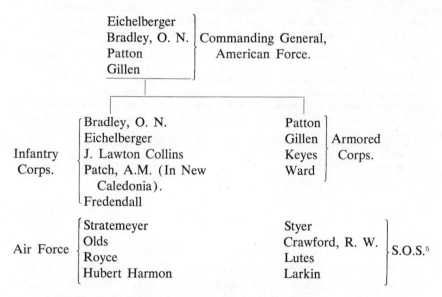

Eichelberger		
Bradley, O. N.	Commanding General,	
Patton	American Force.	
Gillen		

	Infantry Corps.		Armored Corps.
	Bradley, O. N.	Patton	
	Eichelberger	Gillen	
Infantry Corps.	J. Lawton Collins	Keyes	Armored Corps.
	Patch, A.M. (In New Caledonia).	Ward	
	Fredendall		

	Air Force		S.O.S.[5]
	Stratemeyer	Styer	
Air Force	Olds	Crawford, R. W.	S.O.S.[5]
	Royce	Lutes	
	Hubert Harmon	Larkin	

It would appear important to name the principal commanders, at once, and have them start selecting staffs, gathering statistics and studying old GYMNAST[6] Plans. Whoever is selected as C.G. should come over here as soon as firm decisions and Supreme Commander are announced.

I've had long talks with Ismay. General Clark and I go to Chequers Sunday. I've cancelled my Scotland and Iceland plans in anticipation of receiving important instructions before next week.

Thank you very much for sending me the radio about Mrs. Eisenhower. I appreciate your thoughtfulness.

With warm personal regard, *Sincerely*

[1] TORCH was the new code name for the invasion of French North Africa.

[2] SLEDGEHAMMER was an emergency landing on the French coast to be executed only if Russia were on the verge of collapse or if an internal upheaval occurred in Germany.

[3] ROUNDUP was the 1943 invasion of the Continent designed to establish a beachhead from which the Allies could strike the heart of Germany. The code name for the actual buildup of American forces in the United Kingdom was BOLERO.

[4] Brigadier General John E. Dahlquist, former member of the War Department General Staff.

[5] Major General Robert Lawrence Eichelberger; Major General Omar Nelson Bradley; Major General George Smith Patton, Jr.: Major General Alvan Cullom Gillem, Jr.; Major General Joseph Lawton Collins; Major General Alexander Mc-Carrell Patch, Jr.; Major General Lloyd R. Fredendall; Major General Geoffrey Keyes; Major General Orlando Ward; Major General George E. Stratemeyer; Colonel Thayer S. Olds; Major General Ralph Royce; Major General Hubert Reilly Harmon; Brigadier General Wilhelm D. Styer; Brigadier General Robert Walter Crawford; Brigadier General LeRoy Lutes; Brigadier General Thomas Bernard Larkin.

Patton commanded the 1st Armored Corps. He had originally been a cavalry officer but joined the Tank Corps in World War I and earned an impressive combat record. He and Eisenhower had been close friends since 1919. Patton was named to command the Western Task Force which landed at Casablanca, and in February, 1943, to command the American assault force in the invasion of Sicily. His planning for that invasion was interrupted by temporary assumption of command on March 6 of II Corps in the Tunisian campaign. On April 15, planning for the Sicily invasion was resumed. Patton led the Seventh Army in that campaign and throughout the remainder of 1943. He was promoted to lieutenant general on March 12, 1943.

Fredendall had attended West Point from 1901 to 1903 and had fought as an infantry officer in World War I. He had been named the prospective commander of an American force in earlier planning for the invasion of North Africa, and was selected to command the Center Task Force which landed at Oran. In March, 1943, he was relieved of command of II Corps and in June assumed command of the Second Army in the States. He was promoted to lieutenant general on June 1, 1943.

[6] The previous plan for a 1942 invasion into French North Africa.

4 LONDON   *August 9, 1942*

Dear General: A pouch is leaving this afternoon and I am seizing the opportunity to send along the TORCH appreciation as it was developed by the staff planners. It is possible that a copy has already reached Washington, but in any event, I think General Handy's[1] Division would like to have it.

Continuous study of the possibilities has forced us, as is always the case, to seek the best possible compromise between desirable execution of operations on the one hand and definitely limited resources on the other. In view of the ultimate object of the expedition, no argument is necessary to demonstrate the tremendous advantages that would result from an early seizure of Tunisia. However, no air cover of any kind can be provided for an expedition sailing to the eastward of Algiers, because the region is effectively covered by land based enemy aircraft in Sicily and

Sardinia. The original outline drawn up by the planners provided for sizeable expeditions against both Bone and Philippeville, but I ruled this out except for a small effort to be executed by a raiding party of the size of a regimental combat team. It will proceed against Bone where there is only a small garrison, in an effort to capture the airfield there and hold it until we can reinforce the spot. This particular operation will be led by our First Ranger Battalion.

The capture of Oran is vital to the development of air strength along the Mediterranean coast, as well as to give badly-needed additional port facilities. Tentatively, we have assigned the task of capturing Oran to our 1st Division (less one regimental combat team), with certain British reinforcements.

The attack on Algiers will be led by two U.S. regimental combat teams (one, 34th Div.; one, 1st Div.), with British units following some hours later. This attack is a vital one, due to its political implications, and must be decisive in its results.

The attacks at Algiers and Oran are planned as pre-dawn affairs. The result should be that practically every soldier getting ashore during the first day will be an American—thus carrying out effectively the basic purpose of the Combined Chiefs of Staff to give the whole expedition a definitely American tinge. Admittedly, there are administrative and tactical disadvantages to mixing units in this way, but it is believed that it is the best way to accomplish the deception desired.

The problem of timing the Casablanca and North Mediterranean attacks revolves around the question of air. If sufficient numbers of aircraft carriers were available, this question would not be so serious, but under the circumstances it is absolutely essential that Gibraltar be used as a transmitting and "setting up" base for the rapid passing of fighter aircraft into any airdrome that can be captured. The capacity of the Gibraltar airfield is definitely limited; moreover we must be extremely careful respecting any advance preparations at that point because of the fact that every plane arriving at that point is known to the Axis. The airfield there literally lies on the Spanish border and there is no hope of concealing activity from spies and agents. Because of the limitations upon the Gibraltar airfield, planes cannot be passed through at a sufficient rate to meet minimum demands on both the north and west coasts, assuming reasonable successes in seizing airdromes. These facts are leading us toward a plan visualizing a west coast attack some five to ten days later than the north coast attack.[2]

The more I study the operation, the more I am convinced that a high proportion of armored vehicles should be in the assault. Accomplishment of this introduces additional difficulties in the provision of suitable landing craft, but current reports indicate that the greatest weakness of the French at present is in anti-tank equipment.

As radioed to you yesterday, it appears that we should strive to make the initial assault, including the west coast affair, with at least eleven regimental combat teams. General Patton would like very much to have two additional ones on the west coast, but this looks to me to be absolutely beyond our capabilities.

Last night I received your telegram concerning the revision in the August and September BOLERO movements, and will give you a complete answer as quickly as I can consult General Clark and my TORCH planning people. The matter is exceedingly complicated, but I believe we can give a pretty fair answer by Monday night.

As I wired you yesterday, I am convinced that the trained American air units in England must be used in this operation. I think the reasons for this are obvious and will not waste your time enumerating them. When General Doolittle[3] returns he will be prepared to discuss the matter with you and General Arnold in detail.

Planning is proceeding quite rapidly when one bears in mind the very great complexities of the British organization. To date the greatest difficulty has been that the operation, as now conceived, had to be studied from the beginning, with the result that essential points in the outlined plan could not be decided upon except at the cost of considerable time and research. The gist of the plan as it will quickly be submitted to the Combined Chiefs of Staff, is as roughly outlined in this letter. Assuming that it is approved substantially as written, all planning and preparation will take on a more progressive and effective pace, because of the fact that it will be done from there on a command and staff basis. I will, of course, keep you informed on significant developments.

I have a couple of quite difficult problems involving personnel. From time to time over a period of some months, there have been a number of recommendations submitted from here, based upon the needs of the theater and prospective ROUNDUP. The tremendous change in outlook affects a part of this problem very seriously because I consider it inappropriate to fill all positions here when we are certain there will be a five to six months hiatus in the arrival of troops and the whole scale of the fall and winter preparation will be on a reduced basis in this theater. The other matter involves recommendations on the Legion of Merit. I have been in the theater such a relatively short time that it is practically impossible for me to submit absolutely fair recommendations. However, these things are mere details and I mention them only so that you will understand my situation in making recommendations on these subjects, which will be submitted at an early date. *Very sincerely*

[1] Major General Thomas Troy Handy, a 1914 graduate of Virginia Military Institute, had succeeded Eisenhower as Chief of the Operations Division (OPD). The Operations Division was concerned primarily with strategic planning and had broad powers in directing military operations.

[2] On the original and copy, "five to ten" was crossed out, and "few" was inserted by hand.

[3] Brigadier General James Harold Doolittle had led the April, 1942, air raid on Tokyo. He had been named to command the Western Air Command, which became the Twelfth Air Force, the U.S. component for TORCH. He was promoted to major general on December 15, 1942.

Dear General: A short account to supplement what I have been able to tell you in radios of the past couple weeks may be of some interest.

At first we experienced delays because of the British habit of desiring that all agreements be beautifully drawn up, signed and sealed before any further move can be made. The informal exchange of messages between London and Washington that took place while you were still here did not constitute, in the eyes of the British, a sufficiently clear-cut directive to permit immediate initiation of practical planning under my direct supervision. Time was lost in "hanging on the fence" while waiting for more definite approval from Washington. However, we did our best to utilize that particular period, particularly in the development of G–2 studies and in attempting to determine, in detail, the naval and military assets the British were prepared to devote to the TORCH operation.

When tentative understandings were crystallized by the receipt of the President's message agreeing to the plan for command, real work started. It was then that we began to discover the inevitable shortages. I shall not weary you, here, with a repetition of all these. From the instant that I was authorized to assume executive charge of the proposition, I laid down a specific charge to all subordinates that the time for analyzing the wisdom of the original decision had passed—that we were going to accept, without question, whatever the two governments could make available and that our problem was first to make the best possible plan within the framework of visible assets; then by leadership, organizing ability and intensive preparation to do all that lay within our power to insure success. It seems to me that the tougher the prospects, the more necessary it is that superior commanders allow no indication of doubt or criticism to discourage the efforts and dampen the morale of subordinates and of troop units.

Naturally, upon the receipt of your telegram asking for our opinion as to the over-all hazards, regardless of directive, we had temporarily to abandon this attitude, among the few of us concerned. As we pointed out, prospects are not too bright—but right here it may be appropriate to tell you that both Clark and Patton asked me to tack on to that telegram the following sentence: "We unanimously want to assure you that regardless of academic calculations as to eventual success, we have no other thought except that of carrying this operation through to the utmost of our abilities, regardless of obstacles." I declined to include this sentence on the grounds that you needed no reassurance of this particular kind; that unless you took these sentiments for granted you would not have named any of us to our present posts.

To give you one example of the kind of thing we found ourselves up against; the original tentative plan, based on calculated requirement rather than upon estimates of availability of resources, called for at least four fleet carriers and eight auxiliary carriers *inside* the Mediterranean. We found ourselves reduced to the point where we could count upon, from the combined resources of the two countries, two fleet carriers and three auxiliary carriers inside the Mediterranean. This was one reason that led us, in our telegram, to stress so earnestly the matter of initial air support, and the importance of Gibraltar as a staging point for fighter aircraft.

One consideration was not mentioned in my telegram since it applies to the broader strategic situation rather than to the hazards of this particular operation. This involves the shipping situation, with a new line to keep open, not only during the next six, eight or ten months, but throughout the war. When, some time back, you were trying to point out to the President and to others the implications of this project, you stressed this factor insistently, but I wonder whether a full realization of the inevitable consequences has ever been absorbed by the President and the Prime Minister.

Another implication of the operation I have personally brought to the attention of the British Chiefs of Staff. Abandonment of ROUNDUP in favor of TORCH is, I think, based upon a fear that the Russian strength cannot much longer absorb the great bulk of the German power. If we calculate that a large part of the German force will soon be free to act in any direction, we must come back to a serious consideration of the air and ground defensive necessities of England itself. England has just about reached its ceiling in the utilization of its effective manpower. If we remove from this country six additional divisions and place them in an active theater where the replacement problem becomes a serious one and where the building up of base, administrative and supply organizations will be a necessity, we are opening an additional drain upon England's manpower. Merely to transfer American divisions to England does not wholly supply an answer—we cannot provide replacements for British divisions. Moreover, the shipping requirements of TORCH will make impossible, for many months to come, the transfer from the United States to England of large ground formations. In calling this matter to the attention of the Joint Chiefs of Staff, I told them that in my opinion the bulk of the ground forces for TORCH should come from the United States and that the only factor to be weighed against this was the necessity for rapid build-up of TORCH forces. Once the limiting factor in the build-up becomes port capacity and not the rapidity of ship turn-around, it seems to me that, in general, every ground soldier entering the theater should be an American.

The second that I brought General Clark to London to take immediate and direct charge of all TORCH planning, a tremendous upsurge in progress has been noticeable. He is on the ball every minute and his splendid organizational sense, his fine personality and his realism all combine to make him an officer who grows steadily in my esteem and admiration. I have had a few major disappointments here where officers of splendid reputation and who made upon me a fine first impression, have failed to live up to my conceptions of military efficiency. Exactly the opposite is true in the case of General Clark. I know of no one upon whom you can depend with greater confidence and assurance, no matter to what post you may eventually raise him.

Yesterday we were faced with a tough problem. We were anxious to utilize the First Division as the spearhead of the British attack, if this could possibly be arranged. We received a telegram from the War Department which gave us the detailed schedule for the arrival of First Division equipment. The time-tables simply will not click—we must use the Thirty-fourth. On top of this we found that the craft for training combat teams in assault practices will not allow us to prepare more than one regimental team for this purpose. This, in turn, means that the British assaults will each be led by a battalion rather than a regiment of American troops. This is the type of disappointment that we run into daily as actual preparation is instituted to implement academic plans. In this connection, I should like to have the Thirty-fourth Division placed in the highest possible priority for trained replacements in officers and men. The remainder of the division should go to TORCH soon, and I'd like it to be at full strength.

General Patton has shown a definite capacity to absorb the essentials of his problem and has approached all his work in a very businesslike, sane but enthusiastic attitude. I am delighted that you fixed upon him as your choice for leading the American venture.

Major General Gale,[1] the British officer given me to head the Administrative Staff, is the best man in this line in all of England. By the same standards, I regard Colonel Hughes[2] as the best man in the American Army. I have no fears that these two, with their assistants, will do a grand job. Incidentally, their job is an enormous one, even though theoretically each national force is responsible for its own logistics.

Whatever the other burdens and problems that rest upon you, I do hope you will be spared any concern as to the determination of the senior American officers involved in TORCH to carry out your instructions determinedly, enthusiastically and, to the best of their ability, efficiently.

We are delighted that General Handy is coming. He is due today. I will immediately throw him in direct and continuous contact with Clark, so that he can see at first hand exactly what our methods and plans are, as well as the factors that are influencing daily decisions.

With personal regards. *Very sincerely*

[1] Major General Humfrey Myddleton Gale was a Sandhurst graduate and veteran of World War I. He was named Chief Administrative Officer of Allied Force Headquarters, Eisenhower's command in the Mediterranean. He was promoted to lieutenant general on August 9, 1943.

[2] Colonel Everett Strait Hughes (USMA 1908) had been Chief Ordnance Officer under General J. C. H. Lee. He was promoted to brigadier general on September 6, 1942 and to major general on March 18, 1943. In February Eisenhower named him as Deputy Theater Commander to handle American administrative matters.

Dear General: It appears about time that I send you another confidential letter in an effort to present to you some of the more interesting aspects of the developing picture.

General Clark will leave here next Wednesday for a short visit in the States. He will bring with him every detail of the plans, as so far developed, and I anticipate that his visit will be of great value to all concerned, both in London and in Washington. I hope that any schedule that you may fix for him in the way of presentations to the War Department or to the Chiefs of Staff, may be so arranged as to permit his prompt return to this country. He has been doing a most magnificent job and must not be absent from here more than a few days.

I assure you that everyone here has given his whole energy to this enterprise. As you know, the inescapable obstacles and difficulties are tremendous, particularly those involving the proper preparation and maintenance of the Oran attack force. The job that has been laid in front of the U.S. supply and shipping services is most intricate, and I have the keenest appreciation of the tremendous burden placed upon you and General Somervell[1] in the task of solving this problem.

On our side, we are making every concession in the way of eliminating equipment and supplies and assuming every reasonable risk in the effort to conform to what is possible rather than what is obviously desirable. The other imponderables of the operation, including the hoped-for attitude of the French, the probable line of action of the Spanish and weather conditions on the west coast, we have tried to take in our stride and to allow none of these things to dampen our enthusiasm. But last evening, there occurred an incident that has disturbed me more greatly than any other single thing since the initiation of this whole plan. The cause of my anxiety was a newspaper message, concerning which I sent you a radio today (Saturday). In a high-pressure situation, such as now prevails here, the knowledge that all our efforts may be defeated by some damnable and inexcusable act on the part of the press is peculiarly upsetting. It would be a great pleasure to hang the offender!

In one of our radiograms of today, we informed you that we have definitely set November 8th as the date of the attack. I hope that this will never have to be changed and am willing to assume even additional risks, in order not to set back the attack any further.

I have given continuing and intensive study to the matter of United States command in the Eastern Atlantic on and after the start of the operations. As we have tentatively agreed in prior correspondence, I regard it as highly important that I retain an authoritative control over this theater for a considerable period after D-Day, even though the man left in actual charge here operates without referring any of his problems to me. All plans for the tactical utilization of American forces now in Great Britain have been developed under my authority and with schedules laid out so as to meet the anticipated requirements at the scene of operations. However, it is certain that some of these arrangements will have to be changed after D-Day and authority to execute the change must not be dependent upon cooperation or coordination but upon a command relationship. Until all the U.S. troops and supplies that must go from the United Kingdom to the operational area have actually cleared the ports here, the United Kingdom can be considered as nothing but a base which is under the direct command of the officer conducting the American operations. This is exactly as we visualized the matter under the ROUNDUP plan; we have merely increased the length of the water communications. I assure you again that I will not allow any of the responsibilities pertaining to this locality to be shifted to me, but it seems clear that my authority to control all American activities here must, for the time being, be very definitely retained.

General Clark and General Smith, with a small group of staff officers, will leave here about D minus 4 and establish themselves in Gibraltar. I will join them *the day before the attack*. Suitable representatives of my staff will be left in England in a status something like that of a rear echelon of an Army Headquarters. They will have the responsibility of carrying out all planned shipments and, in collaboration with my deputy in this region, of making any changes and additions to those plans that may be found necessary.

I have become doubtful as to the wisdom of making General Lee my local deputy. The principal reason for this is that the S.O.S. operations here have not yet been put on a satisfactory basis, either as to organization or operation. This does not mean that any special blame attaches to any particular individual; it merely means that the concept of the original plan was not such as to permit a rapid diversion of our efforts and equipment to a new objective. Considerable confusion has resulted, which will require the exclusive and earnest efforts of the individual most responsible and best acquainted with the problem—this man is Lee. To saddle him with the responsibilities for the administration of the whole theater would probably operate to the disadvantage of both jobs.

As I reported to you before, I have tentatively set up General Hartle to command the center attack, while both Generals Ryder and Ward are destined for the new region.[2] In this situation I want to use General Gerow,[3] who I understand is soon to arrive here with the 29th Division, as my deputy in command of the U.S. forces in the United Kingdom. I am quite well aware that you do not fully share my very high opinion of General Gerow's abilities. But I submit that his loyalty, sense of duty, and readiness to devote himself unreservedly to a task, are all outstanding. Moreover, he is a very close personal friend of mine and for that reason alone would strain every nerve to meet any requirement I might place upon him. Gerow will not be the senior Major General in the area, but I do not think it necessary for me to request from you any Presidential authority in order to make the plan completely legal, since I intend to

39

designate him as a deputy. All this is, of course, predicated upon your concurrence, but I hope you will give it because I am confident that it will work. I have conferred long and earnestly with both Generals Clark and Smith in these matters and they agree with me fully that this is the best possible arrangement we could make. If you do concur in this proposed scheme, I should like you to direct Gerow to come on over here in advance of the arrival of the 29th Division. In this connection, providing Gerow has a good assistant division commander, I believe it would be best not to change his assignment, since to do so would indicate a permanency in the arrangement which might later prove a bit embarrassing to you. Moreover, from the date the division starts packing in the United States until it is re-established on a definite training basis here, is such a considerable period of time that most anything can happen.

My next subject is merely a personal suggestion that you might like to follow up. During a recent visit to Chequers, the Prime Minister expressed a very great desire to secure a globe of the world of very considerable size. He apparently saw one in Russia of some sixty inches or more in diameter, whereas his own is about thirty inches. He has not been able to secure a larger one in England. It has occurred to me that you might like to have someone make inquiries in the United States and, if a very large-sized world globe is obtainable, you might like to direct its procurement and send it to the Prime Minister as a gesture of the friendship and esteem of the United States War Department. This idea has not been communicated to anyone and I will not make any further mention of it, not even of the fact that I have passed this suggestion to you.

I was very much impressed by Mr. Murphy.[4] We had an afternoon and evening conference on the most secretive basis possible, and I believe much good was accomplished by his trip to this country.

Smith has taken a great burden from my shoulders—I truly appreciate the sacrifice you made in his case. *Very sincerely*[5]

[1] Lieutenant General Brehon Burke Somervell (USMA 1914) headed the Services of Supply.

[2] Major General Russell Peter Hartle, a graduate of the University of Maryland, became instead Eisenhower's deputy commander in the United Kingdom.

Major General Charles Wolcott Ryder (USMA 1915) commanded the 34th Infantry Division which landed at Algiers. Major General Orlando Ward (USMA 1914) commanded the 1st Armored Division which landed at Oran. In April, 1943, he returned to the United States to take command of the Tank Destroyer Center and eventually commanded the 20th Armored Division in Europe.

[3] Major General Leonard Townsend Gerow, a 1911 graduate of the Virginia Military Institute, had been Eisenhower's predecessor as Chief of the Operations Division and was now commanding the 29th Infantry Division. Gerow did not become Eisenhower's deputy, due to Marshall's reluctance. E. to M., September 19, 1942, *EP*, pp. 567–68, n.6.

[4] Robert Daniel Murphy was the chief United States diplomatic representative in North Africa.

[5] Eisenhower attached a handwritten note: "If there is anything in this letter that is not clearly stated, General Clark will be able to explain it further when he arrives within a few days. Best wishes, very sincerely."

Dear General: Generals Clark and Smith and I attended a lengthy staff meeting this morning (Monday) with the Former Naval Person[1] presiding, who suggested that I should not attempt to give you the gist of discussions until after he had given me a written memorandum on certain matters. However, I am writing this for your personal information only, with the request that no other person be informed of it.

It appears that for the first time the Former Naval Person and certain of his close advisors have become acutely conscious of the inescapable costs of TORCH. The arguments and considerations that you advanced time and again between last January and July 24th apparently made little impression upon the Former Naval Person at that time, since he expresses himself now as very much astonished to find out that TORCH practically eliminates any opportunity for a 1943 ROUNDUP. Although the memorandum prepared by the Combined Chiefs of Staff, when you were here, and later approved by both governments, definitely states that the mounting of TORCH would in all probability have to be a substitute for 1943 ROUNDUP, while the several memoranda you presented called attention to the effects of TORCH upon the possibilities of convoying materials to Russia and elsewhere, these matters have now to be met face to face, and with an obviously disturbing effect upon the Former Naval Person. He clearly realizes that the cessation of the PQ convoys will be a serious blow to Russia and also realizes that TORCH in itself can give only indirect support to the Russian front, at least for some months to come.[2] PQ–19 *cannot* be run if we are to attack November 8th, and he is so concerned about the Russian situation that I feel he may possibly, though not probably, suggest a two or three weeks delay in the assault in order to permit the running of one more PQ convoy.[3] My impression is that he still believes the early mounting of TORCH to be the most important objective; but since unforeseen factors may possibly force a delay of a certain number of days, he may decide to recommend that we definitely allow a two weeks period for such contingencies and thus permit the British to run through one more convoy to Murmansk. Reports this morning show that in the last PQ convoy 27 ships arrived out of 40 that started, and he considers that this record is good enough to indicate the wisdom of continuing the effort. In connection with the representations that must be made to the Russians, the question arose as to the progress being made by the United States in sending fighters to Russia via the Alaskan route. I sent you a radiogram on this subject today.

Another question discussed at length involved future U.S. intentions with respect to the shipment of troops to the U.K. I outlined briefly the present plan based on 150,000 ground troops exclusive of the S.O.S. formations and stated that this program, including air and S.O.S. units, would probably run to a 400,000 total. However, I was unable to give any approximate schedule of shipment other than that represented by the Queens, by which there can be delivered about 25,000 U.S. troops per month.⁴ Moreover, information presently available here is to the effect that the United States has terminated all shipment of landing craft to the U.K., even including the shipment of landing craft contracted for by the British before the initiation of ROUNDUP plan. This last point is one on which they will soon submit a communication to you.

I stated at the meeting that you had expressed the opinion, while here, that in the event of a TORCH operation, the United States would have to place a considerable defensive strength in England. I said that, for my part, I was re-examining the whole question of divisional equipment in an effort to reduce the cargo shipping requirements for any *defensive* force that the United States might send here. For ground forces with a defensive mission, I would not object to the 25-pounder in lieu of the 105 m.m. howitzer and some other items of British equipment, which may be available here in ample quantity, would be acceptable as substitutes for somewhat similar items of U.S equipment. I also stated that the motor transportation of such divisions could be considerably reduced below T/O figures.⁵ I have previously sent you a message advocating, in the interests of economy, the concentration of U.S. troops in the south of England rather than scattering them throughout the U.K.

The Former Naval Person stated that the United States and United Kingdom had originally been planning to employ *fifty divisions* in ROUND-UP *next year,* beginning in the spring and pouring this number of divisions rapidly into Western Europe. He, therefore, professed to be amazed to find out that the employment of thirteen divisions in TORCH would have such a profound effect upon the original plan. I again went over with him all the additional costs involved in the opening of a new theater, in establishing a second line of communications, in building up new port and base facilities and in the longer turn-around for ships. He repeated his conviction that the United States and United Kingdom *must resume* at the earliest possible moment a concentration of force in this theater, not only to insure the safety of the country by replacing the British and U.S. ground and air units removed from here for the TORCH operation but to provide an intensification of the air offensive against Germany and to be ready to strike heavy blows against Western Europe. He said that the U.S. and U.K. could not possibly confess to an inability to execute more than a thirteen division attack in the Atlantic Theater during the next twelve months. At the very least, he stated, we should be prepared to execute JUPITER.⁶ (He is asking Stalin to cooperate in executing staff studies on this project, without committing either government to its acceptance.) In connection with the subject of resuming the build-up here, I suggest again the critical importance of concentrating air power here, quickly—very quickly—to the maximum possible extent. Spaatz has written to Arnold on this matter.

The conference lasted for more than two hours, with these subjects being examined from every angle. The serious implication is that either the original TORCH decision was made without a clear realization of all its possible adverse consequences upon the military situation of the Allies and upon projects that are considered as of primary importance in the successful prosecution of the war, or that these considerations were ignored in the anxiety to influence the TORCH decision. It is also very apparent that the Former Naval Person has no conception of the terrific influence the situation in the Southwest Pacific exerts on our own strategy.

Incidentally, the Former Naval Person asked me whether or not, in the event of a later JUPITER operation, the U.S. would be able to produce a division trained in Arctic warfare. I told him that, as cover, you were having one division begin preparations for winter operations, and that I would ask you whether this preparation could be made of a nature that would actually make it fit for Arctic operations.

After receipt of the memorandum promised me by the Former Naval Person, I may send you a further message on some of these subjects but I felt you would like to know at once the tenor of these conversations. *Very sincerely*

  1 Winston Churchill.

  2 PQ–19. For its effect on Allied-Russian relations, see Sherwood, *Roosevelt and Hopkins*, pp. 636–40.

  3 In a handwritten note beside this paragraph Eisenhower said, "Have just been informed by Ismay that there is *no* chance of P.M. recommending delay."

  4 The British ships S.S. *Queen Mary* and S.S. *Queen Elizabeth* had been assigned to troop transport duty during the war.

  5 Table of organization.

  6 JUPITER was the code name for the proposed invasion of Norway.

8 LONDON   *September 23, 1942*

Dear General: Admiral Ramsay[1] brought to me a verbal message from you to the effect that you hoped I would not be compelled to make a visit home prior to the opening of TORCH. Frankly, one of the reasons I am sending Clark at this moment is in an effort to clear up any particular questions that might seem to demand my presence there before the opening of the campaign, and thus avoid the necessity of absenting myself from this critical spot.

Nothing could give me greater mental satisfaction than the opportunity to talk over with you, once more, the various contingencies that may arise in the early days of the assault and to discuss with you many of the major problems that later may have to be solved on the spur of the moment. But the situation here is somewhat different than would be the case if my headquarters were exclusively an American one. British officers, regardless of rank, cooperate cheerfully and effectively and accept positions which make them subordinate to their juniors in rank, all with the best grace in the world—but they do like the Commander himself to be on the job day by day and to be available for the discussion of matters of varying degree of importance. They like, admire and respect Clark, but from the Prime Minister on down to the heads of Staff Sections in my own headquarters, there is an obvious desire to get hold of me with considerable frequency and go over the many points involved. For this reason, I definitely believe that I should not come home unless you should come to believe such a visit to be mandatory.

There are several subjects that I have deferred taking up with you because of my uncertainty as to whether or not I will have to come home. While they are of the type that could best be handled in personal conference, nevertheless, if you can give me reasonable assurance that I will not have to come to Washington, I will try to place them before you in letter form. They involve such matters as future possibilities in American high command in TORCH, the desirability for the promotion of one or two of my subordinates as of the date of attack, Allied and American strategy and plans in the United Kingdom, political factors in TORCH, and others of this general category. In my opinion, the advantages to be gained by personal conference on these matters are not sufficiently great to justify my absence from here for a week—which might grow into ten days or two weeks if I encountered bad weather. Consequently, if you could send me a radio saying that the prospects were that I would not have to come home, I will immediately write up all these matters in sufficient detail for you to give me your answers, or at least your views concerning them.

I cannot tell you how strongly and favorably I have been impressed by Admiral Cunningham.[2] I strongly suspect that you may have lent a helping hand toward getting him into this job and, if so, I should like once again to express my appreciation. His frankness, his generous and selfless attitude, his obvious determination and, above all, his direct action methods and impatience with ritual and red tape all come as a refreshing breath of spring in an atmosphere that sometimes seems to grow dreary with conferences, committee meetings, regard for form and concern for papers. From this you will undoubtedly suspect that I like the man. I do.

With best wishes. *Very sincerely*

---

[1] Vice Admiral Bertram Home Ramsay, who had been designated head of the British Naval Forces for SLEDGEHAMMER and ROUNDUP, was the Chief Naval Planner for TORCH.

[2] Admiral Sir Andrew Browne Cunningham had served in the Royal Navy since 1898. He was the Allied Naval Commander for TORCH. He remained the Naval Commander in Chief in Eisenhower's command in the Mediterranean until October, 1943, when he became First Sea Lord.

Dear General: This letter deals with a few subjects that I feel you may desire to have studied by some one of the War Department sections.

The first of these is the basic training and discipline of individuals. Since my arrival in the United Kingdom, I have made this matter one of primary concern and have constantly hammered at subordinates to bring up our standard to the point where we can create an impression of being a top-notch Army. Progress has been slow. I realize that in many instances there has been no opportunity, at home, to do much about this. Many S.O.S. and Air Base units have been organized out of civilians; put in uniform and rushed here. Consequently, not too much can be expected. Unfortunately, the estimated worth placed upon our Army by many observers is often established by outward appearances. In spite of the fact that in all the camps and stations I have visited, I have found a very high degree of efficiency in performance of duty—the appearance and rather careless attitude of many of our men when on pass create an unfortunate effect. We will cure it; but I sincerely believe that additional effort should be placed upon this feature of training at home. To me, it seems of the utmost importance that we neglect no detail that is calculated to inspire confidence of our Allies in our efficiency and fighting ability. We must have a greater toughness, greater regard for absolute adherence to regulations and orders, and increased smartness in appearance and deportment.

Allied to this question, and largely a cause of it, is the extreme inexperience of many of our officers in grades up to and including Major. Not long ago, it was reported to me by the Air Force that 100 officers arrived here in one group with *no* previous military experience. These men are specialists and it was probably considered that strictly military training was not essential in their case. This is not true! Every one of them is an officer and should have at least sufficient basic instructions to discharge the normal responsibilities of an officer in meeting enlisted men. Their example is bad and their instructional and corrective capacity is nil. As soon as I found out about this, I established a program here of going into the past history of every new arriving officer, and in all cases where they did not show satisfactory military training, to put them in a two weeks' course of intensive instruction *outdoors*—with the sole purpose of driving home to them the necessity for maintaining high standards and smartness of appearances and individual discipline. It is my conviction that every newly-commissioned officer should not be allowed to take any assignment to duty until he has had approximately a month of this type of training. He may be a chaplain or an adjutant general, but when he walks out on the street he is an officer to every observer. He should be taught at least to maintain the *appearance* of an officer.

Another subject involves the rebuilding of U.S. strength in the United Kingdom, after the departure of the TORCH forces. As to the strength of the ground force, I believe that, thinking of security only, our original estimate of a total of about six (6) divisions is still correct. Such a force should be concentrated and trained in southern England to be available for expeditionary purposes also. I still believe that some day the ROUND-UP idea *must* be revived: We should plan and prepare deliberately. We are just completing a study on the possibilities of substituting British equipment for some American items in these divisions, all in an effort to reduce the shipping requirements. This project does not look nearly as hopeful as the original British figures made it appear.

The future air program is certainly as important as is the ground. To date we have developed only one real weakness in the daylight bombing program. This is the extreme dependency of this type of operation upon good weather. But this weakness is a serious one. Daylight precision bombing demands such good weather that constant interruptions are to be anticipated. Only the other day we had a mission of forty-eight (48) planes out over the occupied territory, but it had to return without making an attack and all planes had to jettison their bombs. In connection with this particular operation, an entire squadron of Spitfires was lost, apparently due to bad weather. This squadron of Spitfires was piloted by experienced men. Aside from this extreme dependency upon good weather, the high-level bombing program has been rather well justified and I believe that the basic effort should remain as a principal U.S. objective. The establishment of such an Air Force here has the further advantage of providing a mobile and rapidly available support for TORCH and even the Middle East region, as soon as the necessary bases for maintenance, repair, and normal supply are established properly in those areas. In fact, this consideration is of critical importance because by this means we can probably maintain year-round operation of aircraft that, in the winter time in this theater, will be able to execute their normal missions only infrequently.

With respect to the recent War Department study on future air developments, I think there must be considered the factor of *efficiency*. Too great an expansion will be harmful, and we should be content with the largest force that we can bring up to peak efficiency in personnel and in all other ways. Also, we must not neglect night bombing. We hope to keep ahead of German technique, so that we can keep right on developing daylight action to an intense degree. But we must not get into the position of being stymied if the enemy comes along with some weapon or device that makes daylight work too hazardous. It may be that this is well understood and provided for. I'm having an early conference with Spaatz on the subject.

Both the air and the ground programs, on the scale indicated, are going to involve a lot of shipping. Recently we received a telegram that for the rest of this year a total monthly lift of *5,000* was all upon which this theater could count. We had been figuring on having available the bulk of the troop lift provided by the Queens, and felt that at least 25,000 U.S. troops should be transported here monthly. It seems to me that the Operations Division should go into these matters thoroughly in an effort to develop an overall program that will be best fitted to the strategic and tactical probabilities of the coming months.

Suppose we assume that TORCH goes well and the Russians continue to battle next spring on somewhat the present scale; it would appear that opportunity for some form of continental invasion should be presented, and one that could not exist indefinitely. On the other hand, if both of these factors become unfavorable, then the need for defensive support of England should manifest. I realize that our total assets will let us do just so much, and no more. But in alloting available means through the coming months, I think the OPD should satisfy you completely that the allocation conforms to the major probabilities and potential opportunities.

A final subject is the future training, particularly in amphibious operations, of troops coming to the United Kingdom. I believe this should be continued for troops coming here, and hope the Navy will keep a proper detachment in this command to carry out the naval aspects of this work. The detachment need not be as big as originally planned, but the principle and nucleus should be preserved. *Very sincerely*

10 LONDON   *October 12, 1942*

Dear General: As you can well imagine, there have been times during the past few weeks when it has been a trifle difficult to keep up, in front of everybody, a proper attitude of confidence and optimism. Material preparations consume so much time and progress seems often to be so slow that occasionally impatience is almost certain to turn into irritation and irascibility. On the whole, however, I think we have every reason to be satisfied with the way things are moving along. Schedules have been met; and, although in many instances maintenance and supply are not going to be what one could wish, these are hazards that we accepted long ago. If nothing untoward happens, I believe the plan, as finally approved, will develop almost perfectly up to the point of departure.

What will happen as to weather and enemy resistance, as we turn in toward the Straits, only the future can tell. A telegram received this morning from the War Department is disturbing in that it indicates the Germans are apparently moving planes, vehicles and other equipment into the vital area and reinforcing their Air Forces in Sicily. These are developments that we had to anticipate when the attack decision was made. Our great hope is that any such moves are inspired only by nervousness and uncertainty rather than by definite knowledge of what we are going to do.

My own conviction is that, with a decent break in the weather, we should get on shore firmly and quickly and, at the very least, should find divided councils among the French, which should prevent them from offering really effective resistance. After a successful landing, the important factor of the next few weeks and months is going to be the determination with which the two governments, particularly the two navies, bring in our follow-up convoys and get us established on the ground and in the air in a way that will allow us to proceed effectively.

I am sending radio orders today to Patton to make sure that no documents, carried ashore by his people, carry any mention of Spanish Morocco. In addition, I am anxious that no document, which might be captured, will contain anything tending to nullify the effects of the Presidential promises of completely fair and friendly treatment for the French population. I realize that Patton must give his subordinate commanders certain verbal instructions that will apply in specific instances, but *we must take no chance that a document captured or found ashore can be used either to stir up the Spaniards or to convince the French that we are double-crossing them.* In connection with this last thought, we are preparing a follow-up proclamation for use in the Algiers area and to the east thereof, which will explain plausibly the participation of the British in the operation. Since this will impinge on the political field, in which the President is the decisive influence, the draft will be sent to you at an early date for the President's approval.

Our chores here have not been made any easier by the impending visits of civilian notables. While I am trying to assure that neither of the two persons we expect at the end of this week or the beginning of next is allowed to consume the time of Smith, Clark or myself—the timing of their visits is, from our angle, unfortunate.

With the arrival of Smith and the return of Clark, I have succeeded, fairly well, in freeing myself of many details that were getting backbreaking in their volume. Smith's short sick spell was apparently a recurrence of a trouble he has had for many years. He insists that he is in good condition. Naturally, in a large headquarters, he will not be exposed to the hardships that front-line soldiers have to bear. In any event, his organizational and executive abilities are so outstanding that the beneficial effects of his presence are constantly evident.

As I have said several times, I thoroughly believe that the War Department should make superhuman efforts to build up U.S. strength in the United Kingdom after the TORCH requirements have been satisfied. I agree with the air people that a powerful Air Force here will contribute markedly to the eventual defeat of Germany. However, the exact number to come in here, and the exact strength of the entire Air Force throughout the world, are subjects that will require the most earnest examination into available resources—both material and human. If they attempt to expand beyond the point where efficiency in operating squadrons can be properly developed and sustained, they will be making a mistake. For example, in this theater they recommended forty-two (42) heavy groups. General Hansell[1] tells me they believe they can produce this number and maintain efficiency; unless this is assured, I would far rather have twenty to thirty groups thoroughly trained than forty-two partially trained ones. If we are successful in TORCH and can establish effective air bases, we will have gone a long ways toward realizing the true value of the long-range bomber—in that it will be able to operate, at will, from the U.K., from the TORCH area or from the Near East.

A prerequisite to establishment of an expanded Air Force in the U.K. is an increase in the antiaircraft protection. This is an item of primary importance. Finally, our ground forces here must not only be re-built from the standpoint of security, but we must have constantly available an Expeditionary Force on this side of the water, capable of striking a real blow under favorable opportunities.

There is one important matter with respect to TORCH that we are now exploring. Going on the assumption that the British original commitment of six divisions can be cut to four, we are asking the British War Office to set aside and train a composite group (of approximate strength of two divisions) to be ready to come suddenly into the Tangier area if, during the period from D 15 to D 60, serious danger should arise from that direction. Until the planned forces are actually built up, every passing day will be one of critical danger in the event the Spaniards decide to oppose us. However, this danger may be somewhat alleviated if we can have a force in England ready to use combat loaders, returning from the initial assault, to come in quickly in the event of trouble. I will let you know more about this at an early date. *Very sincerely*

[1] Brigadier General Haywood S. Hansell, Jr., commanded the 1st Bombardment Wing of the Eighth Air Force in England.

11 LONDON   *October 20, 1942*

Dear General: I have just returned from a rather difficult inspection trip in Scotland, where I went to see amphibious exercises carried out by the First Division. (Incidentally, I learn that Mr. Morgenthau,[1] who arrived here while I was attending a meeting of the Chiefs of Staff and who could not see me the following day, has been wondering why I have not called on him. I find, upon my return, that he is out of town, but I have arranged to call on him next Sunday morning. This is just an item to illustrate that, try as one will, it is difficult, even in a field command, to perform all the various chores that have to be done.)

The exercises that I witnessed had, as usual, both encouraging and discouraging aspects. The men looked fine and, without exception, were earnestly trying to do the right thing. I spoke to scores of them, in the pitch dark, and found that their greatest weakness was uncertainty! Most of them did not know exactly what was expected of them. This extended all the way from the method of challenging to actions in tactical moves. All this, of course, is the business of the officer—the Major, the Captain, and the Lieutenant. It is in this level of command that we have our most glaring weakness and it is one that only time and eternal effort can cure. We are short on experience and trained leadership below battalion commander, and it is beyond the capacity of any Division Commander or any Colonel to cure these difficulties hurriedly. Time is essential.

I will be somewhat worried until General Clark has gotten back. The mission he is on is full of risks but, more than that, it is crowded with terrific import for the success of the operation. These days, I live and breathe nothing but TORCH and such irritations as I suffer usually spring from things that I seemingly have to do, but which appear to have no direct connection with the real job.

Tonight, Smith and I dine with the Prime Minister. There is nothing unusual to discuss, but I have regular meetings with him twice a week. They have a valuable effect in my daily dealings with the staffs.

I must say that the British have been constantly ready to meet me more than half-way and have been most considerate in their treatment of my opinions, suggestions and recommendations. For example, they recently sent to me a draft of a War Office directive they intended to issue to the Commanding General of the First British Army. I took definite exception to its tone because it emphasized the degree in which the Army Commander would be exempt from the authority of the Allied Commander, rather than insisting upon unity and showing that exemptions would apply only to circumstances of such extraordinary nature that they were not expected to occur. The Chiefs of Staff promptly met my comments with the most considerate of attitudes and, in effect, apologized for the crude way in which they had attempted to express their instructions. They had merely paraphrased the instructions to Haig,[2] written in the spring of 1918, whereas, their convictions in the matter apparently agree with mine. From the day I came over here, I have dinned into the British the fact that you considered unity of command to exist only when the Commander of an Allied Force had the same authority—so far as it was legal to confer it upon him—with respect to all troops involved, as he had to those of his own nationality. I am now benefiting from this crusade because, in many instances, the British are ready to go much further than some American officers in accepting and abiding by the principle.

Yesterday, there were several questions put before me effecting possible Brazilian participation in the operation and the acceptance of a Brazilian Mission at my Headquarters. Frankly, I can see very little good to be derived from the proposals made, with much possibility for later friction. I do believe, however, that a Brazilian endorsement of the operation, expressed at the right time, should have a good effect upon Spain. The more widespread this endorsement could be throughout South America, the better it would appear to be.

Under present plans, Clark and I will leave here about D-minus-5 and from then on I will be in Gibraltar with a small detachment until my headquarters can be established in Africa. Smith will remain in London for a short time thereafter in order to take complete charge of forwarding certain essentials to the new theater—particularly, elements of Allied Headquarters. He will join me as soon as the Headquarters can be established in North Africa.

I do not need to tell you that the past weeks have been a period of strain and anxiety. I think we've taken this in our stride and, so far as I can see, all of my principal subordinates are up on the bit and ready to go! The real strain comes from trying to decide things for which there is no decision—such as, for example, what is to be done if the weather throughout that whole region simply becomes impossible along about the time we need calm seas. If a man permitted himself to do so, he could get absolutely frantic about questions of weather, politics, personalities in France and Morocco, and so on. To a certain extent, a man must merely believe in his luck and figure that a certain amount of good fortune will bless us when the critical day arrives.

Smith seems in excellent shape again. I am most hopeful as to the results of General Clark's mission and will give you a summary of my impressions immediately upon his return. Admiral Cunningham is a fine type, and I am more than delighted to have him in this show. General Anderson,[3] Commanding the British First Army, is a Scot, straightforward, direct and, if he has any fault, it is that he is inclined to be too meticulous. He studies the written word until he practically burns through the paper. My relationships with him have, however, been of the best and I think that he will do a good job. So far, I have been most favorably impressed with Fredendall. He was not one of those in whom I had instinctive confidence, but my opinion of him has become increasingly favorable ever since he came. In no instance, do I now have any key subordinate that I would like to trade off. If I did, I would get rid of him instantly because I am not going to trust any part of this expedition to a person who, in my opinion, is not up to the job. I firmly believe that we have a chance to score a real success, but the extent of that success is going to be measured in the speed, firmness and skill with which we go about our several tasks. Fumbling and hesitation would ruin us—if I see any man exhibiting traits that lead me to suspect he would be guilty in this regard, I would fire him even if he already had loaded his stuff on the ship.

Through Smith I hear that Mr. Morgenthau was quite disturbed about some things he saw in the Twenty-ninth Division. I have not talked to Mr. Morgenthau personally but Smith explained to him that the Twenty-ninth Division was just arriving in the theater, was sent here to complete its training, and was not considered to be fully ready for combat. I've seen only a part of the division myself, but hope to give it a good going-over later this week. It was unfortunate that my trip to Scotland had to take place immediately after Mr. Morgenthau's arrival, but it was either go then or not see the troops at all, and I still think it is important for troops to know that the Commander-in Chief is as interested in them and their work as he is in paper plans and high-powered staffs.

I will send you at least one more letter before leaving here. In the meantime, I hope that things are going well with you and that you remain in the best of health. Whenever I'm tempted to droop a bit over the burdens cast upon us here, I think of the infinitely greater ones you have to bear and express to myself a fervent wish that the Army may be fortunate enough to keep you at its head until the final victory is chalked up.

With cordial personal regard, *Very sincerely*

P.S.—May I request that you pay my respects to the Secretary?

[1] Secretary of the Treasury Henry Morgenthau, Jr.

[2] Sir Douglas Haig, Commander in Chief of British forces in France in World War I.

[3] Major General Kenneth Arthur Noel Anderson, a graduate of Sandhurst, would take command of the land forces once Algiers had been secured and the British troops landed. In the reorganization of the Allied forces in North Africa brought about by the meeting of the British and American attacks, he was named commander of the British First Army. After the Tunisian campaign he returned to England where he took command of the British Second Army.

12　LONDON　　　　　　　　　　　　　　　　　　*October 29, 1942*

Dear General: There is no question that General Clark's visit to North Africa did much good, even if it resulted in nothing more than the acquisition of a lot of information. General Mast[1] gave him exact details as to location of troops, batteries and installations. We have been assured that the air-troops at Blida, Bone and Oran will *not* resist, and we are hopeful of placing paratroops on these fields without compelling them to jump. If we can do this, we will have immediately available a splendid striking force to hit for Tunisia, which, as always, remains of primary importance to our minds.

The opportunity that we had hoped for of getting Giraud[2] and Darlan together on the proposition went glimmering, at least so far as General Mast is concerned. He believes that Darlan is not to be trusted and that Giraud will have nothing to do with Darlan.

It is my conviction that General Mast has committed himself so far that there is no chance of his double-crossing us. This fact, coupled with the length of time it will take him to get his orders out to the outlying posts along the Algerian coast, is why I agreed to give him, on November 4th, the target date for the attack. He cannot use radio and other normal methods of communication but is forced to rely upon trusted officer-couriers to deliver his messages.

The French Navy will resist but it is the general belief that when the Navy finds the Army collapsing behind it and with no place to go except to sea, its resistance will quickly die out. In anticipation of this, we have set up two small commando type of expeditions to enter Oran and Algiers very quickly after H-hour so as to prevent sabotage and the blocking of harbors and piers.

General Mast says that he controls Bone absolutely. For this reason, we are hoping that, with the aid of airborne troops, and by using a floating reserve originally scheduled for Algiers, to secure Bone instantly and without loss. We have put in earnest requests for additional support in the transport type of airplane. We are combing the British resources and have asked our own Air Corps to do its best.

The question of overall command is going to be a delicate one very quickly after we land. If the whole region comes over to us in the guise of an Ally, there will be two or three questions that are likely to become a bit embarrassing. Supreme Command is one of them; the other is a possibility that the French may start trouble with the Spanish and so attempt to commit us to something that would be most unwise. There have been many reports to the effect that in the event of any disturbance in French Morocco, the Spaniards are prepared to move out of Spanish Morocco to seize a favorable line to the south. This might encourage the Frenchman, who would be counting on the support of the Allied Army, to bring on a battle in that region. To take the greatest possible precaution on this point, I am sending a radio to you today (for transmission to Murphy) to warn Mast to allow no hostility to occur there even if the Spaniards should technically violate the International Boundary. In addition, we are asking the British, through their Ambassador, to warn Franco that while we will respect the integrity of his territory, he must do the same with respect to French Morocco.

Unquestionably, if Giraud comes over, he is going to argue that since the battle is on French territory, that since he is a senior and distinguished commander and that since it was through his influence that we were unopposed in our landing, he should be given immediate Supreme Command of the whole effort. To my mind, it is impossible to make drastic change in the command of an expedition that is planned in the most minute detail and which must continue to develop as planned until the important objectives have been attained. I do not suppose the French will claim any right to command offensive operations in the direction of Libya or toward any of the Mediterranean Islands. They are going to press, however, for military command in French North Africa. I will have to ride a rather slippery rail on this matter, but believe that I can manage it without giving serious offense until the time arrives that the defense of this particular region can logically be turned over to French Command.

I have wondered what is in your mind with respect to the possible broader eventualities, assuming that within a reasonable time TORCH has proved a rather definite success and that Rommel[3] has been driven out of Africa or at least is in a bad way. It would seem that, under current naval and shipping conditions, a great number of divisions cannot be used profitably in the Southwest Pacific. In Northern Africa limitations on port facilities will prevent us attempting to use that as a staging point for a *huge* invasion effort, involving the mass of our ground forces now training in the U.S. All the old arguments for ROUND-UP will still prevail as long as Russia stays in the field as a fighting power. Consequently, the spring of '43 may see the ROUND-UP idea revived with the purpose of launching a decisive blow in the spring of '44, with the summer of '43 used for building up the necessary forces in Great Britain, firmly establishing ourselves in favorable positions in the Southwest Pacific and exploiting TORCH to the point that the whole region from Casablanca on—through Cairo to Persia—is safely protected against Axis aggression and is threatening Sardinia, Italy and the Balkans. In any event, all long-range planning is certain to give a great deal of consideration to eventualities along the Eastern Atlantic front, stretching from Trondeheim around through the Mediterranean. I believe that until a firm strategic decision has been made, reaching as far ahead as December of '43, we should be in no rush to reorganize this particular front. For some months to come, the United Kingdom must act as an auxiliary and subsidiary base for TORCH, while the opportunity to make maximum use of the air forces, available through a unified authority in this region, should not be lost. All this implies that a single, overall authority controlling U.S. forces in the region is, for the present, logical and necessary. As you will see from the instructions I have given General Hartle, who is directed to operate directly with the War Department, none of the normal affairs of the U.K. will be referred to me. The system we have set up will work efficiently.

Recently, General Arnold sent a message to General Spaatz questioning him about the frequency of bombing operations out of England. As I stated in a former letter, the one great weakness of daylight precision bombing is its dependency upon excellent weather, which must be continuous, vertically over the target, to great heights. Time after time we have been disappointed in this regard and it is obvious that more than one practicable base should be available to a bomber force that intends to keep pounding away at an enemy spread out as is Germany. Further affecting our bombing operations, about two weeks ago I directed Spaatz to give his primary attention for the next few weeks to the submarine bases in the Bay of Biscay, so as to help us through that dangerous area. I instructed him that until all TORCH convoys were safely through the eastern Atlantic, he was not to use up his bombing power against auxiliary or less important targets to the northward, since to do so would frequently diminish our ability to hit the Biscay ports. The British and American Air Forces have worked out a very effective scheme for helping get our convoys through the submarine-infested zone, and they must not be diverted from this merely in order to take advantage of one or two good bombing days in the more northerly parts of German-occupied Europe or in Western Germany itself.

It must be obvious to everyone that the submarine is the greatest menace to our future prospects. I have directed that priorities in bombing targets, aside from necessary action against hostile air power, should list the submarine as number one—hitting it at sea, in the manufacturing plants, and in its bases. For the moment, the most immediate threat we have is the submarine base in the Bay of Biscay, and I have no intention of dispersing our air assets until we are safely through this portion of the task. Once our great convoys have gotten through this submarine-infested zone, Spaatz will return to our former policy of taking advantage of the weather in any locality we can reach, but always with earnest attention to the submarine, particularly in the Bay of Biscay.

General Arnold should understand that no one is more anxious to keep hammering away at the Hun than I am. There is no single feature, other than TORCH, to which I give so much attention as to air activities. I keep in touch with every projected raid, and confer constantly with Spaatz and other senior air officers. Every one of them is aggressive and a fighter. None of them likes inaction any more than I do, but it is quite obvious that primary objectives must always be kept in mind and everything concentrated to make one thing a success at a time.

Accompanying this letter are citations which I recommend for your approval in the case of the five officers who went on the mission to North Africa. If TORCH initially goes as we anticipate, I'd like to have them published by November 15th. I confess that I sent Clark on this mission with considerable reluctance, and was greatly relieved when he returned safely. While I seriously considered going myself, our experience here has shown that I simply cannot be absent from the center of things for a single day. Actually, I am going to Gibraltar at least three days ahead of the date I should, so far as affairs here are concerned, but I dare not trust the weather. *I must be on the spot* when the thing breaks and to wait too long is merely to invite possible confusion or even worse.

Everything for TORCH is well in hand, except that Doolittle's air force is having a hard time getting here. I fear nothing except bad weather and possibly large losses to submarines. The submarine map today shows a veritable hornet's nest in the region lying to the west of the Iberian Peninsula. Beyond all doubt, the Axis expects us to be sending an expedition from here toward the South and are lying in wait for it. We cannot possibly expect to get through without *some* loss, but I hope these will be small and will not involve critical things. Given a fair break in these two matters, you may rest assured that the entry will go as planned and that we will have good news for you by the morning of November 9th.

We keep hearing rumors, all originating in North Africa, of a very large Axis force concentrated just to the eastward of Tunis. I do *not* believe it is there in the force indicated by these reports. If it is, we shall have a very desperate battle on our hands very quickly but, even so, I am certain we can take care of ourselves if the French go along with us even in a half-way manner. At least we will be killing some Germans and Italians, even though the battleground may not be at the exact spot that we should like it. I would like very much to be able to send a half dozen ships loaded with 75's, machine-guns and ammunition into southern France if the French Armistice Army actually fights the Germans. But we *cannot* do it simultaneously with TORCH.

My latest reports, received this morning, on the Egyptian affair, make it look like the battle is progressing about as visualized by the British Commanders. It is extremely tough going to get through the defensive area, but both Alexander and Montgomery[4] believed they could do it when they started. I have real faith in them as a combination and if they can pierce the main positions within the next three or four days, the Allied preponderance in armor should give us a real tactical victory. Such a contingency would be veritable God-send to TORCH.

In general, the British, including the Prime Minister and all the Chiefs of Staff, are of good heart with respect to the forth-coming operation. I meet with them very often, mostly on an informal basis. I always see the Prime Minister once a week, usually two or three times. Today I call on the king. There is no question about the British determination to support us to the limit.

With best wishes for your continued good health. *Cordially*

[1] Major General Charles E. Mast commanded the Algiers Division and was Giraud's representative.

[2] General Henri Honoré Giraud, a French World War I hero, had escaped from German captivity and was living in Vichy France. He had established communication wth anti-Vichy Frenchmen in Algiers and was thoroughly anti-German.
Admiral Jean François Darlan was the commander of the Vichy Armed Forces. He feared a German move into French North Africa and was ready to come to Africa and cooperate with the Allies in return for full aid and support.

[3] Generalfeldmarschall Erwin Rommel, commanding the German and Italian forces, was engaged by British forces at El Alamein, Egypt, on October 23 and by November 4 was in retreat.

[4] General Sir Harold Rupert Leofric George Alexander, a Sandhurst graduate, had been Commander in Chief of British forces in Burma. Because of the continuing crisis in Africa, Churchill made him Commander in Chief, Middle East, in August, 1942. When his offensive joined Eisenhower's in Tunisia in February, 1943, he was named to command of the ground forces—the 18th Army Group—which included the British First and Eighth Armies and the French and U. S. land forces in Tunisia. He was also named Eisenhower's Deputy Commander in Chief to plan for the invasion of Sicily. As commanding general of 15th Army Group, he commanded the ground forces in that operation. He fulfilled a similar role in Italy.
General Bernard Law Montgomery had commanded the British II Corps at Dunkirk. He now commanded the British Eighth Army opposing Rommel and would retain that command during the Tunisian, Sicilian, and Italian campaigns in 1943.

13 GIBRALTAR   *November 7, 1942*

Dear General: It is now 9:30 Saturday morning. Tonight we start ashore. Since we cannot foretell with certainty what is going to happen, it may be of some interest to you to have, within a few days, a picture of the situation as we saw it just before the jump off.

This morning's radio report to the Combined Chiefs of Staff stated that no attacks had yet been made on any of our convoys, although we know that the enemy has discovered the two heavy convoys inside the Mediterranean, saw Patton's force when it was south of the Azores and KMF–2[1] when it was about one thousand miles northwest of Gibraltar. Beyond all doubt, we may expect a growing concentration of submarines in this region during the next few days.

We have had nothing but silence out of the submarine that is attempting to pick up Kingpin.[2] Last night we sent out orders for the vessel to break radio silence at 4:00 A.M. today and make a report to us. This was *not* done and while the occurrence inspires some fear that Kingpin has not yet left France, or possibly even that the submarine has been lost, we are still hopeful that some less drastic contingency has caused the ship to remain silent. A rather garbled report just received from an airplane indicates that the submarine is still operating.

Recent messages from McGowan[3] clearly indicate that he has a case of jitters. I assume that you have seen copies of all his communications, including the one demanding, as diversions for TORCH, a landing in Southern France of more than 50,000 soldiers, coupled with simultaneous attacks in Norway and Western France. Yesterday, he sent us a telegram to the effect that unless Kingpin arrived in Africa by the night of the 6–7, the success of the operation could not be assured. However, McGowan was well aware that by no possible arrangement could Kingpin reach Algiers on the night of the 6th. I don't mean to say that I blame McGowan. He has a most delicate position and a stupendous job and one that is well calculated to develop a bit of hysteria as the critical hour approaches.

I have been highly pleased with the calm atmosphere that has been maintained throughout the Allied Staff and among all Senior Commanders. The Commander of the British First Army is temporarily here with us. Air Marshal Welch,[4] Admiral Cunningham and General Doolittle are likewise here. All are busy but reasonably confident.

I can scarcely describe to you the terrific congestion that exists in the harbor and on the airfield here in Gibraltar. We are fully aware that the enemy knows all about this and the very congestion here must indicate to him how important a part the functioning of this place plays in the development of our plans—even if he is still unsure as to the details of those plans. You may be quite certain that the second we have any other place to put these planes, they are going out of here on the jump.

You have, of course, seen the reports made by the British Ambassador at Madrid concerning the Spanish attitude toward any operations in Morocco. We are not decided as to how to interpret the Spanish pronouncements, but feel that we must go ahead on the basis of avoiding an open break with the Spaniard, even under considerable provocation. We are simply not in position to undertake a fight with him at this moment.

A portion of the Allied Staff accompanied me when I left England Thursday morning. We had been trying to start since early Tuesday morning and were getting just a bit fearful that weather might delay us indefinitely.

As a consequence, I had to order a take-off under local conditions that were anything but favorable, but five out of the six B–17's that were ready to go made their getaway in good style. It was an anxious moment. The sixth plane had mechanical trouble just before the take-off and was forced to stay over a day. The five original planes came in without incident except that an air alert here kept two of us flying around for an hour and a half, hoping to land. However, when the sixth plane came down yesterday, it was attacked by four German long-range fighters off the northwest corner of Spain. It had quite a battle for twenty-five or thirty minutes, during which the co-pilot was shot in the arm. The plane contained General Doolittle and a number of others. Because of the passenger load, the waist-guns had been dismounted and this allowed the German to come up on the plane with a certain degree of impunity. However, other guns were manned effectively and one German plane was badly damaged. The pilot handled his ship very skillfully, dove to sea level and turned directly out to sea. The Germans were eventually forced to turn back or run out of fuel. The trip was completed without further incident.

General Clark and I are now making detailed plans for getting an advanced echelon of this headquarters into Algiers at the earliest possible moment. Unfortunately, Gibraltar will necessarily remain, for some time, the communications center for the entire area. It is the only spot from which communications can be maintained with the several landing forces and with London and Washington. This fact tends to hold me here until we can get satisfactory installations at Algiers. In the meantime, we are solving the problem by sending Clark with a small operational staff into Algiers, with the purpose of doing everything possible to speed up the eastward advance.

As you know, we have been counting heavily on the use of some airborne troops, in order to forestall Axis entry into the Tunisian area. However, my latest reports on the weather in the Bay of Biscay and in England are very unsatisfactory, and I am not at all sure that we can bring our transporters and paratroops into the area at the time we had hoped. This would be another sad blow, but we will find some substitute, if necessary, for the original plan.

This morning's reports on the Casablanca coastline show a slightly improved condition. If Patton encounters any real resistance, he is going to have a tough time of it because landing problems alone are enough to occupy his full attention. I am quite loath, however, to contemplate bringing him inside and will avoid doing so if I possibly can.

I received your telegram about the promotions I have recommended and am delighted with your suggestion that I recommend either or both the Corps Commanders for promotion in the event that brilliant work so justifies. I also concur in the thought that it would be fine to promote some regimental commander as the result of operational success, and I have instructed all subordinate commanders to be on the lookout for any colonel who does a particularly fine piece of work.

We are standing, of course, on the brink and must take the jump—whether the bottom contains a nice feather bed or a pile of brickbats! Nevertheless, we have worked our best to assure a successful landing, no matter what we encounter. As I look back over the high pressure weeks since July 24th, I cannot think of any major item on which I would now, if I had the power, change the decision that was made at the time. Every member of the staff, British and American, has slaved like a dog, and I truly believe that we have established a pattern for Combined Staff operation that might well serve as a rough model when expeditions of this nature are undertaken in the future. Many things were in our favor. The greatest single feature, of course, was the fact that there was one responsible head. The next thing was that the British government made absolutely certain that commanders and staff officers, detailed to the expedition, had no mental reservations about their degree of responsibility to the Supreme Commander. The third feature was that throughout the preparatory period the Combined Chiefs of Staff, on both sides of the water, preserved the attitude that they had placed responsibility on one individual and refused to interfere in matters properly pertaining to him. Finally, the officers detailed to the Staff and to command positions, were the ablest that could be found.

If, of course, some unexpected development should make this operation appear as a failure, much of the work that has been done will be discredited by unthinking people, and the methods that have been followed will be cited as erroneous. I do not believe that a final success or failure, which is going to be determined by a number of factors beyond anyone's control, should blind us to the fact that before this war is won the type of thing that we have been doing for the past many weeks will have to become common practice between the British and American services. Consequently, experience of this kind will be valuable no matter what the outcome of the particular operation.

While dictating this letter, the *Thomas Stone*—one of the combat loaders for the Algiers attack was torpedoed about 300 miles east of Gibraltar. The flash report gives some hope that the ship may not sink, since she was hit in the stern. However, she is out of the operation and that, of course, is a definite blow to us. Some time during the morning we will have more details and I will send a short report to the Combined Chiefs of Staff. (2 hours later.) Unless the ship is hit again, there is no danger of her sinking. She is carrying a battalion of the 39th U.S. Infantry.

With cordial personal regards. *Sincerely*

4:00 P.M.

P.S.—I sent you a telegram today asking for authority, as Allied Commander-in-Chief, to confer upon Allies those decorations that I am now empowered, as Theater Commanding General, to confer on Americans. Kingpin has just reached here. I will see him in twenty minutes. The boy (British Submarine Captain) that picked him off is the same one that carried Clark on his hazardous mission. I'd like to give him a Silver Star this evening!

10:00 P.M. I've had a 4 hour struggle with Kingpin. He—so far—says "Either I'm Allied C-in-C or I won't play!" He threatens to withdraw his blessing and wash his hands of the affair. I'm weary! But I'll send you a radio later tonight, after this thing is finished.

¹ A fast convoy from the United Kingdom to North Africa. The assault forces from England were divided into a fast convoy (KMF) and a slow one (KMS). Each in turn had two parts, one carrying a division for the Oran attack, and the other, a division for the Algiers attack.

² Code name for Giraud.

³ Code name for Murphy.

⁴ Air Marshal Sir William Lawrie Welsh commanded the Royal Air Force units which made up the Eastern Air Command, the British air component of TORCH.

CHAPTER 3

Commanding in the Mediterranean, November, 1942–December, 1943

D URING THE PERIOD November, 1942, through December, 1943, Eisenhower faced a new challenge—commanding in combat. He directed three major amphibious operations: North Africa (TORCH) on November 8, 1942; Sicily (HUSKY) on July 10, 1943; and Salerno (AVALANCHE) on September 8, 1943. Moreover, the Sicilian campaign had to be planned while the Tunisian one was being fought. It was Eisenhower's task to put theories of command and tactics into practice while overcoming national antagonisms. In doing so, he sent Marshall thirty-five letters. These letters indicate that Eisenhower broadened his education as a commander by passing the new test of combat. As always, he carefully guarded his authority, but since only one serious challenge to it arose, he concentrated on personnel reports. Eisenhower's role in the allocation of resources increased sharply. Grand strategy was mentioned but infrequently, for his involvement in its creation was minimal; he did write about its implementation, however. He wrote often concerning tactical operations and his moves regarding them—especially in periods of tension. In contrast to his London letters there is little reference to diplomatic problems—this in part a result of Marshall's injunction in December to leave diplomacy to his subordinates.

And once again there are personal references in Eisenhower's letters, although they differ from the letters written earlier. Instead of the profuse expressions of gratitude, one striking feature about this period is that Eisenhower seemed often to be discontented—about the French, attempts to tamper with his organization, his British commanders, communications, staff errors, staff sizes, promotion pressures, planning difficulties, problems of logistics, the weather, and unwanted visitors. Many of these complaints seem brought about less by the tension of working with an ally than by the tension involved in putting combat theory into practice.

Eisenhower's letting down his guard under this stress violated his own and Marshall's precept of being eternally stoic. Faced with the necessity of keeping up a good face to his own subordinates he had to unburden himself to someone; that person was Marshall, who would always hear him. Eisenhower demonstrated continuing loyal subordination to Marshall by acceptance in mid-1943 of the fact that his theater would be secondary. He grew more confident as the Allied Army he had put together performed in combat.

COMMAND AND ORGANIZATION

Eisenhower had three principal organizational concerns during this period: (1) retaining his own clear command authority; (2) selecting and removing personnel; and (3) contending with the twin problems of distance and poor communication between headquarters.

During the first weeks of the campaign Eisenhower felt that he had made good progress in achieving unity of command. He had direct control over land and air commanders; and his deputy, Cunningham, transmitted orders to the naval commands. In January he further centralized his authority by having Spaatz appointed Commander, Allied Air Forces, even though he realized this was only temporary, pending a reorganization of the entire Mediterranean when Montgomery's Eighth Army forces moved into Tunisia. But he encountered trouble from Giraud who at first insisted on receiving overall command of the expedition, a demand Eisenhower did not even seriously consider.[1] Later, Giraud balked at serving under a British commander until Eisenhower "peremptorily ordered General Anderson to take charge of the entire battle line."[2]

On January 17 Eisenhower wrote concerning Marshall's suggestion that he name Patton as "a sort of deputy." But Marshall, who had made the suggestion because he had been concerned that other matters were drawing Eisenhower's attention away from military operations,[3] told Eisenhower to disregard the idea. The British forces driving westward from Libya would soon link up with Eisenhower's command, and this would solve the problem. "Alexander will be your man when British Eighth Army joins you after Tripoli."[4]

When the forces merged, a new command structure created by the Com-

---

[1] Eisenhower, *Crusade in Europe*, pp. 99–101
[2] *Ibid.*, p. 135. See also Howe, *Northwest Africa*, p. 383.
[3] Pogue, *Ordeal and Hope*, p. 423.
[4] E. to M., January 19, 1943, *EP*, p. 911, n. 1.

bined Chiefs at the Casablanca Conference in January went into effect.[5] Under the plan, Eisenhower, as Commander in Chief, Allied Force Headquarters, would have three principal subordinate commanders: Tedder would be in charge of a single Mediterranean air force, with three major commands, one for North Africa headed by Spaatz, one for the Middle East, under him, and the RAF Malta Command;[6] Cunningham remained as commander of the naval forces;[7] Alexander[8] was to be Eisenhower's Deputy Commander in Chief and commander of the 18th Army Group which would then have under it the British First Army under Anderson, the British Eighth under Montgomery, and the French and American ground forces in Tunisia. This same arrangement of a single subordinate for air, navy, and ground forces would also apply to the invasion of Sicily (HUSKY).[9] Eisenhower's rather calm initial acceptance of the change was shattered when he learned "that the combined Chiefs were attempting to issue directions as to how and what his subordinates were to do."[10] He had "dictated a hot message challenging such intrusion into the organizational set-up of an Allied Commander,[11] but his staff persuaded him not to send it. Eisenhower was not really opposed to having a deputy for ground operations and, in fact, had already accepted the idea of Patton's filling that position. However, he had balked at giving Patton any title with the implication that he was an overall deputy with a voice in air and sea matters as well as ground. Eisenhower insinuated that others might resent it—the others at this point seemed to include himself. The fact that Alexander was British and therefore less subject to control than Patton would have been also does not seem to have been enough of a factor to have prevented Alexander's commanding tactically. Eisen-

[5] For an account of the Casablanca Conference, see U.S. Department of State, Foreign Relations of the United States, *The Conference at Washington, 1941–1942, and Casablanca, 1943* (Washington, 1968); Matloff and Snell, *Strategic Planning*, pp. 18–42.

[6] Sir Arthur William Tedder has included a full account of the various air reorganizations during the war in his *With Prejudice: The War Memoirs of Marshal of the Royal Air Force Lord Tedder* (London, 1966). Craven and Cate, TORCH to POINTBLANK, is the official record of air activities in the Mediterranean.

[7] The story of the naval command and operations in the Mediterranean is told in Samuel Eliot Morison, *Operations in North African Waters, October 1942–June 1943*, History of the United States Naval Operations in World War II, vol. II (Boston, 1962) and his *Sicily–Salerno–Anzio*, vol. IX (Boston, 1964) of the same series.

[8] For Alexander's reaction to the change and his feelings toward Eisenhower, see Field Marshal Earl Alexander of Tunis, *The Alexander Memoirs, 1940–1945*, ed. John North (London, 1962), pp. 40–41.

[9] Eisenhower, *Crusade in Europe*, p. 138; Albert N. Garland and Howard M. Smyth, *Sicily and the Surrender of Italy*, U.S. Army in World War II, ed. Stetson Conn (Washington, 1965) pp. 10–11.

[10] Butcher, *My Three Years*, p. 258.

[11] E. to M., February 8, 1943, *EP*, pp. 945–46, n. 2.

hower had already accepted Alexander's position in his letter of January 30. He would later name Montgomery as initial overall tactical commander for OVERLORD, and would consider employing Alexander in a similar capacity after the December, 1944, Battle of the Bulge.

What angered Eisenhower was that the detailed directives were clearly designed to push Eisenhower, as Brooke wrote in his diary, "into the stratosphere and rarefied atmosphere of a Supreme Commander, where he would be free to devote his time to the political and inter-allied problems."[12] Brooke thus intended to insure that the experienced Alexander would "deal with the military situations."[13] Accordingly, the directive stated "there must be one Army Commander or Deputy Commander in Chief appointed to coordinate the operations of all three armies in the Tunisian theater. . . ." Regarding Sicily, Alexander would be "charged with the detailed planning and preparation and with the execution of the actual operation when launched."[14] The command of the air forces had left detailed organization to the Air Commander in Chief.

Brooke had misjudged his man. He had forgotten Eisenhower's response to the initial directive to Anderson. For although Eisenhower might appear to vacillate in his tactical handling of this and other campaigns, he would not waver in his insistence that he was the Supreme Commander and that no subordinate be put into a position that was in reality another power center. He hated the word coordinate, and considered internal organization his prerogative. And Marshall agreed with him.

Writing Marshall on February 8, he angrily gave voice to his intention to ignore the directive. When Eisenhower calmed down, he told Marshall that he did not consider the British actions vicious, that they merely reflected the British experience. He assured Marshall, "I am merely trying to say that I believe I have grasped your idea and that I will be constantly on my guard to prevent any important military venture depending for its control and direction upon the 'committee' system of command."

Eisenhower made this stick. Cunningham, Tedder, and Alexander accepted the role of subordinates, albeit subordinates with wide latitude. Eisenhower accomplished this by his own personality, by the willing attitude of the three commanders, by maintaining as close contact as possible with them, and by circumstance—as, for example, when Eisenhower made the final decision on the Sicily invasion plans because the British commanders could not agree. He also restricted Alexander's command

---

[12] Sir Arthur Bryant, *Turn of the Tide: Study Based on the Diaries and Autobiographical Notes of Field Marshal the Viscount Alanbrooke* (London, 1957), p. 455.

[13] *Ibid.*

[14] E. to M., February 8, 1943, *EP*, pp. 945–46, n. 2.

of ground forces to troops involved in actual combat. On February 21 he reported, "The new command organization is functioning and I expect my burden to be much lightened."

This episode was the strongest CCS attempt to interfere with Eisenhower in the Mediterranean, and the final command arrangements—one subordinate for each of the services reporting directly to Eisenhower— became substantially those for the invasion of Europe. Although the details might change, and arguments, especially over air, would continue, he retained the control he felt was essential. Apparently unity of command was not yet accepted at the very top, even though Eisenhower considered Allied unity the great lesson of Tunisia.[15] By its very nature, then, his triumph was a precarious one.

Eisenhower did not again deal at length with overall command structure until informed in December that he had been named to oversee OVERLORD, the cross-Channel invasion of Europe. Because the area of operation in Normandy would at first be rather narrow, he would have a single tactical ground commander (who would be British, preferably Alexander) and a single tactical air commander, who would share the same headquarters. When operations expanded, he would have Lieutenant General Omar Bradley, the U.S. Army commander, assume leadership of an American Army group, thus creating two ground commanders. "By the time we get four armies deployed along the front it is likely that we would have to have two tactical air forces, at which time I would deal personally with each of the Army Group Commanders or make any other arrangement that then seemed best, depending upon the location of the various headquarters." Eisenhower knew that the scope of the invasion would dwarf his previous endeavors and that there was a limit to the size of operation one man could oversee.

His comments also reflected a renewed belief in the necessity of sufficient flexibility in command arrangements. He wanted to avoid the mistake of Tunisia, where the Allies had entered "with preconceived notions of the areas in which British and American troops would be respectively employed."[16] Drastic changes had been required when military requirements differed from the anticipated situation. When CCS interference with his command authority became excessive, he had ignored them. He well knew, however, that this had been possible only because his subordinates had accepted his authority. This knowledge tended to confirm his belief in the need for loyal supportive commanders.

[15] Eisenhower, *Crusade in Europe*, p. 158. In a letter to Marshall of October 1, 1943, Eisenhower reacted strongly concerning a rumor that part of his air force would be placed under the control of a London-based command. He did not send the letter but instead directed Smith and Spaatz to confer with Marshall in Washington on this and other subjects. E. to M., October 1, 1943, *EP*, pp. 1477–79.

[16] Eisenhower, *Crusade in Europe*, pp. 209–10.

Indeed, comments on personnel form the most recurring theme of Eisenhower's letters in the North African and Mediterranean campaigns. He told Marshall of his visits to subordinate commanders, commented on performance, and discussed present and future needs. He had learned that performance under non-combat conditions did not necessarily indicate performance in combat. Worried over the possibility of Eisenhower's lack of tight control over ground operations, Marshall had suggested that Eisenhower appoint a deputy, and Eisenhower had established a command post under Brigadier General Lucian Truscott, Jr., in January. However, he tried in his letters to reassure Marshall that he did have a firm rein on ground operations.

Eisenhower's first enthusiastic description of his commanders' performances came on November 17, 1942, nine days after the landings. By the 30th, amidst praise of several men, he voiced doubt about others, noting that "a commander quickly learns which of his subordinates are to be trusted under all circumstances to do a fine workmanlike job and which ones he has to watch closely and handle by special means in order to get the best out of them." He complained that the British First Army commander, General Anderson, "is apparently imbued with the will to win, but blows hot and cold, by turns, in his estimates and resulting demands."

Eisenhower also knew the value of promoting—but only those who were deserving. On November 30 he angrily withdrew a recommendation for promotion that had been put through despite his own skepticism. On March 11, at a new height of irritation, he wrote to Marshall, "I have recently issued a flat order that no promotion to the grade of Colonel will be made without my personal approval, and I warned that if any such promotion was accomplished and I learned of it, the officer concerned would be promptly demoted and the man who pretended to authorize it would be disciplined." In forwarding a list of recommendations to Marshall on January 5, Eisenhower singled out Brigadier General Alfred Gruenther for his selflessness. Hardly a newly discovered virtue, he emphasized it here to attract Marshall's eye to someone he felt was especially qualified. Marshall had drummed this virtue into Eisenhower who in turn had displayed it in his famous confrontation with Marshall over his own promotion.

Eisenhower also had to accept the unpleasant task of relieving unsatisfactory officers. As the battle for Tunisia became bogged down, Eisenhower wrote Marshall on December 11 of the need to find a way to handle the "reclassification of officers found unsuited in theaters of active operations." On February 4 he made a recommendation for promotion that he was soon to regret; he cited three officers for a third star, among them Fredendall. Earlier he had reserved judgment on Fredendall, whom Marshall had strongly suggested for command of the Center Task Force.

Although Eisenhower claimed his doubts had been resolved, he wrote Fredendall a letter the same day concerning the latter's prior criticism of the British. He warned Fredendall to watch his subordinate generals very carefully to see that they did not stay too close to their own command posts.[17] Obviously, the admonition about command posts was meant for Fredendall himself. Fredendall had established his command post near the front, but had nestled it in a gulch that was barely passable and ordered underground shelters blasted for him and his staff.[18]

During the height of the battle of Kasserine Pass, February 21, Eisenhower had written to Marshall that he was relieving his G–2. Sloppy intelligence work had led Anderson to believe that the attack through Faïd on the 14th was not the primary attack, enabling Generalfeldmarschall Erwin Rommel to force the Kasserine Pass. Rommel failed in his offensive, but a delay in the counterattack by Fredendall enabled him to retreat successfully.[19] Eisenhower shared the shock of what some considered to be a major military defeat.[20] Because Fredendall was a Marshall selection, Eisenhower moved carefully. On March 3 he told Marshall he was thinking of relieving Fredendall. Fredendall's difficulty was in selecting able men "and, even worse, in getting the best out of subordinates; in other words, in handling personnel." Even though he had kind words for him thereafter and again blamed Fredendall's staff, his doom was sealed at this instant, for Eisenhower felt that the shortcoming he described reflected failure in the most important ability of the modern commander. Ironically, Marshall wired Eisenhower while Eisenhower was writing this letter to inquire if Fredendall should not be promoted.[21] Fredendall was relieved on the 5th and on the 11th Eisenhower wrote that he had left for the States.

In letters of April 5 and 16, as the campaign went on, Eisenhower explained his relief of other commanders—these were division commanders. Marshall asked Eisenhower on the 14th that he be given sufficient notice before officers were returned because of the problem of finding appropriate positions for senior officers. Eisenhower replied on the 24th with a detailed explanation as to why he had relieved certain officers and noted, "In the case of very senior officers, decisions are never arrived at suddenly and on the spur of the moment. They are the result of many observations and reports. When doubts arise concerning any of these people, I think that, even at the risk of bothering you with details, I should give you warning of what may transpire." Eisenhower's somewhat defen-

[17] E. to Fredendall, February 4, 1943, *EP*, pp. 939–41.

[18] The performance of Fredendall's command during the battle of Kasserine Pass led to his relief. Martin Blumenson, *Kasserine Pass* (Boston, 1967), pp. 86–87.

[19] See Colonel Vincent J. Esposito, ed., *The West Point Atlas of American Wars*, 2 vols. (New York, 1959), vol. II, map 85.

[20] Butcher, *My Three Years*, p. 268.

[21] E. to M., March 3, 1943, *EP*, p. 1007, n. 3.

sive reminder that these decisions were not lightly taken did serve as an indication to the Chief of Staff that he was in command.

The rigors of the Tunisian campaign prompted Marshall to send General Omar Bradley, Eisenhower's classmate at the Academy, to act as Eisenhower's roving representative, his "eyes and ears."[22] Eisenhower trusted and respected Bradley and needed his help in these tension-filled days. He acknowledged on March 11 that Bradley was a "godsend."

After the victory in Tunisia and until the landing at Salerno in September, Eisenhower's letters show even more references to personnel. On August 24, under the assumption that Marshall would command the cross-Channel invasion of Europe, he gave his impression of several combat commanders for Marshall to use in determining his subordinate commanders. He first talked about Patton: "He has conducted a campaign where the brilliant successes scored must be attributed directly to his energy, determination and unflagging aggressiveness."[23] As for Bradley, "There is very little I need to tell you about him because he is running absolutely true to form all the time." Then Clark. "Clark continues to be what I have always told you—the best organizer, planner and trainer of troops that I have met." He recommended that in the event Marshall needed to take one of his British ground commanders he take Alexander.[24] On September 6, in replying at length to Marshall's request for Eisenhower's comments on a list of permanent promotion recommendations, he singled out Bedell Smith: "Frankly he comes close to being the ideal Chief of Staff."

Eisenhower's last letter from the Mediterranean on December 17, dealt with both the command organization for OVERLORD and the organization of the American theater in the Mediterranean. He told Marshall that he had expected him to command OVERLORD rather than drawing the assignment himself. "However, immediately I learned of this from the President and upon receipt of your telegram from Cairo, I began figuring on the best way to organize the strictly American phases of this theater." This time Eisenhower made clear his choices for his subordinate commanders. Newly confident, he did not defer completely to Marshall, as he had done with TORCH, when he merely listed a multitude of acceptable names.

He also overcame a variety of difficulties involving communication with his commanders, some due to problems of distance and technical capabil-

---

[22] Bradley, who was to become Eisenhower's most valued commander, recounts his experiences in *A Soldier's Story* (New York, 1951).

[23] Ladislas Farago, *Patton: Ordeal and Triumph* (New York, 1964) is a fascinating account of Patton's wartime career.

[24] This is only one indication of Eisenhower's recognition that the personality of his senior ground commander was important. After being named commander of OVERLORD, Eisenhower tried to take Alexander with him but had to settle for Montgomery. Eisenhower, *Crusade in Europe*, p. 211.

ities of communication facilities, and some due to the inevitable combat shakedown.[25] Eisenhower's move to Algiers ended his several complaints about lack of communications in Tunisia. Moreover, he wrote Marshall on February 4, the establishment of a command post at Constantine in January, enabled him to "keep the threads pretty well in my hands." But the problem arose again when he was preparing to go to Malta for the Sicilian invasion. As he told Marshall on June 26, his headquarters would have to be located there temporarily, because it was the only place the Navy could set up communications.[26] Eisenhower pointed out that he would have virtually no contact with Washington and London while there, and that therefore he would return to Tunisia about the 14th of July. In the Italian invasion, Eisenhower was content with his communications because, as he wrote Marshall on September 13, ". . . all of my Commanders in Chief are in the Tunisia area and I have my advanced headquarters here also."

Eisenhower encountered one final problem of organization related to communications and control that also was not easily solved by the textbook—staff size.[27] He had confidently told Marshall on February 8 that he would reduce the size of his staff. By May 25 he was a wiser man—he had been running one campaign and planning another and lamented the number of headquarters and personnel needed to accomplish all of these efforts. After complaining again about trying to plan for post-HUSKY operations, he issued an urgent appeal for staff officers, secretaries, and stenographers. On June 9, he took specific issue with Marshall, and tried to explain to him the difficulty of reducing staff size. Eisenhower's experience in the Mediterranean had convinced him that it was impossible to keep staff numbers down.

In the beginning of his tenure as combat commander, he was aware that Roosevelt and Churchill had decided where he would land in North Africa and that they and most of the CCS had placed only minimal trust in him. Although he felt he had established his own clear internal authority, he soon learned once again that an Allied commander had constantly to guard his unity of command. The nadir had come in January, 1943, when the CCS attempted to divorce him from actual involvement in ground operations and HUSKY planning. In part this was due to the British preference for the committee system of command, but it also represented a clear expression of the British lack of confidence in him. The battle in

---

[25] Eisenhower vividly describes his subterranean headquarters on Gibraltar in his *Crusade in Europe*, p. 95.

[26] Howe, *Northwest Africa*, p. 84.

[27] Dwight D. Salmon *et al.* "History of Allied Force Headquarters," lithographed (Survey Directorate AFHQ, n.d.), is a detailed administrative history of Eisenhower's headquarters.

Tunisia was not yet a success and Alexander and Montgomery were considered tactical heroes.

Eisenhower's reaction to this continuing undermining of his authority was to write Marshall that he was going to ignore the January directives and he proceeded to do just that. His position as allocator of resources was one determining factor. Disagreements among his British subordinates and among the CCS over where to land in Sicily enabled him to wield the final decision-making power over whether and how to invade Italy. But the vital reason why he was selected to make these decisions was that his subordinates had confidence in the fairness and even the wisdom of his judgment. He knew that challenges would again arise to unity of command, even though he strongly felt that the great lesson of Tunisia had been the need for devotion to that concept.

Eisenhower had learned from bitter experience not to mix small units of different nations. His trouble in keeping up with developments in Tunisia convinced him of the need of a single commander for definable areas. His problem of communicating with his commanders made him more aware of the need to keep his headquarters near those of his top subordinates. He had mastered the unpleasant but vital duty of relieving those who failed, and he had developed a set of top battle-tested commanders whose judgment on tactics and men he could trust when dealing with the much larger operations in Europe.

Strategy and Tactics

Eisenhower became more educated in the urgent task of allocation of resources. Although he did not participate in the formulation of grand strategy, he played an expanding role in its implementation. He did set up overall tactical plans for his theater and wrote Marshall often in the tense early days of the campaign, recounting his experiences. Eisenhower would have had little to say about grand strategy in any event, because Marshall had a closed mind on the subject. As far as Marshall was concerned, operations in the Mediterranean were at best irrelevant and at worst harmful to the only effective way of fighting the war—the cross-Channel invasion of Germany.[28]

Eisenhower had some cautious remarks on future strategy shortly after the landings in a letter of November 17, and did not comment again on that sphere until May, 1943, when the TRIDENT Conference of American and British leaders met in Washington.[29] In his letter of May 13 Eisen-

[28] Pogue, *Ordeal and Hope*, pp. 401–3.
[29] For an account of the conference, see Matloff and Snell, *Strategic Planning*, pp. 126–45; and Morton, *Strategy and Command*, pp. 454–60.

hower presented both a sop and a muted plea to Marshall: "While I
will always believe that the correct line is the straight, short and simple
one, I have come to the conclusion that the old adage—'A poor plan
vigorously carried out is better than a perfect plan indifferently executed'
—applies in this case. We must have some arrow that gives guidance
and meaning to all our strategic and tactical effort." Eisenhower was
again demonstrating the qualities that were so essential to the success of
his mission—compromise and tact. In these phrases, he assured Marshall
that he still believed in the cross-Channel invasion, but advised him to
accept for the moment the British strategy of operations in the Mediterranean in exchange for a more definite commitment to cross-Channel invasion as the major effort in the future.

This is precisely what happened at the conference in Washington. The
Combined Chiefs, still in disagreement, but now beginning to trust Eisenhower's judgment more, solved the problem of if, where, when, and how
to invade Italy by leaving the decision up to Eisenhower. The episode
furnished quite a contrast to the debate over the buildup in North Africa
in the summer of 1942 when higher authorities had decided each detail
of the operation. In addition, the Chiefs agreed that the buildup in England
would continue, with seven divisions being withdrawn from the Mediterranean in November for use in the United Kingdom.

After the CCS set a target date of May 1, 1944, for a 29-division cross-
Channel invasion,[30] Eisenhower wrote Marshall on August 24 that he expected his theater would lose considerable forces. On September 6, a few
days after the British had gotten ashore on the toe of Italy, and two days
before the major landing at Salerno, Eisenhower discussed the opportunity raised by the possible surrender intact of the Italian fleet. He proposed to man the fleet's top positions with British or Americans and turn
them over to the U.S. Pacific Fleet. Eisenhower had not forgotten the
pressures on Marshall to place more emphasis on the Pacific. The surrender of the Italian fleet would also free the British Navy to strengthen
its position in the Indian Ocean and off the coast of Norway. Unfortunately
for Eisenhower's plan, the Italian fleet was severely damaged by the
German Air Force as it sailed to Allied ports on September 9. This letter
ended Eisenhower's strategic writing, for once Italy had been invaded
and the cross-Channel decided upon, there was no issue of grand strategy
to debate.

Eisenhower was charged with carrying out the operations in the Mediterranean which had been proposed by the British over Marshall's strong disagreement. He therefore did the wise thing: kept his own counsel, carried
out the operations, pledged fealty to the cross-Channel invasion, and

[30] Matloff and Snell, *Strategic Planning*, p. 242.

gently urged Marshall to accept a certain commitment to existing operations in the Mediterranean.

These tactical operations occupied much more of Eisenhower's letters than did grand strategy. He had to learn a new trade and he had to keep Marshall informed of his progress at it. The new trade was the planning and actual execution of theater tactics. He did not, of course, formulate details of tactical planning—that would have been impossible. He did, however, approve general tactical plans and movements and was informed of the execution of his subordinate commanders' detailed battlefield plans. He wrote a great deal about immediate operational events and plans, shifting of resources to meet each new situation, and supply problems. These references are more extensive in periods of particular difficulty on the battlefield—when initial success was in doubt in mid-November, at the time of the Kasserine Pass debacle in February, 1943, and during the early Italian campaign in September.[31]

The North African invasion forces readily achieved their minimum objectives—"to seize the main ports between Casablanca and Algiers, denying their use to the Axis as bases for submarines, and from them to operate eastward toward the British desert forces."[32] Alexander's British army was 1,200 miles to the east at the opposite end of the Mediterranean, but was rapidly pursuing the Germans retreating westward. The two forces planned to squeeze the German forces between them and reopen the Mediterranean. In order to do this the Axis line of communication and reinforcement into North Africa had to be cut by seizing the two ports in Tunisia most accessible to the Germans—Tunis and Bizerte. The "main strategic purpose was, therefore, the speedy capture of northern Tunisia."[33]

Eisenhower described the opening phase of the campaign in several letters, and by November 30 he wrote optimistically about Anderson's offensive to Bizerte and Tunis. Eisenhower had been aware when he made the decision to rush his forces into Tunisia as rapidly as possible that there were risks involved, such as having the line of communications disrupted by air attack and sabotage. He felt, however, that the risks were justified, and he was optimistic. The disposition and movements of the Allied troops were described to Marshall in great detail. Eisenhower had no motor transport and could run only nine small trains per day, two of which had to haul coal for the railroad. He was able to use the port of Bône, but it lacked air cover. The preponderance of enemy air power and the inadequacy of Allied air fields, with resulting air attacks, were causing havoc among the troops.

[31] To follow the Mediterranean campaigns, see Esposito, *West Point Atlas*, II, maps 81–101.

[32] Eisenhower, *Crusade in Europe*, p. 115.

[33] *Ibid.*, p. 116.

Eisenhower's fears about German air superiority were well-founded. It was further complicating the already serious problem of logistics. On December 3, in the face of German counterattacks, he had Anderson withdraw to a defensive position. Anderson himself told Eisenhower on the 5th that the principal difficulty was German dive-bombing.[34] The North African invasion, with its emphasis on getting ashore and seizing the three major ports (Casablanca–Oran–Algiers), had stinted on motor transport and other administrative and supply necessities. Eisenhower's fighters were 120 miles from the front, while the enemy was only 15 miles away. As Eisenhower himself put it, "We reached the point where practically by air alone the enemy could break up every attempted advance."[35] The difficulty of reinforcement was worsened by the weather—the battleground was a sea of mud. Eisenhower himself blamed the initial lack of French aid, the inferiority of air forces, the shortage of ships—causing the cut in motor transport units and attendant problems of supply, and the weather.[36]

But he felt that the basic difficulty was "the over-all weakness of his [Anderson's] force. . . . General Anderson's plans had to be based upon speed and boldness rather than upon numbers."[37] Eisenhower's views complemented those of the British, who felt that the U.S. Chiefs of Staff had fatally hampered the prompt capture of Tunisia by insisting upon the landing at Casablanca. In later campaigns Eisenhower would insist on an adequate concentrated strength in his landing force. He would also long remember the importance of air power in the immediate tactical situation; this memory would be amplified by the experience on the beach at Salerno, where lack of adequate air support threatened the success of the invasion. Control of the air was essential for close battlefield support.

The campaign in Tunisia remained at a stalemate until mid-February and Eisenhower grew increasingly concerned about his logistics problem. On February 4 he wrote Marshall of the difficulties he faced. On the 8th he warned that he expected an attack, for Rommel had been sending troops from Tripoli to join the forces in the north. Eisenhower thought the attack would come against Pichon, just north of Fondouk, for Pichon was held by the ill-equipped French.[38] The enemy did launch a major offensive a few days later, with the main effort coming at Faïd, to the south of Fon-

---

[34] E. to CCS, December 3, 1942, *EP*, p. 793, n. 1.
[35] E. to Churchill, December 5, 1942, *EP*, pp. 801–5.
[36] E. to Handy, December 7, 1942, *EP*, pp. 811–16.
[37] Eisenhower, *Crusade in Europe*, p. 116.
[38] Marcel Vigneras, *Rearming the French*, U.S. Army in World War II, ed. Kent Roberts Greenfield (Washington, 1959), is the official account of the Allied efforts to equip the French.

douk, but also held by French forces.[39] On the 20th Rommel forced Kasserine Pass and drove westward, capturing the vital airfields at Thelepte.

On February 21, in the darkest hour of the battle, Eisenhower wrote a long letter to Marshall on the situation, desperately making a plea for aid to operations in the Mediterranean and requesting that the area have a very high priority for three months. He then outlined in detail the course of the battle and countermeasures he was taking.[40] The most vital step was to reorganize and reestablish the units as effective fighting forces, "so that we can operate as Divisions and Corps rather than as Regiments and Battalions." In other words, Eisenhower had learned once again the limitations of coalition command. The blending of units at lower levels had resulted in intensifying national differences and in confusion and delay in the execution of orders. Eisenhower would not repeat this mistake again—he would not place units of different nations together in components of less than a division.

In his published account of the campaign, Eisenhower wrote that of all the reasons for the debacle, "the first and vastly most important of these was the inescapable conditions resulting from failure in our long-shot gamble to capture Tunis quickly." He had personally made the decision. "Afterward, dispersed units could not quickly be brought together and prepared for the hostile reactions we were certain would follow."[41] Eisenhower would always remain careful to avoid what he thought was improper dispersion of his forces. He wished to counterattack immediately, but Fredendall did not attack until the 23rd and the delay enabled the Germans to withdraw successfully.[42] This episode represented the ebb of Allied fortune in North Africa. The fighting tide turned, the supply situation eased, and the conquest of Tunisia became only a matter of time.

But success also brought problems. The role of II Corps in the campaign offensive became the focal point of another step in Eisenhower's battlefield education. On March 29 Eisenhower sent Marshall a copy of a letter he had written Alexander, expressing concern at Alexander's battle plans, including the plan to eliminate the U.S. II Corps' role in the campaign. Considerations of tactics had to take a back seat in this instance. American public opinion and U.S. troop morale had been badly bruised by the lackluster performance of the American as compared to the British forces. A closing out of the American troops from the final offensive

[39] Howe, *Northwest Africa*, pp. 398–400, 410.

[40] Eisenhower later called the piecemeal commitment of the 1st Armored Division to the battle—due to faulty G–2 estimates "the most serious defect." Eisenhower, *Crusade in Europe*, p. 142. See also E. to CCS, *EP*, p. 955, n.2. Howe, *Northwest Africa*, pp. 456–74, describes the counterattack.

[41] Eisenhower, *Crusade in Europe*, p. 147.

[42] *Ibid.*, pp. 145–46; Blumenson, *Kasserine Pass*, p. 282; Esposito, *West Point Atlas*, II, map 85.

would have had an abrasive effect on the already strained relations.[43] Eisenhower's pique at Alexander was further shown in this same letter when he referred to Alexander's caution, blaming him for the fact that the 1st Armored Division had not been employed more agressively. Eisenhower was learning that it is as difficult if not more so to live with an ally in success as in difficulty.

The offensive did begin, as Montgomery broke through the Mareth Line and the American II Corps joined Montgomery's Eighth Army north of El Hamma on April 7.[44] The continuing offensive brought more problems between the British and Americans. On April 16, in response to a message from Marshall showing concern for the preponderance of unfavorable publicity about the American divisions, Eisenhower wrote a long defense of their effectiveness.[45] He gave what amounted to a final renunciation of the ill-advised attempts to integrate the Allied units. "On top of this I have made Alexander agree as to the necessity of keeping all four American divisions together as a powerful corps, even if the logistics of the situation should make the arrangement seem somewhat unwise or risky." This statement might appear inconsistent with Eisenhower's later protestations that his decisions were based solely on military considerations. As always, the truth lay somewhere in between. Eisenhower was realistic enough to realize that there were indeed considerations other than military ones. The important thing was to take them into account insofar as was possible without greatly jeopardizing the military situation, but never to admit that he did. Usually he could justify his decision to himself in military terms, but in this instance, American public opinion simply would not allow the exclusion of II Corps. Alexander, Montgomery, and Anderson had firmly established themselves as battlefield leaders; Fredendall had tried and failed; now the Americans had only Patton. The American troops had not particularly distinguished themselves. This was not surprising, since they and their leaders, unlike the British, were inexperienced. But Marshall and Eisenhower feared that Americans at home would not accept this explanation. They were quite right. The only alternative was to accept a less satisfactory military situation.

The final phase of the Tunisian campaign started on April 19th and the American units performed well.[46] On May 5, a week before the campaign ended, Eisenhower brought Marshall up to date on the campaign and praised II Corps, which had taken Mateur the day before. On the

---

[43] While acknowledging the factor of national pride, Eisenhower, in his *Crusade in Europe*, stresses other factors (pp. 152–54).

[44] Howe, *Northwest Africa*, pp. 526–27, 531–40, 576; Esposito, *West Point Atlas*, II, maps 86a and b.

[45] E. to M., April 15, 1943, *EP*, p. 1229–30, n. 1.

[46] For a description of the final campaign, see Esposito, *West Point Atlas*, II, maps 87 and 88.

13th, the last day of the campaign, Eisenhower wrote Marshall at length, satisfied and relieved that his first campaign had ended successfully. He reminded Marshall that he had always guessed the landings would take place on November 8 and that the campaign would end on May 15.

But in this same letter Eisenhower was already outlining to Marshall his views on future operations. One of these was CORKSCREW, the capture of Pantelleria. He told Marshall that he wanted the operation to provide air support for the southern side of the forthcoming Sicily invasion and to determine whether heavy air and naval bombing could render coastal defenses impotent enough to make landing a rather simple affair. Unlike his subordinates, he felt that on completion of bombing the landing party could simply move in without opposition.[47] The importance of the experiment was obvious enough; its success would justify Eisenhower's earlier request for immediate air support in the Tunisian campaign and vindicate his insistence on use of the Air Force to support and interdict an invasion area generally. On June 9 he told Marshall that he had observed the results of the air and naval bombardment and was highly confident that all would go well if the entry of the landing craft into the harbor was coordinated exactly with the lifting of the bombardment. Eisenhower's confidence proved to be well-founded. The British 1st Division went ashore at Pantelleria on June 11 and the Italian garrison immediately surrendered.[48]

But on June 26 Eisenhower admitted to Marshall that "the past two weeks have been a period of tenseness in this headquarters." The tension was largely the result of the approaching invasion of Sicily—Operation HUSKY. Although planning had begun in February, apart from command arrangements, Eisenhower did not refer to the upcoming HUSKY operation until he was certain that the success of the Tunisian campaign was assured, that is, after the blunting of the German counteroffensive in February.[49] In his comments, he made clear that he was determined to retain control over planning for the invasion. He had learned from TORCH the importance of the landings to the remainder of the campaign and this time would not abandon the decision to others.

Eisenhower originally had wanted a concentrated assault on the east and south portions of Sicily. Because the logistics staff protested that the area was too small for sufficient supplies to be brought in over the beach,[50] the planners widened the assault and shifted to an attack in several points from east to west. In turn, Montgomery immediately rejected the new

[47] Eisenhower, *Crusade in Europe*, pp. 164–66.
[48] Garland and Smyth, *Sicily*, pp. 69–73.
[49] Memorandum, July 1, 1943, *EP*, pp. 1230–33.
[50] *Ibid.* Garland and Smyth, *Sicily*, pp. 58–68; Bernard L. Montgomery, *The Memoirs of Field-Marshal the Viscount Montgomery of Alamein, K. G.* (Cleveland and New York, 1958), pp. 153–65; Bradley, *Soldier's Story*, pp. 101–2; Tedder, *With Prejudice*, pp. 425–35, discuss the arguments over planning.

plan, since he feared that the landing forces were too weak at any one point to defend themselves against counterattack.[51] Montgomery finally proposed that both the U.S. and British forces assault the southeastern corner.

The latest developments prompted another lament on March 29, repeating the one made March 3: "The HUSKY planning is onerous and difficult." Eisenhower wrote that he did not really like the new plan but felt he had no recourse. The real difficulty was and would remain throughout the war the lack of ships. Eisenhower's unhappiness with the latest plan was due to the difficulty of supplying troops over a single beach. With Tedder and Cunningham still displeased—they wanted as many attacks as possible in order to seize as many air fields as possible,[52] Eisenhower called a meeting to settle once and for all upon a final plan. The logistics staff, in the meanwhile, was reexamining the supply problem. The recently invented swimming truck—the DUKW (or duck) made it possible to land supplies over beaches, which removed Eisenhower's doubts, and he decided on May 3 to concentrate the attack in the south and east.[53] However, he extended Patton's landings farther to the west than Montgomery had wished.[54]

On May 5 Eisenhower told Marshall of the difficulty of attacking in mountainous terrain. Mobility was greatly impeded and the enemy could make use of the land for more effective defensive emplacements. Since the Sicilian coastline was mountainous, Eisenhower wanted to avoid a series of dispersed landings which might never be able to join each other. Still smarting from an attack by Marshall on the conservatism of the HUSKY planning,[55] he added: "These conclusions have *not* been developed by planners; they are the result of earnest consideration by the ground commanders."

Eisenhower coupled this reminder of his awareness that wars were not fought merely on the drawing board with a deferential refusal of Marshall's suggested immediate *ad hoc* invasion of Sicily to deprive the enemy of valuable needed time to prepare defenses. He agreed with Marshall that "the products of group planners always tend toward the orthodox and the mediocre and that commanders must at times kick the planners out the window and decide on these things for themselves."

Obviously Eisenhower had no intention of doing this. His original plan for the HUSKY invasion had been as conservative as the one finally adopted.[56] Reliance on risky alliance with the Vichy government and the

[51] Garland and Smyth, *Sicily*, pp. 60–61.
[52] *Ibid.*, p. 59.
[53] E. to CCS and BCOS; May 4, 1943, *EP*, p. 1113, n. 1.
[54] Garland and Smyth, *Sicily*, pp. 62–63.
[55] E. to M., May 4, 1943, *EP*, p. 1113, n. 1.
[56] Eisenhower vigorously defended the concentrated assault in *Crusade in Europe*, p. 164.

dismal outcome of the race for Tunis had convinced him that it was as important to insure against defeat as it was to try for victory.[57] Despite his constant claim that he hated conservative tactics, his plans and operations throughout the war would remain conservative. That he had no intention of an *ad hoc* HUSKY was apparent when he continued: "To be ready for some such attempt requires intensive preparation *now*—whereas we are throwing so much of our resources and energy into the current battle that we can do little else." Once again the master Eisenhower tactic of dealing with people was evident—"I agree with you, but. . . ."

On May 13, at the end of the Tunisian campaign, Eisenhower was even more conciliatory. Now that the decision not to do as Marshall suggested— mount an immediate HUSKY invasion—had been irrevocably made, he lamented his lack of rashness. This is not to say that he was insincere; no doubt he was anxious to get on with the campaign and did not look forward to an even larger amphibious operation than the one he had mounted in North Africa barely seven months previously. But he also knew the value of cutting your risks; combat had taught him this. Yet, apparently once again trying to placate Marshall, he said: "I am convinced that if I could undertake HUSKY today with only two divisions, I could gain a bridgehead and an advantage that would make the further conquest a very simple affair." This was written by the man who had first advocated an invasion of Sardinia as a prelude to aid in the invasion of Sicily, the man whose constant concern had been the lack of adequate air fields and support, the man who, only a week before, had pointed out the danger posed by the mountainous coastline! On July 1 he admitted, "Everyone is tremendously keyed up."

Yet Eisenhower was more confident of HUSKY success than he had been of the other landings.[58] He did not write Marshall on the eve of the landings as he had for the North African invasion, nor did he immediately send a flurry of references to the tactical situation. His letter of July 17 indicated that he was still learning in combat operations. Two nights after the original landing, elements of the 82d Airborne Division had been flown in to the rear of the Allied bases. Despite careful coordination, chance had intervened in the form of an attack by the German planes in the same area and at the same moment. In addition, a local counterattack was launched too late to inform the airborne troops. All of this resulted in serious losses. The lesson in this was ". . . that when we land airborne troops in hostile territory, we should *not do so in successive waves,* but should do it all at once."

Eisenhower next referred to the campaign on July 21, informing

---

[57] Eisenhower uses this criterion specifically in a defense of Montgomery in *Ibid.,* pp. 178–79.

[58] Memorandum, July 1, 1943, *EP,* pp. 1230–33.

Marshall of a greater role for the U.S. Seventh Army. The switch in tactics came about because Montgomery was reluctant, in the face of stiff German opposition, to continue his attack on Catania. Alexander allowed Patton's Seventh Army, which had been protecting Montgomery's flank and rear, to attack east along the north coast to Messina.[59] This attack, although it brought fame to the army and to Patton, served very little tactical purpose. It occurred chiefly because Patton persevered in his insistence on having his army on the offensive.[60] Eisenhower mentioned tactical operations only once more during the remainder of the month-long campaign.

With the success in Sicily, Eisenhower's next operational concern was the invasion of Italy, Operation AVALANCHE. In a letter written two days before the landings at Salerno, Eisenhower explained why he had not written before the Sicilian invasion but was writing now. When Montgomery landed on the toe of Italy on September 3 and met little opposition, Eisenhower was not surprised. "However, the AVALANCHE operation is a horse of a different color and I am frank to state that there is more than a good possibility that we may have some hard going."[61] Eisenhower had already been more cautious in selecting the invasion site than Marshall desired. Marshall and the other members of the CCS preferred a landing further north, but Eisenhower insisted on a closer beach that was within the range of air fighter support.[62]

Eisenhower evinced even more concern on the 13th,[63] five days after the landings, maintaining that all hinged on air power. But by the 20th he was much more comfortable about the outcome of the battle. As it turned out, the 13th had been "our worst day."[64] He provided Marshall with a detailed account of his planned order of battle and the disposition of resources he was making. The Germans' vulnerable point was their single line of communication. Eisenhower's hope that air power would completely neutralize this German weakness was not borne out by events, but the close air support did prove crucial enough to convince Eisenhower of the need for interdiction of the battlefield as far as possible, a policy which was to prove successful in France. After the capture of Naples,[65] the Italian campaign bogged down in the mud and mountains of Italy and Eisenhower ceased to refer to it.

[59] Garland and Smyth, *Sicily*, p. 248.
[60] Farago, *Patton*, pp. 301–14; Garland and Smyth, *Sicily*, pp. 208–11.
[61] See also Garland and Smyth, *Sicily*, p. 482, and Eisenhower, *Crusade in Europe*, pp. 185–86 for the dangers inherent in the Salerno landings.
[62] Garland and Smyth, *Sicily*, pp. 260–62.
[63] For the difficulties at Salerno, see Clark, *Calculated Risk*, pp. 183–215 and Eisenhower, *Crusade in Europe*, pp. 185–90.
[64] Eisenhower tells of the gloomy outlook of September 13th in *Crusade in Europe*, pp. 187–88.
[65] The Allies entered Naples on October 1. Clark, *Calculated Risk*, p. 213.

Eisenhower had learned in his new role as battle commander. His great lesson in combat tactics was caution. Having raced and lost in Tunisia, he concluded that he had misallocated his resources. Despite the fact that there were factors present that he could and would change in future operations, he would no longer employ rush tactics. Eisenhower always regarded as the supreme proof of his recklessness his advocacy of the assault on Pantelleria, where he, almost alone, believed that naval and air bombardment would bring about a surrender. That he would so regard this attack on a bombarded, blockaded island is indicative of the generally conservative tone of his tactical approach. He believed that a commander had to guard against the unexpected. In Tunisia, it was the question of command, the difficulty of the terrain, problems of supply, the necessity of close air power, the weather, personality, and nationalistic problems which endangered battlefield success, difficulties of communication, ineffectiveness of equipment, bad leadership, the diplomatic maze, and above all the weakness of the invading force. These same problems arose in other operations in the Mediterranean. There is no wonder that the man who overcame these difficulties became circumspect.

DIPLOMACY

Eisenhower encountered serious diplomatic problems in the Mediterranean, but Marshall felt that he should not spend an undue amount of his time on matters of that nature. Eisenhower's first letter of November 9 was marked by his annoyance with the French. Pronouncing himself "absolutely furious," he lambasted Giraud, on whom the Allies had pinned their initial hopes for an armistice. He then talked about Admiral Darlan, whom the Allies had in protective custody. Eisenhower had sent Clark to negotiate the "Darlan Deal," in which Darlan signed an armistice on behalf of the Vichy forces. This agreement allowing the Vichy French to retain administrative control of North Africa with Darlan in charge,[66] caused a furor in the United States and the United Kingdom because of Darlan's pro-Fascist policies.[67] Eisenhower himself later commented that the U.S. and Britain had "miscalculated" with respect to personalities and their influence in North Africa, as well as the general sympathies of the French population.[68]

The unsatisfactory diplomatic developments had further repercussions. On November 17th Eisenhower expressed his gratitude at Marshall's and Roosevelt's acceptance of the arrangements. Marshall, of course, un-

[66] Howe, *Northwest Africa*, pp. 269-71.
[67] Feis, *Churchill–Roosevelt–Stalin*, pp. 88–92; Howe, *Northwest Africa*, p. 268.
[68] Eisenhower, *Crusade in Europe*, p. 111.

reservedly backed Eisenhower, but Roosevelt was not willing to accept Darlan indefinitely.[69] On November 30 Eisenhower told of developments in negotiations with the Governor General, Pierre Boisson. Boisson had arrived from Dakar to complete an agreement in which he placed himself under Darlan and guaranteed the same type of assistance to the Americans in his area that Darlan had given them.[70] Eisenhower, involved in this tangle and receiving reams of criticism on all sides, had sent Smith to Washington to try to mute the complaints.[71] Smith succeeded, but as one result of the turmoil, Marshall advised Eisenhower on December 22 to leave diplomatic matters to his subordinates and to direct his own attention to the battle in Tunisia,[72] which was going badly, and suffered from command problems as well. Consequently, Eisenhower sharply reduced his comments on diplomacy. When later the opportunity to conclude a potentially helpful arrangement with the Italian Fascists presented itself, he felt it necessary to check first with Washington, leading to protracted negotiations which precluded a decisive victory in Italy.[73]

On January 17, Eisenhower first mentioned Charles de Gaulle, the leader of the anti-Vichy Free French,[74] who was contending with Giraud for French leadership. On February 4 he wrote of Giraud, "He is volatile rather than stable." Roosevelt was afraid that Giraud's diminishing popularity would imperil the rear areas and also objected to De Gaulle's efforts to replace Boisson in French West Africa. Therefore Eisenhower arranged a meeting with the two Frenchmen on June 19 to convey the President's objectives. Although the meeting proved unsatisfactory, the situation improved shortly thereafter when the French Committee of National Liberation named Giraud Commander in Chief for North and West African forces and De Gaulle Commander in Chief for other areas. The two were each responsible to a war committee under the Free French.[75] Few realized it, but this was actually a clear indication of De Gaulle's increasing

[69] Pogue, *Ordeal and Hope*, pp. 420–21. At this time Eisenhower had also received a broadside from Churchill because Eisenhower's staff in London, looking ahead to operations against Italy, had prepared a directive stating that Italians could earn immunity from retribution by withholding support from the Germans. E. to Smith, November 17, 1942, *EP*, p. 727, n.1.

[70] Howe, *Northwest Africa*, pp. 271–72.

[71] *Ibid.*, p. 270.

[72] Pogue, *Ordeal and Hope*, p. 423.

[73] A clear and comprehensive account of the complicated Italian surrender negotiations is in Garland and Smyth, *Sicily*, pp. 435–553.

[74] There are many accounts of De Gaulle's relations with the other Allies in addition to the general diplomatic works. Charles de Gaulle, *The War Memoirs of Charles de Gaulle*, 3 vols. (New York, 1955–60) is his personal record. Milton Viorst, *Hostile Allies: FDR and Charles de Gaulle* (New York, 1965), is a full account.

[75] Feis, *Churchill–Roosevelt–Stalin*, pp. 138–40; Viorst, *Hostile Allies*, pp. 167–82; Butcher, *My Three Years*, pp. 335–37.

control. Eisenhower was no more astute on the point at the time than anyone else. On June 26 he wrote "I am sure that De Gaulle is losing ground, but strangely enough this is not resulting in a strengthening of Giraud." On July 1, he was grateful but wary: "The political situation has been relatively quiet on the surface, but one never knows, with these people, what is going on underneath. We simply must be patient but watchful."

After June, 1943, the Italian surrender dominated the diplomatic activities of Eisenhower's headquarters, although he did not mention it until September 6, just before the armistice was finalized. A week later he told of a proposed meeting with Marshal Pietro Badoglio, who was charged with the surrender negotiations. These are Eisenhower's only references to the affair. As noted previously, the negotiations went through an incredible series of twists and turns, which Eisenhower followed closely but could not have been expected to report in great detail. Having decided that he would not proceed on his own, every quarter-step in any direction had to be minutely supervised by higher authorities. The job at hand was simply one of arbitration from a position handed down by Washington.

The diplomatic problems Eisenhower had encountered in the Mediterranean gave him bitter experience on which to draw. Having made a deal with the Vichy in North Africa and brought a storm of condemnation on his head, he hesitated to act independently in the Italian surrender. The prolonged negotiations brought about a much worsened military situation and the resulting political settlement was much like what Eisenhower would have settled for in the first place. But he realized that diplomatic problems would continue and, as the commander on the ground, he would have to confront them.

VISITING TROOPS

Although he had written to Marshall of his visits to commanders, Eisenhower did not comment on the troops themselves until April 16, 1943: "My great concern is to get for these units the finest possible leadership that we can produce." The way to do this was by putting them into attacks ". . . where they can be assured of local victories and gradually gain that winning spirit that will make them top flight units." Perhaps this remark is the clue to why Eisenhower did not write about the troops—he preferred not to be in the position of constantly criticizing the U.S. units, and there had been nothing exemplary about which he could write. By May 5, about a week before the end of the Tunisian campaign, Eisenhower could at last comment favorably, and on June 26, having visited the 82d Airborne and the 2d Armored Divisions in training for

HUSKY he "found them in splendid shape." In a letter of July 1 he was enthusiastic about the 3d Division. On July 17 he remarked on visiting the Sicilian front, noting that the men were "in good heart."

The brevity of Eisenhower's comments concerning the troops under his command was probably inevitable. Although he was aware of the need for a commander to be seen by his men and often went among them,[76] there were some unavoidable complications—the great distances and the lackluster performances of the U.S. troops. Even so, there was a limit to what he could say about them to a superior. He could ask for more effective training, comment about discipline, decorate, promote, reduce, and praise. Beyond that, he pointed out deficiencies to his subordinates.[77] Eisenhower had not had very much command experience—he had not led troops at a level of command in which he would have mingled on a less ritualistic level than as a Supreme Commander. He and Marshall had been staff officers. When he spoke of personnel, even though he would often comment in personal terms, it was within the framework of command and strategy.

PERSONAL COMMENTS

The Supreme Commander was human and his maturing relationship with Marshall reflected this. Eisenhower was still Marshall's loyal subordinate but had become a battle-tested combat commander, a distinction Marshall could not claim. He was dutifully respectful and concerned about Marshall's views but did not hesitate to complain about his own problems and discuss what he had learned from combat experiences.

Eisenhower's first task was to convince Marshall that he could endure the rigors of battle. Throughout the Tunisian campaign he reassured Marshall that he was physically sound. He learned a lesson—"a full measure of health is basic to successful command."[78] On May 13 when the Tunisian campaign ended, he gave his final reassurance, "Actually, my health was never better." Eisenhower felt that he had demonstrated his ability to stand the stress of combat and so never again mentioned it.[79]

His relationship with Marshall reflected his growing education in other ways as well. He eschewed the almost fawning flattery of 1942, rarely mentioned liaison with the War Department, and no longer eagerly sought

[76] Eisenhower, *Crusade in Europe*, p. 238.

[77] See, for example, *ibid.*, pp. 313–16.

[78] *Ibid.*, p. 132.

[79] Butcher, *My Three Years*, pp. 247–48 tells of Marshall's continuing concern about Eisenhower's health.

War Department staff assistance. Instead he sent back lessons learned in battle. He made very few references to visits from U.S. personnel other than Marshall, and these references to others are often tinged with irritation at their taking up his time. All of this is not to suggest that Eisenhower became Marshall's equal. It does suggest that, while he continued to express gratitude and respect in his personal statements to Marshall, the expressions became more balanced. A fairly complete account of these comments reflects this new relationship.

On November 9 he asked Marshall to express his gratitude to Marshall's principal assistants in the War Department for all their help. On the 17th he noted his delight at the President's message of congratulations. Three days later he asked Marshall to assure the Secretary of State of his cooperation in the matter of civil affairs and thank the Secretary of War for his message of congratulations.

There were four letters in which Eisenhower talked of Marshall's January visit to the North African theater. He told Marshall on January 10 that he was looking forward to meeting him and getting Marshall's reaction to prospects in the North African theater. He felt sure that the CCS would want the review done from the standpoint of the Commander in Chief: "I feel so confident of my complete familiarity with all major factors that I think technicians would be a mere hindrance." This uncharacteristic outburst may have been prompted by the widespread suspicion that he did not have as complete a grip on the sphere of battle as he should have had. On the 30th he referred for the last time to Marshall's visit, saying, "Again I tell you that your visit here did more for us—and particularly for me— than could any other thing." This was probably no exaggeration. Eisenhower, promoted over hundreds of American officers to command, tasting combat for the first time, experiencing the practical difficulties of getting the Americans, British, and French to fight together, losing the race for Tunis, drawing criticism for the Darlan Deal—must certainly have been buoyed by the visit of the man who had selected him for the job, the man who alone kept telling him to concern himself only with making his military decisions, the man who would do his best to shield him.

On January 27 Eisenhower asked a personal favor of Marshall, something he rarely did, requesting that his superior inform Mrs. Eisenhower before the public announcement if he were promoted to full general.[80] Then on January 30 Eisenhower referred to a rug he had given to Mrs. Marshall: "So far as I can recall, I have never before in my service given a personal present to my superior or to a member of his family, and I assure you that I regard this as a real privilege." He discussed the present

---

[80] Marshall, of course, did so. Butcher, *My Three Years*, p. 259.

again on June 26, because Marshall had given the rug to Mrs. Eisenhower as a present from her husband.

On February 21, at the most crucial point in the Tunisia campaign, he told Marshall that a visit to the front had disclosed the necessity for a considerable rebuilding. He wrote, "This was my job." No doubt this reflected his tension—Eisenhower certainly did not have to tell Marshall that his place was in reallocating resources, not in charging with the troops into Kasserine Pass. After the near disasters of late February and the consequent flurry of communications, Eisenhower protested on March 3, "Please do not look upon any communication I send you as a defensive explanation. Not only do I refuse to indulge in alibis but, frankly, I feel that you have given such evidence of confidence in me, that I never experience the feeling of having to defend my actions." On March 11 he rejected a Marshall proposal to transfer personnel between various tested and untested divisions in order to gain experience for as many troops as possible.[81] But he softened the rejection by stating: "However, I hope to apply your idea on a more moderate scale by getting into HUSKY formations a number of seasoned troop officers and non-commissioned officers." Eisenhower complained on the 29th about the lack of shipping for HUSKY, saying that "we seem always to be skating close to the edge of unjustified or at least dangerous risk." He added that Admiral Cunningham had spoken of Marshall "in terms that would have excited the pride of any individual." Eisenhower's plea about shipping for HUSKY made his letter of May 5, in which he said that he wished he could execute the HUSKY invasion immediately, as Marshall had desired, even more fanciful. This wishful thinking was echoed on the 13th. It is hard to believe that Eisenhower really felt this way, and it is important to note that he was nonetheless rejecting Marshall's plan.

On June 26, Eisenhower confessed to tension over the approaching HUSKY landings. He told Marshall on July 21 that he had received his circular letter on indoctrination of troops: "It is a remarkably good letter and one that I feel needed to be written." On September 6 he returned to the subject of his own operations, assuring Marshall, "our commanders and troops are in good heart; and in view of the great prize that may be won and the fact that, if ever, this is the psychological time to strike, I am determined to hit as hard as I can." He noted Marshall's reappointment as Chief of Staff and told him, "I wouldn't even know how to proceed here if I didn't have the assurance of your firm backing and your complete understanding behind me every minute of the day." When the Italian battle was in doubt on the 13th he told Marshall, "con-

[81] E. to McNarney, March 2, 1943, *EP*, p. 1004, n. 2.

sidering for a moment the worst that could possibly develop, I would in that event, merely announce that one of our landings had been repulsed—due to my error in misjudging the strength of the enemy at that place." This letter was the real Eisenhower—he had previously excused himself from various minor errors on matters of promotion and other concerns, but when real disaster loomed he accepted the responsibility. He was to make somewhat the same statement in anticipation of the landings at Normandy, but at that time felt no need to mention it to anyone. He merely put it in his wallet for later use if necessary.[82]

Eisenhower also showed concern for future operations in Europe. On August 24 and September 20 Eisenhower discussed those subordinates he felt Marshall might want to have in his OVERLORD command. He realized that since OVERLORD was now definitely slated for May or June, 1944, his own theater would soon be a secondary one, but he accepted this. Perhaps he felt—he certainly hoped—that he would play a role in the invasion of Europe, but this was not enough to account for the simple acceptance. Eisenhower had the typical American military leader's commitment to the cross-Channel invasion, but this too was not enough. He might be expected to feel that a greater effort should continue to be made in the Mediterranean. After all, he had successfully commanded two amphibious invasions, and was preparing to conduct a third on the mainland of Italy. There had to be something else. The "something else" was that Eisenhower remembered his own analysis in 1942 of the type of man who should be sent to command the American troops. He must be a man loyal to the Chief of Staff and a man able to accept *any* role in the final command structure, even the most secondary one. So the accounting had come. OVERLORD was Marshall's—Eisenhower would give him his best.

Eisenhower did not write Marshall during October and November. Partly this was because Marshall visited the theater for the Cairo Conference in November. But it also reflected a certain uneasiness, for newspapers had manufactured a feud of sorts between the two men over command of the cross-Channel invasion. Both men denied the existence of a feud, and were undoubtedly sincere.[83] But a new strangeness had to exist as the two for a time appeared in the role of competitors. A characteristically thoughtful gesture by Marshall made Eisenhower more comfortable. Prior to leaving the Mediterranean, on December 17, Eisenhower thanked Marshall for "your thoughtfulness in sending me the memorandum, in your handwriting, on which the agreement was made in Teheran that I was to command OVERLORD."[84]

[82] Butcher, *My Three Years*, p. 610.

[83] In his *Crusade in Europe*, p. 209, Eisenhower maintains that it was Marshall's decision more than anyone else's to give him the job.

[84] See also, Eisenhower, *Crusade in Europe*, pp. 207–9.

All the problems overcome, all the lessons learned brought about the growth of a more confident commander. Eisenhower felt that he had handled things rather well. He had landed in North Africa a junior untested American at invasion points decided by others. He had run into trouble immediately, having encountered command difficulties, diplomatic entanglements, deep nationalistic acrimony, and a battle stalemate. But he had made the best of the diplomatic situation, straightened out his command structure, and resisted attempts to change it. He had made the key planning decisions on the invasions of Sicily and Italy and he had been named to command the cross-Channel invasion.

His personal comments to Marshall were rarely fulsome. He still wrote in periods of special tension—the landings in North Africa, the battle at Kasserine, Salerno beach. But he thanked him only occasionally in extravagant terms and his reassurances of will to win were rare. When this is matched against his negative comments—his complaining about the British, the French, problems of communication, command, visitors, staff errors, and everything else—it is clear that, even with the caveat that Marshall no doubt agreed with many of the complaints, Eisenhower did appear at times anything but optimistic. When in London, his only real contention had been in the areas Marshall had already complained about, most notably the British, and he had reversed his criticism of them when Marshall had counseled the need for cooperation. Moreover, by this time Eisenhower no longer minded rejecting, albeit with great tact, Marshall's ideas calling for an *ad hoc* HUSKY or shifting of personnel in divisions. He had even relieved the man whom Marshall had urged upon him to lead the American troops in North Africa. Finally, he had advised Marshall on combat operations in the light of his own battle-field experience. Marshall had responded to all of these things by assuring Eisenhower of his complete support.

Eisenhower reflected this growth in confidence and responsibility in his letters to Marshall. By December, 1943, he was a man willing to take independent positions, a man who had proved worthy of the highest command. Because Marshall and Roosevelt realized this, the President could keep his Chief of Staff in Washington in the most vital army job of all, and name Eisenhower to lead the invasion of Europe.

Dear General: We are in the afternoon of the second day and I don't mind confessing to you that it seems like it's been at least a month since 1:00 A.M. yesterday morning. I found last night, however, and to my great satisfaction, that I slept long and solidly, better than I have at any time in the last fourteen weeks. Undoubtedly, it was due to the apparently good start that we have made.

If we had come in here merely to whip this French Army, I would be registering nothing but complete satisfaction at this moment. I am irritated though to think that every bullet we have to expend against the French is that much less in the pot with which to operate against the Axis. Worse than that, every minute that we lose will mean a week of reorganization and straightening out later, and I am so impatient to get eastward and seize the ground in the Tunisian area that I find myself getting absolutely furious with these stupid Frogs.

Of course, by the time you get this, you will have had so many reports of developments that there is no use taking up your time to try to get the picture as we now have it. I have had no reports either from Patton or Fredendall today, but have directed the Naval Task Forces in those regions to give me the best possible summary as of four o'clock this afternoon. Naturally, any real development will be radioed to you at once.

The Kingpin proved most difficult. Even so, I could have forgiven him if he would have stepped out vigorously to stop the French resistance. Actually he is doing everything possible to kill time until the French have quit of their own accord. After that he wants to step in and become the knight in shining armor that rallies all North Africa and becomes finally the Saviour of France.

Since yesterday afternoon, we have had Darlan in protective custody at Algiers. Clark left for that area today, where he will establish my Advanced C.P.[1] He has been empowered to treat with Darlan and to do his best to get real advantages out of Darlan's influence with the French fleet. But to show you what I have on my hands in the way of temperamental Frenchmen—Darlan states that he will not talk to any Frenchmen; Giraud hates and distrusts Darlan. It's a mess! I get weary of people that have no other thought but "ME".

My biggest operational difficulty at the moment is the slowness in straightening out the Oran region. That is the real key to the development of air power here, and I must get it soon. The trouble is that I have no real reserves with which to intervene. I have one Commando Battalion in Gibraltar that I will send down there very quickly if the matter is not straightened out soon. We have had to be very careful at this point because of uncertainty as to the Spanish situation.

We are laboring mightily to get decent signal communications into Algiers. As soon as I can control the area from there and maintain proper communications with the Combined Chiefs of Staff, I will leave this spot. I want to get closer to the area whose seizure is vital to us.

I trust that Generals Arnold, Somervell, Handy and all your other principal assistants know how deeply we feel obligated to them for the fine support they have given this effort.

With warm personal regards, *Sincerely*

[1] Command post.

15 GIBRALTAR *November 17, 1942*

Dear General: General Clark and I have worked like dogs on this political situation, but I think there is no need to repeat the story here since my lengthy cable of last Saturday told it pretty well. I am pleased that you and the President saw the thing in realistic terms and realize that we are making the best of a rather bad bargain. In any event, the so-called North African Army and Navy are placed under our two best friends, Giraud and Michelier.[1] The chance for the Toulon fleet seems gone—but we might yet get the Dakar contingent!

One thing bothering us is the congestion and damage in the harbors at Casablanca and at Oran. At the latter place, we are making very splendid progress in rehabilitation, which is in some measure due to excellent work by Brigadier General Larkin of our Engineers.[2] At Casablanca, also, we are getting ahead and, luckily, the small ports near there are partially usable.

A particular problem exists in Morocco, where conditions are much different from what they are in the rest of North Africa. First of all, the tribal question there is always a serious one and we must uphold the local French regime or we will encounter great difficulties. In fact, we're forced to keep the French relatively strong, militarily. At first, General Nogues,[3] who commands the French in Morocco, was particularly difficult to handle. At bottom, however, he is a sail-trimmer and he now believes that his best interests parallel ours. His protestations of cooperative intent are most emphatic, but he is unquestionably "slick."

On the military side, there are three main concerns. The first is the early capture of Tunisia, a job that presents peculiar problems. I will not weary you with the details but, since we had to come into this country with a minimum of transport and the distances involved are almost stupendous, you can well see what a headache we have in logistics and in troop movements. We are working our transport planes hard but, of course, cannot use them in advance of fighter cover since the Axis has got quite a bit of air into the Bizerte-Tunis region. I have reinforced Anderson with all the mobile elements that are immediately available. I must say that I have

89

been highly pleased with Anderson's dash and determination and, although we are badly extended down there and operating by driblets, it is my view that boldness rather than numbers is needed and I have encouraged and directed him to keep driving.

The next military problem is the submarine. Recent messages show that the U.S. Navy is getting some extra anti-sub stuff into Casablanca, where it is badly needed, and the British are doing a pretty good job inside the Mediterranean. The approaches to the Strait, however, are our weakest spot and from the chart of submarine locations, which is shown me daily, it looks like the Axis was ganging up on us to take advantage of the opportunity. We have worked frantically to get ships unloaded and started on their return trip but, after the first two days, we began losing more vessels than I had hoped would be the case. It is a problem that requires eternal effort in order to keep ahead of the other fellow.

The third military problem is Spain. I believe that the British diplomatic people have done a good job in the region and our latest advices are to the effect that we have a very sympathetic attitude in the country. However, all are agreed that Spain could offer little resistance if the Germans should attempt to come through in any amount of force and, unless Spain should *attempt* to resist the German, they *might* resist us when we tried to enter Spanish Morocco, and we'd be badly embarrassed. The next sixty days are going to be anxious ones in this regard, but at the end of that time our forces should be sufficiently well concentrated and prepared to give a good account of themselves in the Straits region. In the meantime, I have to watch the French, who would, I think, like to pick a quarrel with Spain.

My own worry is communications. For some strange reason, radio seems to work at its lowest level of efficiency in this area, and I am constantly battling, with airplane messengers and aerial reconnaissance, to keep contact with our scattered forces. Under present conditions, Gibraltar is the best point in the region from which to keep contact and is, moreover, the focus of all incoming communications from Washington and London. These facts tend to tie me rather closely here—sometimes to my tense irritation. The other day I felt that my presence in Algiers was mandatory, and I made a hurried trip down. But now, in an effort to get bombing operations started in the east, I have even deprived myself of my one command plane (B–17), but am expecting more in soon. By day after tomorrow I can again resume making short trips through the region.

In spite of increasing my difficulties in the signal communications line, I am going to establish my headquarters at Algiers as quickly as fairly decent contact between this point and that one can be maintained, by the last of this week, I hope.

When Tunisia is firmly in our hands, I will consider that the second phase of these operations is largely complete and we can begin the third of preparing for further strategic moves. The first one will be the completion of the destruction of Axis forces in North Africa. After that, I favor the Sardinian project, if we are to continue the advance from this sector. But before that is undertaken, a very broad strategic review by the Combined Chiefs of Staff will probably have been made.

From the reports that I have so far been able to gather from the field, our outstanding performers were Major General Fredendall, Brigadier General Oliver,[4] Brigadier General Larkin, and Colonel Robinett[5] of the Central Force; Major General Harmon[6] and possibly Brigadier General Truscott[7] from the West; in the East Colonel O'Daniel[8] of the 168th Infantry seemed to be the man. I have recommended the two Regimental Commanders to you for promotion to Brigadier, and Oliver for advancement to Division Command. I am not quite ready yet to submit my final word on Fredendall because both Clark and I intend to get into that area this week and review the whole affair on the ground. All the British Naval Officers, including the British Naval Commander of the Central Task Force, give Fredendall a very fine send-off. They think he is doing a marvelous job.

As I've told you before, I'm well satisfied with all my people. I don't believe that any commander was ever sent to the field with his principal staff and command subordinates representing a higher average of professional ability and a higher sense of loyalty and devotion to duty than it has been my good fortune to have here. Long hours and incessant work roll off their backs like water off a duck.

It would be idle for me to say that I have not felt some degree of strain. At times during the past fifteen or sixteen weeks, I have definitely felt the urge to play hookey for a day or so. However, I find that I am bearing up very well and, though it seems more like a year since November 8th than merely eight days, I'm sure I am in as good condition as when the thing started.

We were all delighted with the warmth of the President's congratulatory message, and I had it published to the entire command without delay. The British were highly delighted that he included them so generously in his message. I was personally pleased that he commented upon the unification achieved in this Allied venture. I noted, too, in press reports today that you commented on the subject in a speech. I truly think we've done something pretty good in that line, and was particularly happy that you made special note of it.

With best wishes for your continued health and with cordial personal regard, *Sincerely*

[1] Vice Admiral François Michelier commanded the French Naval Forces at Casablanca.
[2] Brigadier General Thomas Bernard Larkin (USMA 1915) was both chief engineer and commander of the Center Task Force's Service of Supply. He became commanding general of the SOS in February, 1943.
[3] General Auguste Noguès was Resident General of French Morocco.
[4] Brigadier General Lunsford Everett Oliver (USMA 1913) commanded Combat Command B (CCB) of the 1st Armored Division; he was shortly promoted to major general and given command of the 5th Armored Division in the United States.

91

⁵ Colonel Paul McD. Robinett commanded a section of Oliver's Combat Command B. He was promoted to brigadier general on November 20 and succeeded Oliver as commander of CCB.

⁶ Major General Ernest Nason Harmon (USMA 1917) commanded the 2d Armored Division which landed at Safi. In April, 1943, he assumed command of the 1st Armored Division.

⁷ Brigadier General Lucian King Truscott, Jr., who had joined the Regular Army in October, 1917, commanded the sub-task force that had attacked Mehdia and Port Lyautey. He was promoted to major general on November 21 and activated the Advance Command Post at Constantine on January 14, 1943, remaining there as Eisenhower's deputy. In March he took command of the 3d Armored Infantry Division.

⁸ Colonel John Wilson O'Daniel commanded the 168th Combat Team in its landings west of Algiers. He was promoted to brigadier general on November 20.

16 ALGIERS   *November 30, 1942*

Dear General: In these crowded days I lose all track of the calendar and have no idea whether it is a matter of three days or two weeks since I last wrote to you. In any event, I have just returned from a trip in the forward areas and felt you would be interested in a review of the current situation.

First of all, you will understand that when I made the decision to rush our forces into Tunisia as rapidly as possible, I did so in full realization that we were assuming the inescapable risk of having bases damaged, particularly by night air attack, of sabotage on lines of communication, and of having some of our small columns get into bad tactical situations. However, I felt that the Axis was startled and upset by our initial landing and that I was perfectly justified in assuming any risks that did not actually jeopardize seriously what we had already gained.

As a result of this decision, Anderson is already well forward. (I am dictating this from my bed where I am confined today with a heavy cold, and do not have the benefit of maps and other aids. Consequently, there may be a misspelled word or two—particularly in names of places.) Yesterday Anderson's right was just east of Tebourba with his light reconnaissance forces reaching out well to the southeast. The left of his main force was at Mateur. He had two Brigade Groups on the general line with the "Blade" Force,¹ of something over a regiment of armor, operating in their support. Working with Blade were two American Tank Battalions—one light and one medium. The mediums were still largely in reserve. Coming up behind is the Guards Brigade of Anderson's 78th Division. One battalion of this brigade has gotten well forward and the remainder is pushing up as rapidly as possible. On top of this, the remainder of Oliver's Combat Command "B" was moving rapidly into the forward areas. At noon on November 29th his tanks were in the region of Souk-el-Arba and his Armored Infantry was marching forward, with its tail just west of Guelma. With luck he should be in position for taking part in the advance by tomorrow morning, December 1st. When Oliver gets on the line, he will take command, under Anderson, of all Armored Forces.

To the south of this general region, French Forces are providing protection for Anderson's right flank. Scattered among these French forces, particularly in the Tebessa-Gafsa region, is a small mixed detachment of Americans commanded by Colonel Raff,[2] who has done a magnificent piece of work. By his dash and skill, and the exemplary conduct of the U.S. Troops, he has vastly raised the morale of the French Forces and we have derived untold benefit from the coverage we have thus secured.

On the airdrome near Tebessa are 54 of our P-38's, of which at least 40 are operational, and a squadron of DB-7's. The British Air Force has two small fields—one at Souk-el-Arba and the other somewhat to the rear of that, from which they are operating Spitfires to give an umbrella to our foot troops. It is in this job we're having real difficulty. (See Note 1.)[3]

Malta Air Forces are working against Axis shipping, Axis ports of embarkation and against the Ports of Tunis and Bizerte. In addition, our B-17's have been attempting to smash the North Quay at Bizerte, where it seems apparent the greater portion of the German debarkation is taking place.

Because of great distances and very poor signal communications, certain errors in operation and execution of combined air-ground plans have taken place. So far as these are avoidable through definite orders and constant circulation of Staff Officers and Commanders, we are eliminating them, so that everything is coordinated to the single objective of taking Tunisia. We are devoting everything to Anderson's support. Over and above forces previously mentioned, the 6th Armored Division (British) will soon come into the forward area. It will not be up in time for the next push but its early entry into that region will furnish a fine reserve that will give Anderson a lot of confidence. Coming up now, from the Casablanca area, are 25 of the latest U.S. medium tanks. They are going by railroad and, if all goes well, should reach the Souk-el-Arba area in a matter of a week to ten days. I ordered them up a week ago, but it has taken time to get rolling stocks, etc.

Under current conditions, the forces I have mentioned represent the maximum that we can sustain in Tunisia. Even by using transport airplanes for supply of critical items, the logistics situation is one to make a ritualist in warfare go just a bit hysterical. From Algiers to the eastward, we can run a total of 9 small trains per day. 2 of these have to haul coal to operate the railroad; 1 is the barest minimum to keep the civilian population from starving. This leaves 6 for military purposes, and since we have been trying both to crowd troops forward, particularly armor, and to supply what we have already there, you can see that reserves of munitions and rations are almost at the vanishing point. The highway is in fairly good condition and strafing by the enemy has not been serious west of Souk-el-Arba. However, motor transport is something we just don't have and, in spite of impressing every kind of scrawny vehicle that can run, we have not been able to do much by road, except in pushing forward parts of Armored Units. So far as we can, we ship by sea to Bone, but the job of providing satisfactory air cover is one that is just a bit beyond our means. However, Cunningham is bold and in spite of some losses we have gotten a lot of stuff forward that way.

My immediate aim is to keep pushing hard, with a first intention of pinning the enemy back in the Fortress of Bizerte and confining him so closely that the danger of a break-out or a heavy counter offensive will be minimized. Then I expect to put everything we have, in the way of air and artillery, on him and to pound him so hard that the way for a final and decisive blow can be adequately prepared. While that preparation is going on, we can clean up the territory to the south. In this plan, our greatest concern is to keep the air going efficiently on inadequate, isolated fields.

In a confused, fluid situation, such as this, rumors flow thick and fast and are so conflicting that it is a real job to separate the true from the false. By the same token, a commander quickly learns which of his subordinates are to be trusted under all circumstances to do a fine work-manlike job and which ones he has to watch closely and handle by special means in order to get the best out of them.

Anderson, Commanding the First British Army, is apparently imbued with the will to win, but blows hot and cold, by turns, in his estimates and resulting demands. Oliver has impressed me more favorably than any other Division or lower Commander I have encountered. Cunningham is a joy to have around. Welsh, the British Air Commander, is a sound statistical planner but rather devoid of imagination and, I think, lacking in drive. Doolittle is a curious mixture; he has certain strong points and fine qualities and I am going to considerable trouble to handle him in such a way as to help him eliminate his faults, in the belief that he will develop into a really brilliant air force commander. Young Raff, 35 years old, is apparently a find. I will want more opportunity to observe before I go completely overboard on him, but I think that he is a natural leader, possesses a very fine tactical sense, has the admirable quality of visualizing his own minor operations within the framework of the whole, and is an energetic, resourceful officer.

Yesterday, during my absence, my Headquarters had the embarrassing duty of asking you to hold up the promotion of Colonel Duncan, Air Corps,[4] whom we had previously recommended for Brigadier General. Since last June, this is the second time a thing like this has happened and, in both instances, I was originally skeptical of the individual and held up for several weeks the recommendation of the man's immediate superior. In both cases, I finally felt compelled to go along with my immediate subordinates, but I assure you that when anything like this happens my face gets extremely red. I try to be most conservative and sure of myself in submitting to you recommendations for promotion to higher positions.

Boisson[5] arrived from Dakar yesterday and conferences started with him immediately. He has obviously come here, according to Mr. Murphy, to complete a definite written agreement that places himself under Darlan, and in which he apparently expects to subscribe, generally, to the same type of assistance to the Americans that Darlan has agreed to give in this region. In accordance with the general understanding I have with you by radio, I had hoped to secure here only an agreement as to principle and to have all other negotiations take place in Dakar, carried on for the United States by a mission specially selected in Washington. So far as it is possible to do so, I will still observe this principle; but I feel that we cannot possibly throw cold water in Boisson's face, when he has come here in an attitude of going overboard for us. In any event, the presence of an American Mission in Dakar will be necessary, both to develop details of agreement and to supervise the execution of the cooperative effort. I will keep you fully advised as to developments here.

This morning I received your telegram concerning the functions of the State Department in developing the economy of this particular theater. I agree with every word of it and I can assure you that no trouble whatsoever will occur in the execution of the plan. I shall be obliged if you will assure the Secretary of State of my desire to assist him in every possible way. The sooner I can get rid of all these questions that are outside the military in scope, the happier I will be! Sometimes I think I live ten years each week, of which at least nine are absorbed in political and economic matters.

Upon my return from the east this morning, I was handed a most commendatory message sent me by the Secretary of War. I answered immediately but, if it is not imposing upon you too much, would you please assure him, in person, of my intense satisfaction in receiving word of his official approval of what we've done to date.

With best wishes for your continued good health,

[1] A mixed mobile and armored unit.
[2] Colonel Edson D. Raff (USMA 1933) commanded a small parachute detachment on the south flank.
[3] Note (1), written at the bottom of page 2 of this letter, noted: "A message received from Anderson since writing this letter states he must cease large-scale effort until we can reduce Axis air activity—strafing, etc." The original is in the Marshall Papers, Eisenhower Correspondence.
[4] Colonel Claude E. Duncan headed the 12th Bomber Command.
[5] Pierre Boisson, the French Governor General of Dakar.

Dear General: I enclose herewith recommendations for promotion just received from General Clark, and with which I concur.

A special word about General Gruenther. There is no better type of officer, and one of his *great* attributes is selflessness. He apparently never thinks of himself or his personal fortunes—a quality that I assure you has come to be one that means much to me in any officer. He is one of the ablest men I have met and I have allowed him to leave this headquarters to become Clark's Chief of Staff only because I felt in the latter position his sphere of usefulness would be enlarged. Of all the men I have recommended to you for promotion I place none above him in professional qualifications, complete devotion to duty and in the integrity of his motives and character. *Sincerely*

18 ALGIERS   *January 17, 1943*

Dear General: All the way home on the plane I turned over in my mind the idea you gave to me of using General Patton as a sort of deputy. I am discussing the matter a bit further with some of my staff, but I have tentatively come to the conclusion that I am going to name him as "Deputy Commander for Ground Forces." This will give him the necessary authority and will allow me to use his great mental and physical energy in helping me through a critical period. On the other hand, it will avoid the difficulties that might be involved should I call him "Deputy Commander-in-Chief", which would imply an influence in Naval and Air matters, and might be resented.

Today, I sent Mr. Hopkins[1] a telegram giving the gist of a conversation with Peyrouton.[2] It was important only in the conviction expressed by this particular Frenchman that a De Gaulle[3]–Giraud agreement would create a great uplift in French morale.

I am looking forward to your visit here. Twenty-four hours notice will be sufficient and, in view of the change in our operational plans, it is almost certain that I will be here during the period of your visit, without neglecting any slightest duty that will devolve upon me.

Would you please tell Admiral King that in the rush of conferences which involved my time while at your Headquarters, I inadvertently failed to extend to him, personally, an invitation to come to this Headquarters. I should very much like to have him come, either with you or at another time if that suited his convenience. Certainly, he will be most welcome and I can make him comfortable. All ranks here would like to see him.

With personal regard, *Sincerely*

[1] Harry Lloyd Hopkins was a key adviser to the President.
[2] Marcel Peyrouton had been serving as Vichy Ambassador to Argentina. He had just been named Governor General of Algeria.
[3] Charles André Joseph Marie de Gaulle was the leader of the anti-Vichy Free French.

19 ALGIERS

January 30, 1943

Dear General: The letter you wrote me from your plane on January 26 reached here this morning.

I am delighted to know that you believe Mrs. Marshall will like the rug. Frankly, I was afraid to mention the subject to you personally, for fear that you would discover some objection to taking the rug from my bedroom. So far as I can recall, I have never before in my service given a personal present to my superior or to a member of his family, and I assure you that I regard this as a real privilege. So I fervently hope that Mrs. Marshall's judgment will justify your prediction.

A telegram from General Alexander arrived this morning. After discussion with the CIGS, he has decided to accept the command arrangement set up for HUSKY,[1] although I know he is not particularly happy about it. I immediately replied, asking him to name his Chief of Staff and to come here in person as quickly as he can. These two campaigns have definitely merged into one, and it is high time that Alexander got on the job and took the tactical reins in his hands.

I am not going to give up my advance CP, and will, during the weeks to come, pay many visits to that area. Tedder[2] is due tomorrow morning, Sunday, and, immediately after he arrives, I hope to take off for another three day tour of the front. I particularly want to visit Fredendall's area, because I am quite sure that in that sector we must keep up a bold, aggressive front, and try to keep the Axis forces back on their heels.

Again I tell you that your visit here did more for us—and particularly for me—than could any other thing. I hope that your future schedules will include another trip to this area.

With warm personal regards, *Very sincerely*

[1] Code name for Allied invasion of Sicily in July, 1943.
[2] Air Chief Marshal Arthur William Tedder had fought in World War I and transferred to the Royal Air Force in 1919. He was serving as Air Officer Commanding in Chief, Middle East. In the reorganization of the Mediterranean command made at the Casablanca Conference, he was named Commander in Chief of the Mediterranean Allied Air Forces, thereby becoming Eisenhower's senior air officer.

Dear General: It has occurred to me that part of the difficulty in securing Presidential authorization for decentralization in the issue of the Legion of Merit may arise from a possible failure to differentiate between the Legion of Merit and the Medal of Merit.[1] I had a talk with General Patton, who discussed this subject at Casablanca with Mr. Hopkins, and since Patton himself did not know of the difference between the two, it is possible that some misunderstanding on the subject exists in the White House. It would certainly be a great help if the lower orders of the *Legion* of Merit could be awarded by commanders in the field.

We have had a busy several days on the battlefront. The German attacks, although in no single case of very great strength, always make rapid progress when they strike the French because of lack of proper defensive equipment in the French forces. We have been kept on the jump to stabilize the situation and to maintain some mobile striking power as a general reserve both from defensive and local offensive affairs. Giraud visited me night before last in a very agitated frame of mind. He, of course, blames all the French troubles in the front line on alleged slowness by us in supporting his detachments, and he keeps talking about an imminent breaking up of French civil and military morale and is, in general, very pessimistic. He is volatile rather than stable. I have reassured him to the best of my ability, but our equipment status is so low that I simply cannot turn loose anything of particular value to him at the moment.

Yesterday, I visited Anderson at my forward C.P. and am convinced that we are doing everything possible to establish a situation that will facilitate operations by the combined First and Eighth Armies. Because of the anticipated arrival of the Eighth Army on the Mareth Line,[2] the southern part of our front assumes a much greater importance than would be the case if we were merely concerned in protecting the right flank of the Tunisian forces. I now have assurance that Alexander will be here by the 8th, and I am sure that he will see the tactical part of the problem exactly as I do. In the meantime, if nothing happens to our special convoy of trucks that Somervell and Admiral King cooked up between them, we will rapidly ameliorate our precarious situation in front line supply. Moreover, if we get the fighters we need, we'll be O.K.

The troops in the west are almost completely immobile. I have stripped them ruthlessly. For example, one division, which is supposed to have more than 800 trucks, has approximately 100. I am vastly concerned with restoring the tactical power of these divisions, not only because of training necessities but because of the ever present possibility of action. I have been trying to get one of the regiments of the Second Armored Division prepared for a rapid move to the east, but there just simply is not enough equipment left in the division to get a regiment ready for action.

I hope that the promotion of three officers to Lieutenant General will not be too much of a chore to handle in one bite. Spaatz really should be promoted quickly to establish the importance of his position in this new organization, which I do not want to see played down in the slightest. He is and must be recognized as my "Chief of Allied Air Force." On the other hand, I think that Fredendall and Patton should be handled together with no distinction between them and, purely as a matter of morale in this Army, I should not like to see Spaatz promoted ahead of them. This leaves me with no suggestion to offer except to try it simultaneously, with rank in the order of Fredendall, Patton, Spaatz. However, if this is too much, I believe I should prefer to see the first two promoted, with the understanding that Spaatz would come along as soon as you could arrange it.

Agent[3] is due to visit me day after tomorrow. Two days after that, Alexander gets here and naturally I must leave my headquarters for early conferences with him. You can see what difficulty such visits create when I attempt to plan a trip lasting four or five days along the Tunisian front. Luckily, the airplane makes it possible for me to hop back and forth rather frequently to my C.P. at Constantine, where I can keep the threads pretty well in my hands.

I have taken to heart most seriously your talk about caring for my health, and my system is to take about two hours for lunch and, except when it is unavoidable, I will not make my luncheon period a business hour. We have been blessed with a bit of sunlight and I have been getting about an hour's sun at least three times a week. This has a very relaxing influence on me, and I believe I am already feeling and looking better than when you were here. Moreover, I am getting in an occasional bit of exercise, since Commander Butcher[4] has found a back way to walk to the office. *Sincerely*

[1] The Medal of Merit was awarded only to civilians; the Legion of Merit was an Army award with four degrees.
[2] The Mareth Line was a defensive position first built by the French on the southern Tunisian border. Rommel was strengthening the fortification.
[3] A code name for Churchill.
[4] Commander Harry Cecil Butcher (USNR) was a personal friend of Eisenhower's who had worked for the Columbia Broadcasting System before the war. When Eisenhower learned of his appointment to command, he requested Butcher's services as naval aide.

21 ALGIERS   *February 8, 1943*

Dear General: Today I sent you a telegram on the matter of publicity that will emanate from England upon the transfer of the British Eighth Army to this command. I think that the telegram explains the situation sufficiently and there is no use belaboring the point. But it brings up another subject that is also closely related to one you discussed with me while you were here.

I am thinking of the inevitable trend of the British mind toward "committee" rather than "single" command. It is reflected in two recent papers from the CC/S, one dealing with the establishment of the Air Command in this theater and the other with the overall command for HUSKY. In each case the influence of the British tendency toward reaching down into a theater and attempting to compel an organization along the lines to which they are accustomed, is readily apparent. For example, in the Air paper the statement is made that after following out the general organization prescribed, further details will naturally be left to the *Air Commander in Chief*. As far as I am concerned, no attention will be paid to such observations. It is my responsibility to organize to win battles and while I do not anticipate, ever, any difficulty with a man of Tedder's ability, it is still quite evident that only a man of Portal's turn of mind would have thought of inserting such a statement.

In the HUSKY paper, the CC/S directed Alexander to take over planning details, yet they expect Alexander to *cooperate* with Cunningham and Tedder in executing this project. Manifestly, responsibility again falls directly on me and though, in this particular instance, since all the senior commanders will be British, my tendency will be to follow the methods to which they are accustomed, I would consider it a definite invasion of my own proper field if they attempted to prevent me, for example, from setting up Alexander as a Task Force Commander for the tactical phases of the operation. Naturally, there are many broad naval and air problems that will be solved by the respective Commanders in Chief under my direction, but it seems impossible for the British to grasp the utter simplicity of the system that we employ.

I do not consider that there is anything vicious or even deliberate in the British actions; they simply reflect their own doctrine and training just as we do ours. But when the two governments accept the principle of unified command—which means a Task Force Commander—in a partcular theater, I not only believe that they must leave him a considerable freedom in organizing his own forces as he sees fit, but that when it becomes necessary to organize subordinate task forces, he should be free to do it under the principle of unified command, if he so chooses.

By no means am I proposing or suggesting that anything be done with respect to the examples I have just quoted. I am merely trying to say that I believe I have grasped your idea and that I will be constantly on my guard to prevent any important military venture depending for its control and direction upon the "committee" system of command.

We have just received notification that Gruenther's name has gone to the Senate for promotion. While admitting certain serious mistakes with respect to personnel, I venture the prediction in this case that there will never be further disappointment. I have watched him under conditions of strain and stress and long hours of work, and he is really a grand, self-effacing officer.

The enemy attack in the Pichon area that we have been expecting for several days is probably due to hit day after tomorrow. I think we are in position to deal with it effectively.

As a matter of interest, I am sending along to you copy of a letter I recently wrote Fredendall. It now looks as if I could get up to his headquarters tomorrow or the day after. If I uncover anything new, I will write you upon my return.

The time has come to organize upon definite lines the American administrative matters in this theater. Naturally, I must keep final power of decision in my hands, but I am now setting up a line of communications or S.O.S. organization. Alongside of this will be a command for static defense installations and another for handling routine administration with the War Department. Over the whole thing will be a Deputy Theater Commander and I have picked Brigadier E. S. Hughes, who I brought down from London for this purpose. In a very short time I will probably recommend him for a second star, which recommendation will be accompanied by one in the case of Brigadier Thomas Larkin who, as I now see it, will be the actual head of the S.O.S. organization. I am merely telling you this so that you will understand my telegrams when they come in. It is quite apparent to me that I must organize to get further details, particularly American administrative details, off my shoulders and out of this headquarters. It is my present intention to set up this particular groupment in Oran. I am constantly impressed by the fact that the tendency of all staffs to crowd around the center of local power is especially noticeable in this theater, and I am determined to kick out of here all matters that involve petty patronage, which make staff officers so reluctant to devote themselves to their own operational duties in preference to administration.

I am sure my staff thinks I am getting tougher and more arbitrary day by day but, although I admit the impossibility of working without adequate staffs, they do seem to develop diseases that include obesity and elephantiasis. Apparently only a sharp knife, freely wielded, provides any cure. *Sincerely*

22   ALGIERS   *February 21, 1943*

Dear General: I have had a crowded two weeks, starting with the visit of the Prime Minister on the 5th and 6th. Providing for his protection was quite a mental burden upon us, since we had received a message from London indicating that a definite attempt would be made here to knock him off.

After a series of important conferences here I got away late on the 11th for a trip to the front. I was particularly concerned with our south flank, where it seemed to me that dispositions made were not completely in accord with my general instructions. While it would naturally be a delicate matter for me to interfere directly into tactical dispositions, I am always free to satisfy myself that policies and general principles that have been laid down are being executed correctly.

As I told you when you were here, my great effort was to hold the Thelepte airfields and, so far as possible, to confine the enemy to a narrow corridor from Fondouk southward, by keeping small detachments in his most likely channels of exit, and then stationing the bulk of the First Armored Division in rear of this extensive line so as to be ready to launch a vigorous and powerful counter-attack against any force thrusting its way through the hills. Due to faulty G–2 estimates in this and lower headquarters, the First Army did not become convinced, until too late, that the attack through Faid was really the main effort. Consequently, the bulk of the First Armored Division was held out of action until considerable portions of its forward detachments had been used up, and this naturally resulted in piecemeal action.

The night before the attack I visited the exact spot through which it came and thereafter remained in the east until it became evident that the new line would have to be established west of Sbeitla-Feriana and that considerable rehabilitation and rebuilding of formations would be required. This was my job.

I came back here in time to meet Alexander who immediately left for the front, where he has been ever since last Thursday morning. We are cannabilizing the Second Armored Division and the Third Infantry Division to rebuild as necessary, while we get ourselves established to stop further advance and get our units sorted out all along the line.

Although the materiel and personnel losses in the First Armored Division and in part of the 165th Infantry are very severe, the real tragedy is the loss of the Thelepte airfields. It was on my responsibility alone that we attempted to operate along a forward line, which it was obvious could not be held passively against any concentrated, determined attack. The only chance was a vigorous active defense, featuring mobile counter-attacking strength. To me it seemed, as always before in this campaign, that the risks involved, assuming reasonable tactical efficiency on our part, were fully justified. Now we have the picture of the enemy, on our side of the valley, doing as much, and trying more, than we did on the other side. Yet altogether we had, for employment in the region, the First Armored Division, which had 188 runners in mediums alone, 2 additional Infantry Regiments, and many supporting units. Among other things, our troubles came about because we are still too weak in A.T. and A.A.,[1] and we don't yet know exactly how to handle the Mark VI tank. We are pushing up some of our Mark X, with 3″ guns.

In the broad aspect of the campaign, I realize that this affair is only an incident, but I am provoked that there was such reliance placed upon particular types of intelligence that general instructions were considered inapplicable. In this connection and for your eyes only, I have asked for the relief of my G–2. He is British and the head of that section must be a British officer because of the network of special signal establishments he operates, but Paget has agreed to make available a man in Great Britain who is tops in this regard.

I think it must be obvious to all that, for the next three months, considering the job we have of throwing the enemy out of Tunisia, of doing something concrete in the way of rehabilitation of the French Army, and of preparing for the next operation, this theater must have a very high priority in all shipping and escorting facilities and in other assets, including Air Force. By concentrating to the utmost, we will get the job done much sooner and save time, tonnage and troops in the long run.

I suppose you keep in rather close touch with our situation through the means of the daily reports submitted to the CC/S by our Operations Section. I will not weary you with them here. The materiel losses in the First Division involve as major items about 112 medium tanks, some 80 half-tracks, 11 self-propelled 105's, and 10 self-propelled 75's. There were also quite a number of 2½-ton trucks lost. All the evidence goes to show that most of this stuff was destroyed in actual battle and that we took a heavy toll from the enemy. However, some of it was overrun through surprise action; and while I do not believe that any of our tanks will be particularly valuable to the enemy, he undoubtedly picked up a considerable amount of transport, which he badly needs.

I just called Alexander on the phone, since I thought I would run up to see him this afternoon or tomorrow morning. He has gone down to the southern end of the line himself, as he is worried as to further enemy capability there. All of us are, since a general attack northwestward would seem logical for him. I have a date to meet Alexander on Tuesday morning. We are leaving no stone unturned to give him everything possible so that we may not only reestablish our formations, but will get this front tidied up once and for all, so that we can operate as Divisions and Corps rather than as Regiments and Battalions. I am determined that progress along this line will take place, subject only to the necessity of preventing any major advance by the enemy, while we are waiting for the Eighth Army to get closer to a threatening position.

The new command organization is functioning and I expect my burdens to be much lightened. I was able to maintain for almost 48 hours the personal regime you so earnestly advised. Since then I was temporarily thrown off stride by events but will soon, I hope, get back on to a more reasonable rate of living. It happened that when the late battle opened, Smith and Patton were in Tripoli, Clark was sick and Alexander and Tedder had not arrived. I was really busy!

With sincere personal regard. *Cordially*

P.S. Since writing the above, yesterday afternoon, the enemy has made an advance into Kasserine Pass. We are supposed to be counter-attacking as quickly as possible. Evidence increases that he may try a major stroke attempting to get in rear of 5th Corps. We have enough to stop him

—at the very least to foil any such purpose—if we can only use it effectively. I've heard some really discouraging reports about our M–3 (Grant) tanks. Sometime I'll write to you in detail about it. In the meantime, I am disappointed but nothing worse. We'll do it—even though it is obviously a major job.

¹ Antitank and antiaircraft.

23 ALGIERS   *March 3, 1943*

Dear General: Please do not look upon any communication I send you as a defensive explanation. Not only do I refuse to indulge in alibis but, frankly, I feel that you have given such evidence of confidence in me, that I never experience the feeling of having to defend my actions. My communications, therefore, whether in letter or in telegraphic form, spring simply from my belief that in higher echelons the common understanding of problems is the most certain way to insure smooth functioning.

Today I am writing about personnel. The problem plagues me all the time. As you know, I have had my moments of doubt about Fredendall and I have spent much time in travelling just to assure myself that he was doing his job successfully. Alexander likes him, and by every yardstick that can be produced for measuring an officer, he is tops—except for one thing. He has difficulty in picking good men and, even worse, in getting the best out of subordinates; in other words, in handling personnel. He is too good to lose; but his assignment is critical at this moment because Alexander is depending on the II Corps, as an *independent* American organization, to conduct a speedy attack. I have discovered that a man must take the tools he has and do the best he can with them, but in this case I must either find a good substitute for Fredendall or must place in his command a number of assistants who are so stable and sound that they will not be disturbed by his idiosyncrasies.

• • •

Terry Allen seems to be doing a satisfactory job; so is Roosevelt.¹ I am enclosing a letter that Allen wrote me about Roosevelt. I have not seen Ryder in some time but have good reports of him.

We have gone so far down the line in picking good men for young Brigadiers, that it is getting exceedingly difficult to find a good staff for a Corps or Division. Fredendall's staff I consider weak and I am searching the theater to pick him up a good man or two to reinforce him. I want him to have every single thing that it is possible for him to have.

HUSKY planning is most involved and difficult. Since, by direction, we are using for the operation the British system of command, the whole arrangement—in higher echelons—presents intricacies and difficulties that cause me a lot of headaches.

I am feeling well. The battle period, during which I was alone, was very strenuous, and since then I have made one rather extended trip into the southeast. Now I have caught up with myself and have things on a fairly even keel. Our bombing is going well and we are making the enemy suffer.

With cordial regard, *Sincerely*

P.S. Since writing the above, I received your wire reference Fredendall and Lieutenant Generalcy, just as I was sending you one on the same subject. For some curious reason, Fredendall has shown a peculiar apathy in preparing for a big push as an independent corps. Luckily, I have had Bradley[2] with him for the last four days and I am rushing up there tomorrow to settle this matter once and for all. Originally, Alexander thought the world of Fredendall, but I have had word today through Alexander's Chief of Staff that he is quite worried about Fredendall's apparent inability to plan the next operation. My own real worry is his apparent inability to develop a team, and in this war the team must be developed before any of these large organizations will work.

[1] Major General Terry de la Mesa Allen commanded the 1st Infantry Division. Brigadier General Theodore Roosevelt, Jr., Theodore Roosevelt's eldest son, had been twice wounded as an infantry officer in World War I. He had returned to active duty in April, 1941, as a regimental commander and was presently Allen's second in command.

[2] Major General Omar Nelson Bradley was a close friend and classmate of Eisenhower's whom Marshall had sent at Eisenhower's request to be Eisenhower's "eyes and ears." He became deputy commander and then on April 15 commander of the U.S. II Corps, which position he retained until September, when he was sent to England as the American Army commander for the cross-Channel invasion. He was promoted to lieutenant general on June 2.

24 ALGIERS   *March 11, 1943*

Dear General: Fredendall has left in response to your telegram of instructions, which were shown to him. I am quite certain that you are making the best use of him; he has the physical and nervous energy to keep on producing for a very considerable time and has very clear and specific ideas as to additional requirements in our training program. Under conditions of strain, he is not particularly successful in developing a happy family and complete teamwork, and I have personally cautioned him about one or two personal faults that have had a bad effect in the past. I believe he will be the most successful of any of your Army Commanders in obtaining the results you want.

Bradley and I had a long conference yesterday, extending well into the night. We are quite clear in our minds that, desirable as it would be to make a transfer of personnel between the First and Third Divisions and between the First and Second Armored Divisions, the project is an impracticable one at this time. The offensive operations that the First and First Armored Divisions will undertake are scheduled to begin within a few days, and the involvement of these divisions in that affair will extend over a sufficient length of time that HUSKY training for the Moroccan troops will have proceeded too far to justify wholesale transfers. However, I hope to apply your idea on a more moderate scale by getting into HUSKY formations a number of seasoned troop officers and non-commissioned officers.

Lately, the weather has almost stopped our heavy strikes against shipping. The Axis is getting into the ports much more equipment, supplies and personnel than I like—however, his present success in this line may lead him into a serious mistake. He may think that he can continue it and will, therefore, be counting on greater maintenance possibilities in the future than he will actually be able to sustain. Some such reasoning must lie behind his continuous effort to attack us all along the line from Bizerte to Mareth. These attacks are, of course, costly in ammunition and fuel as well as equipment, and I am secretly hoping that he is miscalculating in his estimates as to how much of this he can afford. I believe that with a return of good weather we can cut down his supply capabilities very drastically.

Our own plans contemplate a rising scale of offensive operations, and it will be the role of the II Corps to draw all possible strength from the south, so as to help Montgomery through the Gap. Once we have the Eighth Army through that bottleneck, this campaign is going to assume, rapidly, a very definite form, with constant pressure and drive kept up against the enemy throughout the region.

When you were here, you will recall that I was getting rather impatient with the constant pressure put on me by subordinates to promote people. Since that time, my ideas have become even more emphatic and more firmly fixed. By taking advantage of various emergency delegations of authority and through misguided zeal, there have been too many promotions made, particularly in staffs, up to and including the grade of Colonel. I have recently issued a flat order that no promotion to the grade of Colonel will be made without my personal approval, and I warned that if any such promotion was accomplished and I learned of it, the officer concerned would be promptly demoted and the man who pretended to authorize it would be disciplined.

I cannot tell you how fortunate it was for me that Bradley arrived here at the time he did. He has been a godsend in every way and his utter frankness and complete loyalty are things that I count on tremendously.

The visitor question is getting a bit vexatious. As I told you in a telegram, I believe that Bureau Chiefs and Division and Corps Commanders should take every reasonable opportunity to visit this place and to absorb everything possible, so as to assist them in their own work. But American Legion Commanders, Princes, and others of that stripe are nothing but a deadly bore. You will probably be told sooner or later that I am becoming a discourteous boor, but, except for the briefest of meetings, I am cutting everybody off my list that has not something specific to do in the job of winning this war.

With personal regard, *Most sincerely*

Dear General: I am enclosing a copy of a letter I recently wrote General Alexander. In the main, it is self-explanatory. It was brought about by the fact that his outline plan for the continuation of the Battle of Tunisia seemed to me to be a bit on the slow, methodical side and, in addition, appeared to contemplate the eventual pinching out of the U.S. II Corps. I have taken up both these matters verbally, and Alexander sees eye to eye with me in principle; however, I felt that a letter, which could be circulated among members of his staff, might have a wholesome effect.

The First Division continues to give a very good account of itself. The First Armored has also done lots of good work, but there seems to be a feeling that it has not been employed quite as aggressively as it might have been on several occasions. I am not at all certain, however, that this can always be attributed to lack of aggressiveness in the Divisional Command, because on two occasions I have been present with Alexander in II Corps Headquarters when he constantly emphasized his purpose of avoiding pitched, indecisive battles in the Maknassy-Gafsa area where, as he expressed it, "we might get into trouble" and clearly directed the employment of threat coupled with caution rather than actual seeking of heavy fighting.

A few days ago I sent you a wire about Colonel A. N. Stark.[1] Apparently my first radio on this subject had gone astray or had not been brought to your attention. His experience and general record on the front seem to me to indicate a real value in the training army at home and I think that he will be a very fine Assistant Division Commander. In his case, my only word of caution would be that you may have to think of his possible "ceiling". He may not be of the caliber to go higher, but there is no doubt that as a training influence in a Division he will be very fine.

We have had a flood of great and near-great visitors and at times some of the incidental chores grow irksome. However, I try to be officially courteous, but make myself rather inaccessible at other times. Recently the aides found a place in the country where they have accumulated four horses, and I have gotten three short rides in the past week. I cannot tell you what a tremendous exhilaration I got out of it. I sincerely hope I can keep on with the practice.

The HUSKY planning is onerous and difficult. I reported to the Combined Chiefs of Staff the changes I had to make in the plan in order to satisfy Alexander and Montgomery that they had a chance of taking the southeast sector, which is of course vital to us. I didn't like it, but it seemed to me there was no other recourse. As always, we have to think in terms of ships. It is a matter of ability to place our strength where we want it at the time we want it, and this one factor practically governs everything we do. If we had the necessary shipping, particularly in combat loaders, I would have no fears about the outcome of the HUSKY operation. As it is, we seem always to be skating close to the edge of unjustified or at least dangerous risk.

It would have warmed your heart to have heard what Admiral Cunningham, who dropped into my house last evening on a piece of business, had to say about you. He brought up your name and spoke of you in terms that would have excited the pride of any individual. He particularly stressed your standing and prestige in the British Empire. Prince Bernhard[2] did the same, but I think so highly of Admiral Cunningham that I cannot help making special mention of that incident.

With personal regard, *Very sincerely*

[1] Colonel Alexander Newton Stark, Jr., had commanded a miscellaneous group known as Stark Force in the battle of Kasserine Pass.

[2] Prince Bernhard was the Consort of Crown Princess Julianna of the Netherlands and a leader in the affairs of the Dutch government-in-exile.

26 ALGIERS   *April 16, 1943*

Dear General: I returned from a two-day trip to the front last evening to find waiting for me your telegram reference the adverse stories published concerning certain of our American units. The knowledge that such stories had gotten out in such a definitely critical vein was practically a body blow because many weeks ago I had foreseen the effect at home of discouraging reports and had been working like a dog to insure a reasonable utilization of American troops and the presentation of a proper perspective in reports. Moreover, I have made Alexander and others concerned see the great damage that would result from unfair or caustic criticism of any tactical failure of the kind indicated.

On top of this I have made Alexander agree as to the necessity of keeping all four American divisions together as a powerful Corps, even if the logistics of the situation should make the arrangement seem somewhat unwise or risky. For the past few days we have been gathering statistics to show the accomplishments of all our forces to date, and to evaluate properly the American ground and air contributions to the results so far achieved.

In spite of all this, to find myself defeated by the stupidity of a subordinate censor, was perfectly infuriating. I do not often get even temporarily discouraged, but I must say that last night was a bad one.

The excuse given by the censor was a curious one. I have issued the most stringent orders that *no personal criticism of me or of my actions is ever to be censored.* The fool censor extended this to include troop units, although how he reasoned that one out is beyond me.

As I told you in my telegram, the matter is one in which I am now going to do a little bit of propagandizing and I hope you will find that the situation rapidly improves.

Curiously enough, the First British Army has been suffering somewhat

108

from the same difficulty. The units in that force feel that their efforts have been minimized in the press and that all the glory has gone to the more spectacular advances of the Eighth Army. Yesterday afternoon I went over that part of the British First Army front that lies to the east of Beja and where some of the fighting around March 26th took place. In one area I counted 27 completely destroyed German tanks, including, in one spot, three of the big Mark 6's. It was a lovely sight. All through the area is evidence of the fiercest kind of fighting and it is easy to see why some of the Divisions of the First Army felt that full credit has not been given to them.

Our Ninth Division has already taken over its sector in the North and the First Division was beginning to move in while I was there yesterday. The II Corps Headquarters moved to Beja yesterday. The 34th Division will follow immediately, and it will be followed by the First Armored.

To get down to the actual facts of the case, both the First and Ninth Divisions did a very workmanlike job in the Gafsa area, with the First Division definitely showing the results of its greater experience and consequent greater successes. On the other hand, its task was not as difficult as that facing the Ninth Division. Quoting from memory, in the Gafsa operations the Second Corps took something over 5000 prisoners, damaged at least 60 tanks, of which almost half were completely destroyed, captured over 100 guns of various caliber, and inflicted many other casualties on the forces opposing them. In one area our troops counted 800 enemy graves. The 34th Division had the task of attacking the southern part of the Fondouk pass. Originally that Division had been badly scattered along the lines of communication and was assembled on the battle front piecemeal, to help stop gaps in the line during our critical days of late January and early February. It finally was gotten together as a Division, with a defensive mission covering such a broad front that it was practically tied down to passive action. Such advances as it made were of a demonstration character, directed by the 18th Army Group, and the troops were expected in each instance to withdraw after having made short advances. As a result of all this the Division had never really gotten a chance to get itself together for an advance or to produce an offensive spirit. The task given it in the latest operation was very difficult tactically and required advance under most difficult conditions of terrain and enemy domination.

Under these circumstances the forward troops did not do well, but they did far better than has frequently been the case in the early stages of a war where relatively untried troops are pitted against veterans. For example, the British experience in the desert during the first two years reveals many instances that were far more susceptible of criticism than was the 34th Division.

In the long run, of course, facts are going to speak for themselves. My great concern is to get for these units the finest possible leadership that we can produce. Alexander is sincere in his efforts to launch them into attacks where they can be assured of local victories and gradually gain that winning spirit that will make them top flight units. It is for these reasons that I go so frequently to see Alexander or one of our American commanders and keep this problem before them in the plainest possible terms.

Harmon has relieved General McQuillen[1] from the First Armored Division. I inclose a copy of the letter General Harmon sent me about McQuillen. Harmon also has written to General McNair.[2]

To this long letter I naturally do not expect any reply. I just happened to be a bit garrulous this morning. *Sincerely*

---

[1] Brigadier General Raymond Eugene McQuillin commanded Combat Command A of the 1st Armored Division.
[2] Lieutenant General Lesley James McNair (USMA 1904) was chief of the Army Ground Forces.

27   ALGIERS   *May 5, 1943*

Dear General: Today, I sent you a telegram telling of some of the difficulties in planning formal HUSKY; also replying to your radio concerning the great desirability of a modified, immediate operation. You will recall that you mentioned this latter possibility when you were here in January, stating that you believed that if we could follow into Sicily on the heels of the withdrawing Axis forces from Tunisia, we might take advantage of the confusion and consternation to get a great success very cheaply. Since that time, this possibility has been a constant objective in our studies and plans. Cunningham and Tedder are particularly ardent advocates of some such attempt, always assuming that once the final crumbling of the Tunisian front begins, it will go with a rush. I agree that the products of group planners always tend toward the orthodox and the mediocre and that commanders must at times kick the planners out the window and decide on these things for themselves. To be ready for some such an attempt requires intensive preparation *now*—whereas we are throwing so much of our resources and energy into the current battle that we can do little else.

The fighting since April 23rd has had a definite influence on our thinking and calculations. Even the Italian, defending mountainous country, is very difficult to drive out, and the German is a real problem. At this moment, I am certain that the Axis cannot have more than a total of 150,000 men in Tunisia. We outnumber, out-tank and out-gun him, and are infinitely stronger in the air. He has had great breaks in the weather and for days on end our superior air force has been practically tied to the ground. Yet this factor alone has not accounted for the slowness of our advance. The difficult and mountainous terrain in itself imposes very slow and laborious cross-country movement; while the enemy with his use of innumerable land mines and skillful utilization of the ground for emplacing

110

machine guns and mortars, has made our task a tough one. Anticipating similar conditions in the mountainous coastlines of HUSKY, all of us have come to believe it best to attack in the strongest possible force on the vital southeastern coastline and avoid dispersed landings, which might leave us in a series of small pockets all around the coastline and with no real possibility of operating rapidly toward a common junction. These conclusions have *not* been developed by planners; they are the result of earnest consideration by the ground force commanders.

As to the current battle: Yesterday, the II Corps took Mateur, continuing the good work and great improvement that began with the assumption of command of the II Corps by Patton in March. Bradley is bringing the whole force along in fine style. While we still have certain deficiencies in the battle coordination of the various arms, and in speed of action, these things are showing steady improvement. That whole Corps must soon be classed as an outstanding tactical organization. As you know, the Third Division is now just about ready to enter the battle. Due to anticipated shortening of the line through yesterday's successes, I hope that the Third Division can relieve the First on the battleline and allow the latter to come back for immediate amphibious training. I would like to use the First, Third and Forty-fifth Divisions as the assault units for HUSKY.

Tomorrow morning we start the big drive which we hope and believe will see us in Tunis in a day or so. I believe we can clean up the Bizerte angle very quickly, but the Bon Peninsula may be a different matter. Incidentally, the necessity for sending the Third Division to the front (while a great advantage from the standpoint of obtaining combat experience) threw further difficulties in the way of a sudden, modified HUSKY.

Just a word about the matter of uniform. I have no doubt that you have been impressed by the virtual impossibility of appearing neat and snappy in our field uniform. Given a uniform which tends to look a bit tough, and the natural proclivities of the American soldier quickly create a general impression of a disorderly mob. From this standpoint alone, the matter is bad enough; but a worse effect is the inevitable result upon general discipline. This matter of discipline is not only the most important of our internal military problems, it is the most difficult. In support of all other applicable methods for the development of satisfactory discipline, we should have a neater and smarter looking field uniform. I suggest that the Quartermaster begin now serious work to design a better woolen uniform for next winter's wear. In my opinion, the material should be very rough wool, because such material does not show dirt and is easily kept in presentable condition. Something on the order of the British battle-dress would be indicated, although I think our people should be able to design a garment that would be distinctive. The matter of head-covering is more easily solved. Our helmet is splendid, and its inner lining is suitable for wear when not in the actual combat zone. For pass and office work, the overseas cap may have to be good enough. I suppose something on the beret line would be unacceptable to the American public but, where I have seen troops in this type of headgear, I must say they have given an impression of morale and elan. All such things as fatigue hats and mechanic's caps should be instantly abolished. Most soldiers prefer them to decent headgear. I am issuing orders prohibiting the wear[ing] of such things in this theater.

Another subject that has been somewhat on my mind is that of suggesting a re-survey of the so-called over-age officers and determining whether or not we cannot salvage from that group a number of good regimental commanders. One big advantage of using such a man, particularly in the early days of regimental development, is that he thoroughly understands the need for discipline and on the average is tough and hard enough to enforce orders. Such men, if useful only up to include the first few weeks of campaign, would prove of enormous value because we would get fairly well prepared regiments before the first battle. While the older men might last only long enough to allow division and other higher commanders to determine the natural leaders in the regiment, this would be a great advantage. We have already gotten extremely thin in experience—I mean just normal disciplinary and training experience as opposed to battle experience—in all divisions. With added expansion coming on and the certainty that you will be calling on all units to return battle trained men to the United States, we will be progressively worse off in this regard. I hope you will have someone study this idea very carefully because we have discovered that the older man—that is the 50 to 55 year old fellow—does not wear out *physically* as quickly as might be imagined. Occasionally, there would be developed—from among such a group—an individual capable of going on up.

I find this letter has stretched out a bit longer than usual. However, I had a number of things on my mind this morning, concerning which I wanted to talk to you. *Very sincerely*

28 ALGIERS   *May 13, 1943*

Dear General: Sometimes I think it would be most comforting to have a disposition that would permit relaxation—even possibly a feeling of self-satisfaction—as definite steps of a difficult job are completed. Unfortunately, I always anticipate and discount, in my own mind, accomplishment of the several steps and am, therefore, mentally racing ahead into the next one. The consequence is that all the shouting about the Tunisian Campaign leaves me utterly cold. I am so impatient and irritated because of the slowness with which the next phase can unfold, that I make myself quite unhappy. I am convinced that if I could undertake HUSKY today with only two divisions, I could gain a bridgehead and an advantage that would make the further conquest a very simple affair. Just as I suffered, almost

112

physically, all during January, February and March while the enemy was fortifying his positions in Tunisia, so now I resent every day we have got to give him to perfect and strengthen HUSKY defenses. I have gotten so that my chief ambition in this war is finally to get to a place where the next operation does not have to be amphibious, with all the inflexibility and delay that are characteristic of such operations.

Statistical details of the present campaign have been furnished you by now and there is no use repeating them. One little element of personal satisfaction for me is that I have predicted ever since January 1st, that May 15th would see the wind up of this affair. I find that in letters to you and in recorded conversations with Alexander, with newsmen and with my own staff, I have always stuck to this date. I must confess that it was more a hunch than anything else—but so was the selection of November 8th a hunch; another lucky one.

I hope that out of your present conversations in Washington will come some final agreement as to the specific line the Allies are to take in winning this war. While I will always believe that the correct line is the straight, short and simple one, I have come to the conclusion that the old adage—"A poor plan vigorously carried out is better than a perfect plan indifferently executed"—applies in this case. We must have some arrow that gives guidance and meaning to all our strategic and tactical effort.

Colonel Smith[1] of the War Department General Staff just arrived with a letter you wrote to me on May 6th. That was the day we began our final attack, and I know that every day since then has brought you increased satisfaction. Von Arnim[2] was captured yesterday and is passing through here today on his way to London. All the German Generals are being evacuated by air via London, from which point the rest of their journey to the United States will be as determined by the War Department.

Your story of the man who was concerned about my drinking cold water with my meals gave me a chuckle. I am still, I think, a bit of a puzzle to my British confreres because I refuse wine, but this is the first time that any comment has been made about my drinking water. Actually my health was never better. For the past three weeks, I have been getting in some five or six hours a week of rather vigorous riding, which represents the only exercise I have had since the war started. The only difficulty I have at all is sleeping in the later hours of the night. I have developed a pernicious habit of waking up about 4:00 to 4:30, and finding that I am sufficiently rested to begin wrestling with my problems. Once in a while I have been able to put myself back to sleep.

Spaatz has suggested that this theater would offer a very fine region from which to use some of the new B-29's. Because of their range, they could reach Berlin from this area, while the prevalence of good weather from now on would make their employment practically continuous. In addition, from this direction, there would be avoided the great belt of fighter and antiaircraft defense, which the enemy has been establishing across western Europe. This point is one that the Air Force should study.

I want to make the capture of Pantelleria a sort of laboratory to determine the effect of concentrated heavy bombing on defended coastline. When the time comes, we are going to concentrate everything we have to see whether damage to materiel, personnel and morale cannot be made so serious as to make landing a rather simple affair. From what we were able to learn of the fall of Corregidor, artillery pounding on one section certainly seemed to have that effect, and now I would like to see whether the air can do the same thing. Fortunately, the British First Division is not included in the HUSKY allocation and is trained amphibiously—it is assigned to the taking of Pantelleria.

General Kuter[3] returns in the morning and will carry this letter. He has been a standout in his job and will be included in a list of recommendations for suitable award. I sent a telegram to the War Department this morning on suggested general policy in awarding the Distinguished Service Medal and various degrees of the Legion of Merit. Actually, I sent the telegram to Smith, who will give you my suggestions. *Cordially*

[1] Probably Colonel Joseph Smith (USMA 1923) of the Air Corps.

[2] General Juergen von Arnim, commander of the German forces in Tunisia.

[3] Brigadier General Lawrence Sherman Kuter (USMA 1927) commanded the 1st Bombardment Wing of the Eighth Air Force.

29 ALGIERS   *May 25, 1943*

Dear General: I am constantly appalled by the number of headquarters seemingly required to run this sprawling theater and its several tactical efforts, and the size that each of these headquarters tends to assume. I battle on the matter constantly and yet the proof brought to me of overworking staff officers is conclusive. In my own headquarters here, I have men definitely showing signs of continuing strain and we are way behind in the development of certain plans, which we would like to have ready in spite of the fact that some of them will never be used. For example, my directive requires me to do what I can in the exploitation of HUSKY. This means the preparation of a number of *detailed* as opposed to general plans. Because each of these is an amphibious operation, the building of plans is a most laborious business and requires a number of officers. You can see that the requirements finally appear to be insatiable.

From every source there is a constant cry for trained staff officers, secretaries and stenographers. I have come to believe that we had better make the most liberal interpretation we possibly can in the employment of WAACs. It has become almost impossible to find a satisfactory clerk or stenographer among the enlisted men. I understand that one of the difficulties about sending the WAACs overseas is the type of accommodation given to them on ships. I would have no foolishness about this matter, but would pack them in exactly as I would a troop unit whenever it was necessary to ship them to a theater. I realize that our personnel people here are constantly dealing with your staff on such matters, so I am not making any specific recommendation—I am just expressing an opinion.

The CORKSCREW operation,[1] while almost a vital preliminary to HUSKY, is certainly far from an easy one. In fact, some of the people carrying responsibility toward it, are shaking their heads. Briefly the plan is to blast the place with an increasing crescendo of air from D–5 to D–day, and then put down a very intensive naval bombardment on the port area and make a daylight landing at the port under cover of a smoke-screen. The reason for this is that there is no other place where anything except a scrambled landing can be made. Personally, I believe that it will work. If it won't, when everything except the character of the beaches is in our favor, we had better find out—once and for all—just what is involved in operations of this kind.

I am putting in this letter a copy of a paper that was written by a private of the 34th Division. Copies have been sent to the Army Ground Forces and I do not recommend that you read the whole paper; but if you will glance at a few points I have marked in pencil, you will see a participant's idea of the subjects on which I have labored so long and so earnestly—namely, battle discipline, mental attitude, and thorough training of our soldiers. Correction calls for a prodigious amount of work by all of us, and people who haven't the nervous energy to keep on working and working in spite of slow progress and seeming failure, must be relieved. You might send the attached paper on to the OPD. *Sincerely*

P.S.—One criticism I have of all the schools where they tried to pound into my head some military erudition, is that I was never given a hint of what a headache could come out of a quarter of a million prisoners of war, when transportation facilities are clogged and evacuation from the theater can be at the rate of only about thirty thousand a month. The 36th Division will be down to nothing in order to provide static guards and escorts; the 1st Armored Division cannot get its equipment back to Morocco, and soon again I will be in my old position of nothing protecting my rear. . . .

[1] Code name for the operation against Pantelleria.

30 ALGIERS   *June 26, 1943*

Dear General: The past two weeks have been a period of tenseness in this headquarters. The main subjects of our concern have been the approaching HUSKY operation and the constantly recurring problems of the local political mess. However, during the period, I did get to make a three-day inspection of Clark's layout in the Oujda area, and I was highly impressed. I saw large portions of the 82nd Airborne and the Second Armored Division, and found them in splendid shape. Clark's schools are efficient, and the discipline in this area is the best in the region.

A whole series of "ifs" present themselves when one begins to calculate the extent of success we should anticipate in HUSKY. The risks are great but the thing I am counting on more than anything else is that the Italians really have no great stomach for fighting and, moreover, the HUSKY garrison has had no battle experience.

Newspaper comment on our Pantelleria success is, as usual, rather undiscerning. The fact that we were able to pour into Pantelleria so many bombs that we made the garrison surrender, is too easily interpreted as a forerunner of what will happen in other areas. Although every factor, except the single one of the character of beaches, was overwhelmingly in our favor in the Pantelleria operation, there were a number of long faces in this headquarters when the matter was merely a project. If we could give HUSKY a pounding that could compare remotely with that we gave Pantelleria, I would have no slightest doubt of the outcome; but this is not even a faint possibility.

At the beginning of this week, I had all the principal commanders of Ground, Sea and Air in here for a two-day conference. We went over all plans with great thoroughness; and I know that everything that careful preparation and hard work can do, has already or is being done. I count confidently upon success but do not blind myself to the fact that a bloody nose is always a possibility.

Undoubtedly, my telegrams have kept you rather familiar with the developments in the political situation. I am quite sure that De Gaulle is losing ground, but strangely enough this is not resulting in a strengthening of Giraud. I sense a rather growing weariness by the majority with the bickerings of individuals. We have been making this thing work for a number of months, and I have no reason to doubt that we can keep on doing so. However, it does constitute a constant strain and there is no obvious setup that would eliminate worry and watchfulness. My two strongest and ablest assistants in this matter are General Smith and Mr. Macmillan.[1] They are both sound, respected by everybody, and are not hysterical.

My present plans call for my presence in FINANCE[2] from about July 7th to an estimated July 14th. During that period my communications with Washington and London will be almost nil. While normal staff communications will be exchanged as usual, only the most pressing things can be sent to me because of the need for reserving signal communications for operational matters. Along about the 14th, I should be able to get back to Tunisia, from which point I will be in reasonably close contact with the main headquarters here. If all goes swimmingly, I will quickly return to the main headquarters, in order to implement exploitation plans.

Assuming that one or more of the operational possibilities discussed when you were here will become realities, it is certain that one of our greatest needs for the remainder of the year is going to be for transport

116

aircraft. I have heard that a number of our B–24's, now coming off the line, are to be transformed into troop carriers. I wonder if this is true. The staff is now sending forth an estimate of our needs in transport aircraft for the months following upon the HUSKY landing. I sincerely hope that these can be met, because I am certain that if we once get to going good in this region, nothing will be more valuable.

The King's visit was well received and now that he is safely back in England, I am glad he came. However, while he was here, his presence threw an additional burden upon all of us. An astounding number of man hours are required in order to plan such a tour as he made and to see that it is properly and safely executed. While here, he personally conferred upon me the Grand Cross of the Order of the Bath—a compliment which I admit was most pleasing to me.

One other item: I hope you have found no personal objection to acceptance by Mrs. Marshall of the rug that Mamie[3] presented to her. The actual fact is that when you carried the original one home, I was then negotiating for a rug for Mamie that I wanted very badly. I finally obtained it and, at the cost of considerable duty payment, got it to her, so it is my earnest hope that the original one can go for the purpose which I intended.[4]

With continued personal regard. *Cordially*

[1] The Right Honorable Harold Macmillan, as the British Minister Resident to Allied Force Headquarters, was Eisenhower's principal British political adviser.
[2] FINANCE was the code name for the island of Malta.
[3] Mrs. Mamie Eisenhower, the general's wife.
[4] Marshall replied on July 3: "The rug gratefully received . . ." E. to M., June 26, 1943, *EP*, p. 1213, n. 4.

31   AMILCAR, TUNISIA   *July 17, 1943*

Dear General: This has been a busy week. I have been away from Algiers for eleven days, but important messages from Washington and London have reached me in a reasonable time.

All the initial invasion moves were carried out smoothly, and an astonishing lack of resistance was encountered on the shoreline. Captured Italian generals say we secured complete surprise. The airborne operations, which were executed about three hours ahead of the landing, were apparently the first real notice the defenders had of what was coming. Our parachutists and the British glider troops got fairly well into their positions in spite of the very high winds and bad navigating conditions. The landings on the east coast were not greatly troubled by the weather, but the 45th and 1st Divisions had an extremely bad surf. Admiral Cunningham told me that he considered the United States Navy landing operations, under Admiral Kirk[1] (with the 45th Division), to be one of the finest examples of seamanship he had ever witnessed.

Beginning on the morning of D–day we had some trouble with enemy bombers hitting our shipping on the western flank. It seems obvious the enemy had expected us to come into the western tip of Sicily and, for that reason, was in better position to strike us on that flank. In later days, enemy bombers and submarines have been sniping at us. Yesterday a submarine damaged a British cruiser, and an aerial torpedo hit a merchant ship. Both went into Malta. U.S. naval losses, so far reported to me, are 1 destroyer and 1 cargo ship sunk, 2 destroyers and 2 combat loaders damaged. Yesterday an ammunition ship blew up in the harbor of Algiers (cause unknown) and set two gasoline ships ablaze. I do not yet know the full extent of the damage.

Morale in the Italian Army is low and we have some evidence on which to base a belief that the population, generally, is very friendly to us. However, we have had some cases of sniping in the rear areas. One night three soldiers had their throats cut almost on the beaches. I hope that the Rome bombing (day after tomorrow) does not work in reverse, so far as morale is concerned.

Patton is doing well and, so far as I can determine, all the troops are handling themselves satisfactorily. He has grouped the 3rd and 82nd Divisions together as a provisional corps, under Keyes.[2]

Last Monday morning I made a quick tour along the American beaches, in order to get a visual picture of unloading operations and also to have a personal visit with Hewitt[3] and Patton. I must say that the sight of hundreds of vessels, with landing craft everywhere, operating along the shoreline from Licata on the eastward, was unforgettable. I went ashore in the Canadian sector merely to welcome the Canadian Command to this Allied Force. Everybody I saw was in good heart and anxious to get ahead.

The most difficult thing we have to solve is to work out methods whereby friendly aircraft can work over our troops and vessels with safety. Take for example one operation: We were quite anxious to assemble all the fighting elements of the 82nd Division in the rear of Patton's line as a general reserve, since all the evidence showed that he might receive some rather serious counter attacks. Two nights after the original landing, we laid on a very carefully coordinated plan for bringing in the remainder of the 82nd Division. Sea lanes were established with the Navy and all troops were carefully warned as to what to expect. In spite of this, the troop-carrying planes encountered some fire before they got over the shore and from then on we had a very unfortunate experience. Some German night bombers came in at the same moment that our troop-carrying planes did and the dropping of bombs and flares made all the ground troops open up a maximum fire. In addition to this, a local counter attack, which took place at too late an hour to warn the airborne troops, apparently allowed the enemy to establish a fire zone near the selected landing ground. The combination of all these things resulted in quite serious losses. My present reports are that we lost twenty-three planes, while personnel losses as yet are unestimated. A later operation on the British front brought out the

118

lesson that when we land airborne troops in hostile territory, we should *not do so in successive waves*, but should do it all at once. In the first wave, where we had surprise, losses were negligible, but in the two succeeding waves they were very large. Even in the daytime we have great trouble in preventing our own naval and land forces from firing on friendly planes. This seems particularly odd in this operation, where we have such great air superiority that the presumption is that any plane flying in a straight and level course is friendly. Spaatz has written Arnold at considerable length on this subject and he is convinced, as I am, that we are going to have to do some very earnest basic training in both ground and naval forces. Otherwise, we will finally get our air forces to the point where they will simply refuse to come over when we want them. Generally speaking, we are on the strategic offensive, which means we *must* have air superiority. Therefore, we should teach our people not to fire at a plane unless it definitely shows hostile intent.

Latest evidence is that the German is pushing forces into the toe of Italy with the intention of pushing them over to Sicily. My own guess is that he will largely abandon the western part of the island and attempt to take up a line running northwestward from Mount Etna. This line would be one that, with German troops alone, he might believe he could hold for a considerable time. I rather think he has given up hope of making the Italians fight effectively. Nevertheless, we did not get ahead materially yesterday, Friday.

The hostile air force in Sicily is practically destroyed. Such planes as he is still operating are principally based in Italy itself. This allows our strategic air force to go for his lines of supply and other targets of that character. His present reinforcement of Sicily is somewhat immune from interference by our strategic air force because of the fact that he is using landing craft from beach to beach. However, I suspect that the Admiral's patrols will soon be interfering with that plan to some extent.

I expect to have a Commanders-in-Chief meeting Saturday afternoon, after which I will hope to send the Combined Chiefs of Staff my tentative recommendations concerning future operations. *Sincerely*

[1] Rear Admiral Alan Goodrich Kirk (USNA 1909) commanded Task Force 85 which carried the Scoglitti Attack Force, the 45th Infantry Division (and other troops making up the Cent Force), plus General Bradley and the staff of II Corps. Kirk had been serving as commander, Amphibious Force, Atlantic Fleet, since February, 1943.

[2] Major General Geoffrey Keyes (USMA 1913) had commanded the Provisional Corps, which had overrun all of western Sicily. He became commander of the II Corps in Italy in September.

[3] Vice Admiral Henry Kent Hewitt (USNA 1907) was in command of the Western Naval Task Force. Hewitt in turn was under Admiral Cunningham, the overall naval commander.

Dear General: When things are going rather badly, the troubles of an Allied Commander-in-Chief are wholly at the front. At such times his commanders in his rear are providing him with everything a ship can carry and his great concern is to satisfy, as speedily as possible, demands for supplies, replacements, reinforcements and additional units of all kinds. When things get going rather well, the people in front are quite self-satisfied, but some of the individuals who are responsible for running the war begin to take an enormous interest in its detailed direction. I have in mind just now the recent activity of the Prime Minister in firing telegrams here and to the President about every little detail, particularly where it applies to the propaganda effort. I wrote you a long telegram on the subject, and I think it fully explains the incident concerning which he has most recently wired the President.

Actually, Mr. Macmillan is very much irritated by the occurrence, and apparently feels that it implies lack of confidence in him on the part of the Prime Minister.

I am enclosing a letter from General Spaatz. It is on the old subject of promotions and is completely self-explanatory. In a recent wire to the War Department, we asked whether it were possible to give us a general expression of policy with respect to staff promotions. Some of these recommendations have been submitted to me time and again during the past eight months, but I have always felt that staff promotions, in general, should follow some definite plan to be applied appropriately to comparable positions in Ground and Air Forces. In a letter about a week ago, I sent to you a somewhat similar list involving theater positions, and it is my thought that the two might be used by the G–1 Division in determining exactly what we should do in those cases.[1]

The Seventh Army has been performing magnificently. It has marched over long distances, supplies itself under most difficult circumstances, fought many sharp and successful engagements, and is now in a prominent place on the battleline hammering away to drive the enemy from the island. It is really difficult to give it sufficient credit for its accomplishments to date. I see no reason why it should not continue its fine performance. *Sincerely*

[1] Marshall sent a representative to review this matter with Eisenhower. E. to M., August 4, 1943, *EP*, p. 1317, n. 3.

Dear General: Foreseeing a future need of yours for senior U.S. commanders who have been tested in battle, I have been watching very closely and earnestly the performance of American commanders here and I have been trying to arrange affairs so as to give a number of them opportunity to demonstrate their capabilities.

To give you a brief picture:

First, Patton. He has conducted a campaign where the brilliant successes scored must be attributed directly to his energy, determination and unflagging aggressiveness. The operations of the Seventh Army in Sicily are going to be classed as a model of swift conquest by future classes in the War College in Leavenworth. The prodigious marches, the incessant attacks, the refusal to be halted by appalling difficulties in communications and terrain, are really something to enthuse about. This has stemmed mainly from Patton. He had fine division and corps commanders, but it is obvious that had he been willing to seize on an excuse for resting or refitting, these commanders could have done nothing. He never once chose a line on which he said "we will here rest and recuperate and bring up more strength." On the contrary, when he received an order from Alexander that made it look as if he was to remain rather quiescent in the Enna region, he immediately jumped into a plane, went to Alexander, got the matter cleared up, and kept on driving. Now in spite of all this—George Patton continues to exhibit some of those unfortunate personal traits of which you and I have always known and which during this campaign caused me some most uncomfortable days. His habit of impulsive bawling out of subordinates, extending even to personal abuse of individuals, was noted in at least two specific cases. I have had to take the most drastic steps; and if he is not cured now, there is no hope for him. Personally, I believe that he is cured—not only because of his great personal loyalty to you and to me but because fundamentally he is so avid for recognition as a great military commander that he will ruthlessly suppress any habit of his own that will tend to jeopardize it. Aside from this one thing, he has qualities that we cannot afford to lose unless he ruins himself. So, he can be classed as an army commander that you can use with certainty that the troops will not be stopped by ordinary obstacles.

Next, Bradley. There is very little I need to tell you about him because he is running absolutely true to form all the time. He has brains, a fine capacity for leadership and a thorough understanding of the requirements of modern battle. He has never caused me one moment of worry. He is perfectly capable of commanding an Army. He has the respect of all his associates, including all the British officers that have met him. I am very anxious to keep him in this theater as long as we have any major operations to carry out.

Clark. Clark continues to be what I have always told you—the best organizer, planner and trainer of troops that I have met. Unless something unforeseen occurs, he will shortly have a chance to prove his worth in actual operations. I have every confidence in him. The one trait concerning him that you and I discussed last January has been suppressed. He inspires an intense loyalty in all his staff and in his subordinates, and I have the earnest conviction that if success is possible in the next operation he will achieve it.

For Corps commanders any of the above three, I am sure, would do a magnificent job. Among others that could also command a corps, I would recommend the following: Middleton,[1] Truscott, possibly Dawley,[2] who has not yet been tested, and to this list (although I place his good judgment and common sense far lower than I do his ability in actual battle leadership) I would also add Harmon. My reports on Keyes as an acting corps commander in the Sicilian affair were most favorable.

A special word about Lucas.[3] He has not had combat responsibility but he has had combat experience. He spent the entire month in Sicily, and is well acquainted with battlefield conditions and requirements. I think he would command a combat corps most successfully.

Of course, I have not yet been informed of what operations will be expected in the Mediterranean theater during the coming months. From what I have heard of the present trend, we are not only to lose seven divisions and certain other troops but a very considerable amount of landing craft and some air force. Consequently, our theater will probably not be so important in your calculations and you will not have to worry so much about the commanders that are assigned to me. If you are forced to take one of my present British ground commanders, I would suggest you take Alexander. He is broad-gauged and should perform excellently in the very senior position that would likely be given him. He works on the "Allied" basis. On the other hand, I would be perfectly content to accept Montgomery in Alexander's present place because during these months I have learned to know him very well, feel that I have his personal equation, and have no lack of confidence in my ability to handle him.

I hope this letter does not strike you as being just a waste of your time; I felt that you might like to have some of my thoughts concerning these things. *Very sincerely*

---

[1] Major General Troy Houston Middleton had been a career officer; he resigned in 1937 and was called back to active duty in January, 1942. He commanded the 45th Infantry Division in the Sicilian campaign.

[2] Major General Ernest Joseph Dawley (USMA 1910) commanded the VI Corps in the Salerno invasion in September.

[3] Major General John Porter Lucas (USMA 1911) had served for a time as Eisenhower's "eyes and ears." He replaced Dawley as commander of VI Corps in September.

Dear General: First, I will take up the subject of the permanent list referred to in your telegram # 6595.

Speaking generally, I think you are doing a very gracious and wise thing and, moreover, I must agree in general with the list as you have made it up.

Concerning Stilwell,[1] there can be no shadow of doubt about him. He took a very unattractive looking job, has carried on in the most discouraging kind of circumstances, and has apparently kept his head and done his share in preserving a workable team in that region. He seems self-effacing and effective.

With respect to Patton, I do not see how you could possibly submit a list for permanent Major Generals, on combat performance to date, and omit his name. His job of rehabilitating the Second Corps in Tunisia was quickly and magnificently done. Beyond this, his leadership of the Seventh Army was close to the best of our classic examples. It is possible that in the future some ill-advised action of his, might cause you to regret his promotion. You know his weaknesses as well as his strength, but I am confident that I have eliminated some of the former. His intense loyalty to you and to me makes it possible for me to treat him much more roughly than I could any other senior commander, unless my action were followed immediately by the individual's relief. In the last campaign he, under stress it is true, indulged his temper in certain instances toward individual subordinates who, in General Patton's opinion of the moment, were guilty of malingering. I took immediate and drastic measures, and I am quite certain this sort of thing will never happen again. You have in him a truly aggressive commander and, moreover, one with sufficient brains to do his work in splendid fashion. So I repeat that on the basis of performance to date, I concur completely. Incidentally, I think he will show up even better in an exclusively American theater than in an allied one.

I agree also with respect to *Somervell*. Although all the other individuals named, excepting Handy, are men who have been on one of the various battle-fronts, certainly no one could object to this distinction coming to a man who has carried the burden Somervell has. I think it wise, also, for the moment, to keep the Major General list quite small because you can always, later, promote a Brigadier; whereas, of course, the reverse process is impossible in the regular army.

I do have one or two points to make with respect to your Brigadier list. I think that *McNarney*[2] by all odds should head the list; but I think that Bradley, Handy and Bedell Smith should follow, in order, after him. You have already designated *Bradley* as an Army Commander and he is, in my opinion, the best rounded combat leader I have yet met in our service. While he possibly lacks some of the extraordinary and ruthless driving power that Patton can exert at critical moments, he still has such force and determination that even in this characteristic he is among our best. In all other things he is a jewel to have around and I cannot tell you with what real distress I see him leave this theater. Concerning *Handy*'s work and its value, you are in much better position to judge than I; but the mere fact that you have kept him on that job for the period you have, is evidence enough to me that he is doing it to your satisfaction. But so far as the responsibility resting upon him is concerned, I feel I can speak from experience and I think we should be always ready to assert that the people who are carrying the load in Washington are doing just as much— often far more—to win this war than are those whose names most often appear in the papers. With respect to *Bedell Smith*, I feel a great deal like I do about Handy, except that I have more intimate knowledge of the daily good he is accomplishing. Frankly, he comes close to being the ideal Chief of Staff, and his standing with the British is so high that General Montgomery not long ago remarked to someone that General Bedell Smith was one of the two American generals under whom he, Montgomery, would willingly serve at any time. He is in the job for which he is ideally suited and the contributions he has made to Allied success in the past ten months simply cannot be exaggerated. Concerning the rest of your list, the order in which I would put them would be: *Spaatz*, *Kenny*,[3] *Eichelberger*,[4] *Harmon*[5] and *Eaker*.[6] I clearly realize that in my field, which is restricted as compared with yours, I am not in as favorable position as you from which to judge the value of the contributions these men have made. However, I give you my honest opinion for what it may be worth to you.

I assume that, from time to time, an additional recommendation of this kind could be made to you. I have in mind, for example, Clark, in the event that his leadership of AVALANCHE[7] is up to the best standards.

The Italian negotiations have temporarily reached their culmination and I hope that something real will come from it. If we can only produce a situation that will force the Germans in the south to become fearful and retire rather than to counter attack us quickly and seriously, my greatest concern will be alleviated. Beyond this, if the Italian fleet and merchant ships will sail out of their harbors on the evening of September 8th and head for the places that Admiral Cunningham has designated, we will have at one stroke secured an advantage that will be felt throughout the world. For example, the Admiral tells me that several of these Italian battleships are really firstclass, with some of them having a speed of thirty knots. The armistice terms I insisted upon leave no doubt that the United Nations can do with these ships exactly as we please. We have captured some battleship ammunition at Messina and are hopeful of getting a lot of it at Naples and Taranto. Moreover, I suppose it would be possible for a couple of the United States factories to machine up so as to produce the calibers necessary for the guns of these ships. Suppose, then, within a very short time we could man some of these big ships, at least in their key positions, with either British or American officers and ratings and turn them over to Nimitz[8] in the Pacific; that—it seems to me—would not only be a tremendous advantage to us in the Pacific but would certainly go a long ways to show that the United Nations are not forgetting the Pacific while we are turning our first attention to the European campaign. Moreover, since a great British battle fleet here will be relieved of the necessity of watching the Italians, our position in the Indian Ocean as well as off the coast of Norway should be immediately and decisively strengthened. There is one ship for which our mouths are fairly watering! We hear that in Genoa there is a brand new aircraft carrier, I believe it is called the Roma. If that ship comes out and we get our hands on it, you will probably get a very hysterical sounding telegram from me.

Montgomery had no opposition at all getting ashore in the Toe—a week before the attack I told him he wouldn't have any. I visited Messina with him and looked over the ground on which the attack was to be made and felt sure that there would be no trouble about the matter at all. However, the AVALANCHE operation is a horse of a different color and I am frank to state that there is more than a faint possibility that we may have some hard going. But our Commanders and troops are in good heart; and in view of the great prize that may be won and the fact that, if ever, this is the psychological time to strike, I am determined to hit as hard as I can. I only wish our build-up could work out at a faster rate.

Little by little there seeps in to me rumors as to how you are setting up your European command. Our hearts are in that show and we only hope that we can do everything possible to increase its prospects for success.

Bradley has selected a group of about thirty officers and some twenty enlisted men that he would like to take with him. Upon receipt of your latest telegram on the subject, I told him to go up to the U.K. with only his Chief of Staff and aides, get a real conception of what has been done and of his requirements there, and then, after his visit to the United States, give us his ideas of what he wants. I have promised him that from every Corps and Division Headquarters we will produce some good individuals to help him in his very great task. We will hold nothing back whatsoever, and I am sure you understand that when I do send you a telegram or message concerning our own requirements here, it is only in the thought that when we are risking great resources we should make such provision as is humanly possible to give ourselves a reasonable chance for success.

As a last item, let me say that notice of your reappointment as Chief of Staff came to me as a bit of a shock, for the simple reason that I had not realized that your first four-year term was near its end. Time certainly goes by on speedy wings. My only other thought in connection therewith was that at least here was one action that no one in this world could question. I wouldn't even know how to proceed here if I didn't have the assurance of your firm backing and your complete understanding behind me every minute of the day.

I apologize for this long letter and add only my best wishes for your continued health. *Very sincerely*

[1] Lieutenant General Joseph Warren Stilwell (USMA 1904) was serving as commanding general, U.S. forces in China–Burma–India. He was also commander of the Fifth and Sixth Chinese Armies in Burma. Along with everyone else on this list, he was promoted to the permanent rank that Marshall requested.

[2] Lieutenant General Joseph Taggart McNarney (USMA 1915), an air officer, served as Marshall's Deputy Chief of Staff from March, 1942, until October 21, 1944.

[3] Lieutenant General George Churchill Kenney, a 1911 graduate of the Massachusetts Institute of Technology, was commanding general, Allied Air Forces, Southwest Pacific.

[4] Major General Robert Lawrence Eichelberger (USMA 1909) was commanding the 77th Infantry Division.

[5] Major General Millard Fillmore Harmon (USMA 1912) was commanding general, United States Army Forces, South Pacific area.

[6] Major General Ira Clarence Eaker was the bomber commander of the Eighth Air Force in England. He was promoted to lieutenant general on September 13, 1945. In December, 1943, he became Commander in Chief of the Air Forces in the Mediterranean.

[7] Code name for the invasion of Salerno.

[8] Admiral Chester William Nimitz (USNA 1905) was Commander in Chief, Pacific Fleet.

35 AMILCAR   *September 13, 1943*

Dear General: We are very much in the "touch and go" stage of this operation. Internally the Italians were so weak and supine that we got little if any practical help out of them. However, almost on pure bluff, we did get the Italian fleet into Malta and because of the Italian surrender, were able to rush into Taranto and Brindisi where no Germans were present. Our hold on both places is precarious but we are striving mightily to reinforce.

Our worst problem is AVALANCHE itself. We have been unable to advance and the enemy is preparing a major counter-attack. The 45th Division is largely in the area now and I am using everything we have bigger than a row boat to get the 3d Division in to Clark quickly. Ships that are unsuitable for going to Clark will carry reinforcements into Taranto. Unfortunately the 18 LST's[1] finally given to us temporarily were already loaded for departure to India and it will be tomorrow night before the first eight are ready to move. It will take additional time to get the others unloaded. Many of them were carrying steel rails. In the present situation our great hope is the Air Force. They are working flat out and assuming, which I do, that our hold on southern Italy will finally be solidified, we are going to prove once again that the greatest value of any of the three services is ordinarily realized only when it is utilized in close coordination with the other two. Clark has built a landing strip in the AVALANCHE area but we cannot use the established airdrome there because of hostile artillery fire. We are planning to put three squadrons of fighters on the landing strip this afternoon. That will do something to ease the protective job but will not give us the facilities for operating Fighter-Bombers and P–38's from close up. If we could do this I think we'd begin to advance, even if slowly.

Recently I sent you a telegram about my P–38 situation and I hope that we will quickly get the necessary replacements. I have kept in very close touch with the operations of this Air Force and I assure you that every man is working like a dog to make this thing a success. From a command standpoint this operation is easier to handle than was HUSKY because all of my Commanders in Chief are in the Tunisian area and I have my advanced headquarters here also. We meet daily and it is astonishing how much we can get done to keep our staffs operating at full tilt to execute needed projects.

Montgomery is going up the toe as hard as he can but progress is very slow because of demolitions. As soon as we have sufficient strength in the Taranto area that force will operate to the westward to threaten the Germans operating against Clark. The next week will be one of anxiety, but our Air Force can keep major hostile reinforcements from coming too far south, so if we can only solidify the Naples–Foggia line, the first big crisis will be over.

The Sardinian and Corsican situations show how helpless and inert the Italians really are. In both those places they had the strength to kick the Germans into the sea. Instead they have apparently done nothing, although here and there they do occupy a port or two.

Badoglio[2] wants to see me and has suggested Sicily as a meeting place. I am telling him he has to come here. He also wants to bring along some of his general staff but I can't make out what his general staff can possibly be directing just now. A few Italian artillery units are supporting the British Airborne Division in Taranto. Aside from that there has been some local battling throughout the peninsula. This has, of course, served to keep the Germans preoccupied, but there has been nothing like the effect produced that was easily within the realm of possibility. I have sent a military mission to Badoglio headed by General Mason Mac-Farlane,[3] whom I brought from Gibraltar after getting authority from the CIGS.

The course of this battle may force me finally to change the designation of some of the divisions now earmarked to leave here, beginning in November. However, I cannot see where this will be of any great moment as long as the ones I send are battle-tried. Under present orders they are to come without heavy equipment, which is extremely fortunate, as the hard campaigning in Tunisia, Sicily and in Italy has consumed or partially worn out a lot of it. I have not been back to main headquarters for some days and I do not know what the staff has developed concerning the possibilities of bringing in two green divisions. Taking the long view, it seems to me that we would want to keep strength of this kind in Morocco. Depending upon the situation next summer, they could be used either here or in the north.

I went out the other day with Admiral Cunningham to watch the Italian Fleet sail by. It was a grand sight.

Considering for a moment the worst that could possibly develop, I would, in that event, merely announce that one of our landings had been repulsed—due to my error in misjudging the strength of the enemy at that place. But I have great faith that even in spite of currently grim reports, we'll pull out all right. Our Air Force, the fighting value of our troops, and strenuous efforts by us all, should do the trick. Besides, the Germans must still be worrying some about sabotage and unrest in his rear. I wanted to visit Clark tonight but when Alexander also felt he should go, I had to stay back, because of Alexander's immediate command responsibility, and the fact that we should not both go at once.

With warm personal regard. *Cordially*

[1] Landing ship, tank.
[2] Marshal Pietro Badoglio had formed a new Italian government after the overthrow of Mussolini.
[3] Lieutenant General Frank Noel Mason-MacFarlane was the Governor and Commander in Chief of Gibraltar.

36 AMILCAR   *September 20, 1943*

Dear General: On a visit on the 16th to General Clark's headquarters I found things in reasonably good shape. Some trouble had arisen in the 36th Division during the very hard fighting on the 13th (our worst day). It was struck in the left flank and four battalions were rather badly mauled. My own hasty attempts to trace the cause led me to place a portion of the blame on Dawley. However, this had nothing whatsoever to do with his relief which had been decided upon by Clark and which Alexander (who saw Dawley forty-eight hours before I did) believed to be absolutely necessary. It seems apparent that when the going is really tough he ceases to function as a commander. In my telegram to you I recommend that I be authorized to reduce him. This is a hard thing to do but I believe it to be necessary unless you have special need for him in his present grade.

As matters now stand, the only American Division that I will have to withdraw from *Italy* to meet my U.K. commitments is the 82nd Airborne. The matter of replacements for American Divisions allocated to U.K. service is one that will have to be carefully planned out. Naturally it would be best if all divisions could have all replacements at once. But since it appears that each of these Divisions will have a considerable training time in the U.K. before it is committed to action, considerations of trans-Atlantic and local transportation, together with present resources in replacements, *may* make it advisable for you to ship replacements directly from the United States to the U.K. A hasty estimate given me this morning on our replacement situation is that we now have in Africa about enough to provide for the succeeding month's wastage in Italy. This would provide us none to bring the First and Ninth Divisions, both of which are considerably down, back to strength. I will have the Staff study this matter further and report more formally to the War Department.

While I have no exact information as to how you are going to organize in the U.K., I did receive word, possibly in one of your telegrams, that the new U.S. divisions would be used to *lead the landing* while the experienced divisions, coming from here, would go into the follow-up forces with the idea of going through your beachhead for the initial drive to early objectives. I gather that you are to have *two* Armies. I think you should consider Patton for the command of one of those Armies. Many generals constantly think of battle in terms of, first, concentration, supply, maintenance, replacement, and, second, after all the above is arranged, a *conservative* advance. This type of person is necessary because he prevents one from courting disaster. But occasions arise when one has to remember that under particular conditions, boldness is ten times as important as numbers. Patton's strength is that he thinks only in terms of attack as long as there is a single battalion that can keep advancing. Moreover, the man has a native shrewdness that operates in such a way that his troops always seem to have ammunition and sufficient food no matter where they are. Personally, I doubt that I would ever consider Patton for an army group commander or for any higher position, but as an army commander under a man who is sound and solid, and who has sense enough to use Patton's good qualities without becoming blinded by his love of showmanship and histrionics, he should do as fine a job as he did in Sicily.

Events have progressed here in such a way that it looks like Clark would be my American Army Commander for the fall and winter. He is not so good as Bradley in winning, almost without effort, the complete confidence of everybody around him, including his British associates. He is not the equal of Patton in his refusal to see anything but victory in any situation that arises; but he is carrying his full weight and, so far, has fully justified his selection for his present important post. This leaves Patton as surplus in this theater, so far as an important battle command is concerned. I feel that his talents should not be wasted although naturally I could use him as a "rover" for me if there were no other job in the offing for him.

Tomorrow the three B–24 groups, which came here at a reduced strength of twenty planes per group, will start operating on the communications in north central Italy. Likewise, the eighteen LST's that the Combined Chiefs of Staff temporarily loaned me are now operating to get the 78th Division into Taranto. By the end of the month our picture should be somewhat as follows: In the west the Fifth Army will have the II and VI American Corps and the British X Corps. The British X Corps will be two infantry and one armored division. The two American corps will include the 36th, 45th, 3rd and 34th Divisions with a major portion, by that time, of the First Armored. The 82nd Airborne may still be in action but along about that time it will have to begin concentrating preparatory to its transfer to the U.K.

To digress for a moment. I do not believe in the Airborne *Division.* I believe that airborne troops should be organized in self-contained units comprising infantry, artillery and special services, all of about the strength of a regimental combat team. Even if one had all of the air transport he could possibly use, the fact is that at any given time and at any given spot, only a reasonable number of air transports can be operated because of technical difficulties. To employ at any time and place a whole division would require dropping over such an extended area that I seriously doubt that a division commander could regain control and operate the scattered forces as one unit. In any event, if these troops were organized in smaller, self-contained units, a senior commander with a small staff and radio communications could always be dropped in the area to insure necessary coordination.

To follow up on the general picture: Montgomery's Eighth Army will have the 13th, 30th and 5th Corps. The Fifth Corps is on the right and has now established in that area the First British Airborne Division. The 78th British and the 8th Indian Divisions will make up the rest of this corps, the 78th landing at Taranto and the Indians at Brindisi. There are no Germans to speak of in the heel, up to include the Foggia area, and once these troops can be disembarked with a moderate amount of transportation, they should advance rapidly to a line to the northwest of Foggia. The 13th and 30th Corps, comprising about four divisions, will be the remainder of the Eighth Army, advancing up the center. The rear areas will be organized and protected partially by Italian forces which will operate under Allied control.

I believe that the German, as he sees these forces moving toward him, will fight nothing but delaying action since he will always fear that we will again land a force of about three divisions on his flank, and our reinforced heavy bombers will so constantly pound his communications that he will be too nervous to stand for a real battle south of the Rome area. The German is wily and tough and knows how, with little cost to himself, to make an advancing enemy pay for every foot it gets. Nevertheless, I am still hoping that our reinforced air will create such difficulties in his rear that we can bring sizeable formations of his to decisive action and destroy them. I do not subscribe to the "push back" theory, but my only chance of bringing his southern troops to battle under terms advantageous to us is by intensive use of the Air Force. I am sure we could do something rather effective along this line if the divisions which we are now waiting for, namely, the British 78th and 8th Indian, and the American Second Armored, 3rd and 34th Divisions, were already on the mainland. As it is, I can only hope that the German will wait too long.

A small French Corps of about two divisions is due to begin moving in about the middle of October to serve as part of Clark's Fifth Army.

The above presents the general picture of the next month as nearly as I can analyse it at this moment.

You can see from the above that the period from now until early October is largely one of building up as rapidly as we possibly can, while we content ourselves on the ground with seizing unoccupied points, following up withdrawal, and seeking opportunity to launch sharp attacks against any isolated portion of the enemy. I personally believe that we will have Naples before the end of the month. It is even possible that we may get naval possession of the place before that time. I hear that the place is apparently starving, and the first ships going in there will have to take a load of flour and tinned meats. I hear, also, that cholera and typhus fever have broken out in the city and this will mean a terrific job of inoculation of such of our own soldiers as may have to operate in that particular area.

With personal regard, *Cordially*[1]

[1] Eisenhower added a postscript: "If you can conveniently do so I should like very much for you to pay my respects to the Secretary and the President. I appreciate the obviously solid support they have given to decisions that possibly looked, at the time, as very risky." E. to M., September 20, 1943, *EP*, p. 1442, n. 9.

37 ALGIERS   *December 17, 1943*

Dear General: Yesterday I wrote you an official letter on the subject of promotions. This one is more of a personal nature.

First, let me tell you how very deeply appreciative I am of your thoughtfulness in sending me the memorandum, in your handwriting, on which the agreement was made in Teheran that I was to command OVERLORD.[1] Of all possible assignments this was the one that I least expected, since I had assumed that the decision was firm that you were to take that job on personally. However, immediately I learned of this from the President and upon receipt of your telegram from Cairo, I began figuring on the best way to organize the strictly American phases of this theater. Several combinations are possible. My first idea was as follows:

Bring Clark back as Theater Commander and assign Lucas to command the 5th Army. This would have made Patton about the only choice to plan and execute the early stages of ANVIL.[2] I did not like this solution for several reasons. First, Clark's presence with his 5th Army I regard as a virtual necessity until the Rome line has been secured. He is doing a very good job and is in the middle of the problem. It is impracticable for any man to be an active Army Commander and to be at the same time administrative Theater Commander because this latter individual is in constant communication with Washington over matters of varying importance and which cannot possibly be handled except with the aid and assistance of the American staff of Base Headquarters. Another reason for rejecting this solution was that I believe Clark should be the man to plan and execute ANVIL if we can work it out, because of his particular skill in that sort of work. If he were made the American Theater Commander, the same reasons that prevent him from doing both jobs at present would prevent him from carrying out ANVIL.

While working in the dark to some extent because of lack of knowledge of your plans for particular individuals, I finally came to the conclusion that the best possible arrangement would be to bring Devers[3] down here as the American Theater Commander. It would appear that he will be superfluous in U.K. Since, by the SEXTANT[4] decisions ANVIL is to become a rather formidable attack rather than a mere bluff, it will require, from this minute onward, a headquarters that can work in the closest possible collaboration with Naval and Air commanders. This means that the 7th Army headquarters must stay here. However, because of my knowledge of the personalities involved, I believe that Patton himself should be brought to England. This solution would permit Clark, at the proper time, to take active command of the 7th Army headquarters and turn over the 5th to Lucas.

With regard to organization in OVERLORD I have some positive ideas that may be a bit modified when once I reach there or possibly even before that. Briefly they are as follows:

At the beginning of the operation and for many weeks following that—in fact up until the time when the ground front becomes so broad as practically to compel the utilization of two *separate* tactical air forces—there should be a single ground commander. If the British would give him to me, I would like to have Alexander. My conception of his job would be that his eventual assignment would be in command of the British Army Group but that until the time for employment of two complete army groups arrived, he would be my single ground commander. Under him a British Army and an American Army will carry out the direct assaults and will expand as rapidly as possible, each in its own sector. This arrangement to my mind is absolutely necessary because of the compelling necessity for complete coordination between tactical air and ground forces. The front is so narrow that the employment of two separate tactical air forces at the beginning is unthinkable. This means one tactical air force man in control, and this means also one ground commander in control. I would therefore see the developments somewhat as follows:

We would go into the operation with an operational organization set up largely according to the one we now have here. Tedder would be my chief air man and with him I would have Spaatz who would have control of the Strategic Air Forces. Under Tedder will be one officer in charge of coordinating the tactical air forces. This tactical air force commander will be in the same headquarters as Alexander and they will operate as they have here. Bradley will have command of the First U.S. Army and as quickly as another army can begin to come in alongside of him, Bradley will move back to U.S. Army Group, giving his Army to the best man that is then available. In this connection, while we might look forward to a Corps Commander developing into the Army command, I would have no objection whatsoever to taking one of your younger army commanders at home and letting him go in with Bradley and become experienced in the problems that he will meet. By the time we get four armies deployed along the front it is likely that we would have to have two tactical air forces, at which time I would deal personally with each of the Army Group Commanders or make any other arrangement that then seemed best, depending upon the location of the various headquarters.

With respect to the administrative side, I expect the S.O.S. Commander to be also the Deputy American Theater Commander. I will compel him to take off my hands all of those details of administration that consume so much time and thought.

Under this whole arrangement we will be most economical in the constitution of headquarters, while command will be simple and direct.

I would want Patton as one of my Army Commanders.

With respect to the whole Patton affair, there was a bad mistake made in the staff here when the matter first broke into public print. However, this mistake was made by my ablest and finest officer and there is nothing for me to do except to keep still and take the brunt of the affair. I hope it has died out by the time you arrive, as I have no intention of throwing valuable men to the wolves merely because of one mistake. Actually the mistake here occurred late one evening just as I had returned from a long trip, suffering from a heavy cold. I was in bed for a day and knew little about it except by constant telephoning. However, I think that more important news will soon distract public attention.[5] *Sincerely*

---

[1] Plan for the invasion of Northwest Europe, Spring, 1944. It had a broader connotation than NEPTUNE. The former included the entire operation, air, sea, and ground; the latter, the Channel crossing, the seige of the beachhead, and the breakout from the beachhead.

[2] The invasion of the south of France in August, 1944.

[3] Lieutenant General Jacob Loucks Devers (USMA 1909) had been serving as commanding general of the European Theater of Operations since May, 1943.

[4] The international conference at Cairo in November–December, 1943.

[5] Eisenhower added a postscript in longhand which read: "I'm having the memo framed that you sent me from Teheran."

CHAPTER 4

Preparing OVERLORD, January–June, 1944

Eisenhower arrived in London on January 15, 1944, to prepare and mount the cross-Channel invasion of northwestern Europe, Operation OVERLORD. Both his status and the Allied situation had considerably improved since his previous stay in 1942. In 1942 he had been an uncertain and untested protégé of Marshall's. By 1944 he had borne out Marshall's judgment and was the successful battle-tested commander of a coalition army. Eisenhower had confidently assumed control of an army that would total over 4,000,000 men before the end of the war.

The balanced tone of Eisenhower's eighteen letters to Marshall of this period reflect his confidence. Most of his comments on organization concern personnel and show little uneasiness about command arguments. His comments on strategy show that he played the most crucial role in deciding one of the great strategic questions of the period, whether or not to launch an amphibious assault on southern France (Operation ANVIL) in conjunction with OVERLORD. In addition, he supervised the planning for the OVERLORD assault, and in all of this had an important part in the allocation of resources, particularly landing craft. Eisenhower himself was fully aware of the contrast to the situation he faced in 1942.[1]

COMMAND ORGANIZATION

As always, Eisenhower was determined to insure clear lines of authority and to select the most effective subordinates. The principle of unity

---

[1] Eisenhower, *Crusade in Europe*, p. 220.

of command was not fully accepted, but discussions of personnel rather than command organization itself dominated his writings at this time.

As in 1943, Eisenhower had to continue his fight for control of air operations. The struggle was closely related to the dispute over where the strategic or long-range bombers ought to concentrate their attacks.[2] Eisenhower and Air Chief Marshal Sir Trafford Leigh-Mallory (who had been tentatively selected to direct OVERLORD air forces) wanted the heavy bombers to attack the railroad network in France, western Germany, and the Low Countries. This would effectively interdict the battle area and thus hamper the movement of German supplies and reinforcements. Air Chief Marshall Arthur Harris and General Carl Spaatz, supported by Churchill, wanted to continue the strategic bombing assault on Germany's industrial capacity, especially factories producing fighter aircraft and refined petroleum. This disagreement over operations made the British, especially Churchill, reluctant to give Eisenhower and Leigh-Mallory control of the RAF bomber force.

Yet Eisenhower sent Marshall only infrequent references to this struggle. The reasons were several. Eisenhower did not have to set up a brand new structure as he had to do in 1942. He knew Marshall wanted him to insist upon command of the air forces, so his direction was clear. As long as he and his chief agreed, there was really no need to write Marshall about it, unless Eisenhower felt especially threatened. It is apparent that he did not. Operations in the Mediterranean had demonstrated the necessity of the use of air power in close support of ground operations and Eisenhower had no intention of wavering on that issue.[3] In fact, he told Churchill he was prepared to "go home" if he did not obtain control of the air for the period of the invasion.[4] He had never been so emphatic before and there is no reason to believe that he was being melodramatic. Eisenhower had at first felt that he had Churchill's support for his control of the air forces.[5] Thus, feeling that there was no real threat from above, knowing Marshall's insistence on this point and agreeing with him, Eisenhower felt that the problem would eventually be solved to his satisfaction. After all, in contrast to TORCH, when he made frequent references to setting up the proper command lines, he had written Marshall only once from the

---

[2] For a discussion of the issues and personalities involved, see Pogue, *Supreme Command*, pp. 123–37; John Ehrman, *Grand Strategy*, vol. V, History of the Second World War, ed. J. R. M. Butler (London, 1956), pp. 286–304; Wesley Frank Craven and James Lea Cate, eds., *Europe: Argument to V-E Day*, The Army Air Forces in World War II, vol. III (Chicago, 1958), pp. 67–83.

[3] Eisenhower, *Crusade in Europe*, pp. 221–22.

[4] E. to Tedder, February 29, 1944, *EP*, p. 1756, n. 2.

[5] Churchill had told Smith previously that he felt that control of operational aircraft should go to Eisenhower. Butcher, *My Three Years*, p. 276.

Mediterranean concerning this matter. This occurred when the CCS at Casablanca had diluted his authority and Marshall seemed to accept the arrangements.

Eisenhower had been aware from the start that disagreement over control of the strategic air force might become an issue. In his first letter, January 17, he told Marshall that among the various questions to be settled was "the exact pattern of command." On February 9, Eisenhower wrote that he expected shortly a draft of the plan for air operations, which would lay priorities and fix dates for the passage of control of the strategic air forces to Eisenhower. He did not refer again to the problem until March 3, when the fight had ended in his favor. Although there was one further argument over the precise wording of Eisenhower's directive and he had to agree to certain reservations, nonetheless control was secured.[6] He did not have power over the British coastal command; the CCS could give him additional bomber forces; and the British could withdraw their forces if the safety of Great Britain was in danger—but nonetheless the CCS on April 14 formally turned over control of the strategic air forces for the invasion period[7] to Eisenhower. On April 29 he reported that the British had made one more effort to change his air plans, but Eisenhower did not waver in his insistence on the need for overwhelming air support of the assault area.

Eisenhower had no major problems with naval or ground command, although there was a minor encounter over naval representation in the SHAEF command. Admiral King had pointed out to Eisenhower that Admiral Chester Nimitz, commanding in the Pacific, had naval officers in charge of personnel, plans, and operations, but had army officers in charge of intelligence and logistics. He was concerned over the lack of adequate naval representation on Eisenhower's staff, where all the section chiefs were army officers. Eisenhower did agree on May 5 to add an American as Assistant Chief of Staff to the naval commander, who was British.[8] But the next day Eisenhower complained to Marshall that the true integration at his headquarters was not "completely understood" in Washington.[9] He did not have any arguments during this period concerning the ground command. This was largely because he had Montgomery as the single ground commander. However, he intended to place the American ground commander, Bradley, on an equal footing with

---

[6] E. to M., March 3, 1944, *EP*, pp. 1758–60; E. to Tedder, March 9, 1944, *EP*, pp. 1765–66; E. to M., March 21, 1944, *EP*, pp. 1781–82; Memorandum, March 22, 1944, *EP*, pp. 1782–87.

[7] Memorandum, March 22, 1944, *EP*, p. 1787, n. 9.

[8] E. to M., April 25, 1944, *EP*, p. 1832, n. 3.

[9] See also Pogue, *Supreme Command*, p. 66, for the role of SHAEF staff in planning, and Eisenhower, *Crusade in Europe*, p. 221, for Eisenhower's own defense of this organization.

Montgomery once the beachhead was established and separate zones of operations were clearly in order. At that point, trouble in this area would begin, and Eisenhower knew it.[10]

Trying to obtain the people he wanted and assessing the contribution of the personnel he had were always both frustrating and enlightening. On January 29 and February 9, he dealt at length with selection of combat commanders.[11] He confessed to being "a bit uneasy about our failure to get a greater leaven of combat experience among our formations," and indicated that he was still bitter about not having been able to bring everybody from the Mediterranean theater he would have wanted. Eisenhower quite naturally recalled the experience of the green U.S. troops in the Tunisian campaign and had commented to Marshall upon the difference in performance brought about by the development of leaders tested in battle.

Eisenhower had to deal with the commanders he had as well as obtain new ones. This often meant resolving a dispute over Patton. April 29 found him commenting on the latest unfortunate public statements. Marshall wrote that the newspapers had been filled with Patton's statements referring to Britain and America's rule of the world.[12] Eisenhower considered simply sacking Patton and sending him home, and Marshall assured his support no matter how heavily or lightly Eisenhower treated his subordinate. Ultimately, Eisenhower decided that Patton's experience and ability would be sorely missed and contented himself with an official reprimand.[13]

Eisenhower had to contend with other personnel problems as well. On May 6 he complained about "things that need never to have arisen," referring to three incidents. The first was that involving Patton; the second was that of a high-ranking air force officer who had stated in a public dining room that the invasion would come before June 15; the third, that a staff officer had made a number of purchases for Eisenhower's living quarters which Eisenhower considered "exorbitant."[14] By May 21 he had

---

[10] Eisenhower, *Crusade in Europe*. p. 223. Eisenhower was aware that the principle of unity of command was not wholly accepted. In a private memo of May 22, he wrote that the teamwork on the SHAEF staff had been easier to accomplish than that on the TORCH staff. This no doubt reflected the fact that many of them had been with Eisenhower in the Mediterranean. "On the other hand, complete devotion to the principle of unity of command has been more difficult to establish among these Commanders-in-Chief than it was among Cunningham, Tedder and Alexander, when all three came under my command about February 3d or 4th of '43." Memorandum, May 22, 1944, *EP*, pp. 1880–82.

[11] Marshall had sent him a list of those available. E. to M., January 28, 1944, *EP*, p. 1694, n. 1.

[12] E. to M., April 29, 1944, *EP*, p. 1838, n. 1; Farago, *Patton*, pp. 416–23.

[13] E. to M., April 30, 1944, *EP*, pp. 1840–41; E. to M., May 3, 1944, *EP*, p. 1846; E. to Patton, May 3, 1944, *EP*, pp. 1846–47.

[14] See Butcher, *My Three Years*, pp. 536–37.

been informed of "the most serious breach of security of which I have yet heard." The case involved a key naval officer. He raged, "Sometimes I get so angry at the occurrence of such needless and additional hazards that I could cheerfully shoot the offender myself."

All was not bleak, however. Eisenhower was quite pleased with the readiness of the OVERLORD force. His last letter before D-day, written on May 24, showed that his thoughts were focusing on the men with responsibility for carrying out all the planning—the combat commander and his troops. He asked for authorization of a special distinctive marking on the uniforms of combat troops.[15]

STRATEGY AND TACTICS

As reflected in his letters during this period, Eisenhower's principal concern was planning. Grand strategy and theater planning for OVERLORD were intertwined, and he now played a more positive role in their determination. The great strategic debate concerned whether to have a landing in southern France, Operation ANVIL,[16] in conjunction with OVERLORD. There were three basic attitudes. The British argued from the first that ANVIL could not be brought about without weakening the OVERLORD assault and critically jeopardizing Allied forces in Italy. The American Chiefs, especially Marshall, insisted to the last that it was possible to mount ANVIL, even though they acknowledged the effect of events in Italy in the design. Eisenhower's position was the most flexible and the most reasonable. Remembering similar difficulties in the Mediterranean, he maintained that his overriding priority was to insure that OVERLORD had the necessary resources, especially landing craft, to get ashore and stay ashore. Although he initially favored ANVIL, he acknowledged much more readily than Marshall that the Anzio operations in Italy would require prolonged use of landing craft to prevent total disaster and to break out of the stalemate. Therefore, Eisenhower believed that ANVIL as a simultaneous assault should be abandoned and planning proceed on the basis that OVERLORD be correspondingly strengthened to make up for the lost ANVIL. He told Marshall this but loyally insisted to the British that planning for the southern France invasion continue.

Eisenhower's first letter to Marshall from London on January 17 dealt almost entirely with this problem. He said that he was hesitant to accept reduction of ANVIL because of the commitment to the Russians on this operation and because ANVIL represented the only profitable way to

---

[15] Eisenhower's idea was approved. E. to M., May 24, 1944, *EP*, p. 1888, n. 1.

[16] For the debate, see Pogue, *Supreme Command*, pp. 108–17; Ehrman, *Grand Strategy*, V, pp. 225–70.

employ the French forces, in which the Allies had placed considerable investment. This did not mean that Eisenhower was prepared to give up OVERLORD for ANVIL. Sicily and Salerno had taught him the importance of landing in sufficient strength. When he had first seen the OVERLORD plan calling for a three-divisional assault, even before he knew he was to command it,[17] he had immediately expressed the belief that it needed to be widened.

Eisenhower submitted his estimate of the needs for OVERLORD and his views on the feasibility of ANVIL (simultaneously with OVERLORD) to the CCS on January 23. He made a strong plea for maintaining a two- or three-division ANVIL. However, if mounting such an invasion concurrently with the northwestern European invasion should seem unfeasible, he felt that ANVIL should be reduced to a threat—to be employed later at an appropriate moment of enemy weakness. Still, such a solution should be adopted only as a "last resort." Both the Americans and the British accepted Eisenhower's broadening of OVERLORD, and the American chiefs delegated authority to Eisenhower for ANVIL discussions with the British.[18]

The two sides remained at odds about ANVIL during February, and Eisenhower was in the middle of the fray. While still pressing the case for ANVIL to the British, Eisenhower had sent a message to Marshall that "late developments in Italy create the possibility that the necessary forces there cannot be disentangled in time to put on a strong ANVIL."[19] This comment had drawn an angry response from Marshall, who accused Eisenhower of falling victim to "localitis." He denied the charge, pointing out that his conclusions had been reached independently and that he was still pressing the case for the invasion of southern France. Eisenhower stressed the requirements for OVERLORD, stating that this was his overriding concern.[20] He did not specifically rule out ANVIL, although he had written a private memo on the 7th in which he said, "with Italy requiring an allotment, it looks like ANVIL is doomed."[21] On February 9, he wrote Marshall that his response to Marshall's charge had been the first time he had been "on the defensive in explaining my views to you." He said that the reason was that there appeared to be an implication on Marshall's part "that I might, merely in the interests of local harmony, surrender my convictions as to operations. I hope I cleared up that point."

In the same letter, Eisenhower commented on the operations in Italy on the basis of his own experiences, and said that he had told Churchill

[17] Memorandum, February 7, 1944, *EP*, pp. 1711–13.
[18] E. to CCS and BCOS, January 23, 1944, *EP*, p. 1676, n. 8; see also Gordon A. Harrison, *Cross-Channel Attack*, U.S. Army in World War II, ed. Kent Roberts Greenfield (Washington, 1951), pp. 168–70.
[19] E. to M., February 6, 1944, *EP*, pp. 1707–8.
[20] E. to M., February 8, 1944, *EP*, pp. 1713–15.
[21] Memorandum, February 7, 1944, *EP*, pp. 1711–13.

that bad weather would "create a continued demand for landing craft which we could not afford, and would possibly place the landing forces in a precarious position." Eisenhower realized that the plight of the troops at Anzio contained a lesson to be appled to the ANVIL debate—namely, that the OVERLORD landing had to be made in sufficient force to quickly achieve success, particularly in capturing ports. The lack of a good port at Anzio necessitated supply by means of landing craft. This situation would continue from January until May 25 when the Anzio forces at last linked up with Fifth Army.[22] Since planning for a simultaneous OVERLORD-ANVIL had posited that no landing craft would be needed in Italy after the end of January, the ultimate fate of a simultaneous ANVIL was clear.

Eisenhower continued to urge the British Chiefs to at least plan for ANVIL[23] and to counsel Marshall that ANVIL as planned was probably not possible.[24] On February 22, while continuing to insist on planning for ANVIL, Eisenhower agreed that Italy must have first call on resources for the moment. These two ideas were embodied in a draft agreement by Eisenhower and Ismay and the arrangements were to be reviewed on March 20. Basically, planning proceeded much as Eisenhower advocated, but in the meantime events required that specific decisions be made. On March 3 Eisenhower told Marshall that he had received an emergency request from Alexander on February 28 to retain in the Mediterranean some British LST's which were slated to leave immediately for England.[25] The LST's were needed to get another division into the beachhead. Eisenhower suggested that the request be approved, but that 26 new LST's slated for the Mediterranean be sent instead to England.[26]

In this same letter, Eisenhower once again pointed out, "It becomes daily more apparent that a 2 Division ANVIL is out of the question." By this time Eisenhower was also willing to convey this thought to the British, which he did at a meeting on that same day.[27] Finally, on March 17, three days before the review of commitments was to be made, Marshall acknowledged that it was unlikely that the Allies would take Rome in the near future. Everyone had agreed that this must occur before

---

[22] E. to M., February 6, 1944, *EP*, p. 1708, n. 5. For the difficulties at Anzio, see Martin Blumenson, "General Lucas at Anzio," *Command Decisions*, ed. Kent Roberts Greenfield (Washington, 1960), pp. 323–50.

[23] E. to BCOS, February 18, 1944, *EP*, pp. 1732–34.

[24] E. to M., February 19, 1944, *EP*, pp. 1735–36.

[25] Ehrman, *Grand Strategy*, V, p. 244.

[26] The U.S. Chiefs objected to Eisenhower's proposal, although not to the delay in the departure of the LST's from the Mediterranean. They proposed instead that the LST's in the Mediterranean be allowed to remain there and join the OVERLORD forces in May. They argued that the 26 new U.S. LST's had been especially designed for use in the Mediterranean. E. to M., March 3, 1944, *EP*, pp. 1759–69, n. 3; and Ehrman, *Grand Strategy*, V, pp. 243–45.

[27] E. to M., March 3, 1944, *EP*, p. 1760, n. 4.

ANVIL could be launched. Marshall said that the most reasonable thing was to cancel a simultaneous ANVIL and he assured Eisenhower that he would support his wishes.[28] Although this move eased the deadlock, the problem was not yet solved. The British wished to cancel ANVIL entirely while the Americans wished only to postpone it, with that operation to have priority over a continuing offensive in Italy once the main forces and the Anzio bridgehead had joined.[29] Eisenhower complained about the continuing debate on March 21.

The new deadlock was broken in April. On April 17 Eisenhower told Marshall that he had received Marshall's cable agreeing that ANVIL be indefinitely postponed and that the battle in Italy would have current priority in the Mediterranean.[30] Eisenhower realized that this represented only a temporary solution and did not deal with future developments. On May 6, in telling Marshall of his talk with the commander in the Mediterranean concerning forthcoming operations, he noted, "I dread the possibility of strong Allied Forces in the Mediterranean becoming immobile and useless at the very time when they should be fighting full out."

Among other elements in planning which concerned Eisenhower, the most significant was a brief but meaningful debate on OVERLORD assault tactics involving the use of airborne troops. Eisenhower stated on February 9 that he envisioned their use in close support of ground operations. Marshall had a much bolder scheme, writing on February 10 that he had directed studies to be made in Washington concerning the use of airborne troops in OVERLORD. Among several alternate plans presented, he had approved one that envisioned the establishment of an airhead south of Evreux, with four airfields that could be fully developed within forty-eight hours. "This plan appeals to me because I feel that it is a true vertical envelopment and would create such a strategic threat to the Germans that it would call for a major revision of their defensive plans." He pointed out that the operation had the asset of being a complete surprise, would threaten the Seine crossings as well as Paris, and would be a rallying point for the French underground. He felt that the only argument against the plan was "that we have never done anything like this before, and frankly, that reaction makes me tired." He added that he was sending the authors of the plan over to see Eisenhower personally, and did not wish to put pressure on Eisenhower but only wanted to assure that Eisenhower was seriously considering the operation.[31]

Eisenhower replied on the 19th, and he rejected the plan. He agreed

[28] E. to M., March 18, 1944, *EP*, p. 1773, n. 1.
[29] E. to M., March 21, 1944, *EP*, p. 1779, n. 6.
[30] E. to M., April 17, 1944, *EP*, pp. 1825–27.
[31] E. to M., February 19, 1944, *EP*, p. 1739, n. 1.

with the idea but disagreed with the timing: "As I see it, the first requisite
is for the Expeditionary Force to gain a firm and solid footing on the Continent and to secure at least one really good sheltered harbor. . . . To
meet this *first tactical crisis* I intend to devote everything that can be
profitably used, including airborne troops." Eisenhower's second reason
was also based upon his experiences in the Mediterranean. He said, that,
no matter how superior Allied air forces were, they could not totally
prevent the movement of troops and supplies—thus the enemy retained
the capability of massing his forces at a given point. "There must exist
either the definite capability of both forces to combine *tactically*, or the
probability that each force can operate independenely without danger of
defeat."

Drawing on his experience at Anzio, Eisenhower said that the Germans did not fear the strategic threat of envelopment, for conventional
military tactics at Anzio would have dictated a rapid German withdrawal.
"But the German decided that the thrust could not be immediately translated into *mobile tactical action*, and himself began attacking." He pointed
out that the Allied force that had landed south of Anzio "was immobile
and could not carry out the promise that was implicit in the situation then
existing." The situation had been saved only because complete command
of the sea had made possible the supply and reinforcement of the beachhead. According to Eisenhower the lesson to be learned was: "An airborne landing carried out at too great a distance from other forces which
will also be immobile for some time, will result in a much worse situation." He then pointed out that the landing force would meet strong opposition and that the role of the airborne forces in close support of the
ground forces was crucial. He did not agree that large-scale use of airborne troops would be impossible if not done in coordination with the
OVERLORD landings. However, he tried to soften the rejection by claiming,
"I instinctively dislike ever to uphold the conservative as opposed to the
bold. You may be sure that I will earnestly study the ideas. . . ." Later,
on May 21, he told Marshall that he was trying to "visualize an operation" in which he could bring to bear a large armored attack from the
beachhead in conjunction with "a deep and very heavy penetration by
airborne troops."

This caveat notwithstanding, Eisenhower's refutal of Marshall's idea
was complete. This was the Chief's greatest effort to contribute to the
overall tactics of the assault that everyone, including Marshall, had thought
he would command. His protégé, Eisenhower, more conservative in his
tactics, citing the realities and quarreling with the myths of combat operations, rejected his contribution. Eisenhower had also questioned Marshall's
position on the great strategic problem, the debate over whether or not to
launch ANVIL. The difference between 1942 and 1944 was considerable.

DIPLOMACY

Eisenhower's letters showed an increasing consideration of diplomatic problems. An Allied commander could never be above these and other problems of a political nature. As much as Eisenhower repeatedly averred his distaste for such matters, he had discovered that they were often as important as military concerns.

Yet Eisenhower did not refer at all in his letters to his most pressing diplomatic problem—the setting up of channels for dealing with the French.[32] This was probably caused by several factors: Eisenhower's Chief of Staff Bedell Smith handled most of the detailed working out of arrangements which culminated in an agreement with General Pierre Koenig on April 19,[33] just as Smith had handled most of the details of the Italian surrender negotiations. Marshall had specifically told Eisenhower to leave such matters to Smith and others, and the Chief himself left political affairs to Roosevelt and Churchill after the Darlan Deal.[34] Consequently, Marshall seemed to act, in the main, as a relayer of information between the President and Eisenhower's headquarters.[35]

On February 15 Eisenhower offered a solution to the problem of the postwar occupation of Europe which had left the British and Roosevelt at odds.[36] Both wanted to occupy northwest Germany, containing the rich Ruhr region. Churchill argued that the only zonal division that made sense was for the British to take the northwest, as the British would be to the north in the landings and then throughout the campaign. On the other hand, Roosevelt said that he was not going to police France, Italy, or the Balkans.[37] Eisenhower's solution was simple: "Refuse to take specific American responsibility for any area." He wanted to avoid a conflict by keeping SHAEF in existence, thereby administering western Germany on an Allied basis. Eisenhower later made another long and more detailed exposition of this idea in a letter of May 27, but it was not adopted.[38] Eisenhower's suggestion of May 16 to aid the Communist guerilla army of Marshal Josef Tito in Yugoslavia was accepted. Tito's forces were waging far more effective warfare against the Axis than was the non-Com-

---

[32] For the problem of relations with the French at this time, see Pogue, *Supreme Command*, pp. 138–57; Ehrman, *Grand Strategy*, V, pp. 318–31.

[33] E. to M., April 26, 1944, *EP*, p. 1835, n. 2.

[34] Pogue, *Ordeal and Hope*, p. 424.

[35] For Eisenhower's description of his difficulty in establishing relations with the French, see Eisenhower, *Crusade in Europe*, pp. 247–48.

[36] See Pogue, *Supreme Command*, pp. 348–58; Feis, *Churchill–Roosevelt–Stalin*, pp. 358–73, 530–34, 619–21; Frederick Morgan, *Overture to Overlord* (New York, 1950), pp. 104–22.

[37] Pogue, *Supreme Command*, p. 349; Feis, *Churchill–Roosevelt–Stalin*, pp. 360, 363.

[38] E. to Smith, May 20, 1944, *EP*, pp. 1872–76.

munist army under General Draža Mihailović, but they desperately needed supplies of all kinds.[39] Therefore he asked that obsolete U.S. planes be found to transport Yugoslav supplies from southern Italy to Yugoslavia.[40]

These letters, along with several references to Churchill, constituted all of Eisenhower's occupation with diplomacy. While quantitatively they are small, they do show a willingness to give opinions on matters that even Eisenhower had to admit were not military. Further, they help to reinforce the view that, while disclaiming that political factors played a part in his decision-making, he was well aware of their existence and would take them into account even while proclaiming that he did not.

VISITING TROOPS

Continuing the earlier pattern, there is little mention of visits to troops. On March 21 he did write Marshall of such a visit saying that he "got real recreation and a lift out of it," and that he planned to see several outfits the same week. He reported on April 17 that he had been busy inspecting troops, and noted that they were "in good heart." Perhaps because the invasion date was drawing near, on May 21, he commented at some length on these visits. He said that he recognized the desire of the troops to see their commander but that he had had to sandwich the task between important appointments in the London area.[41] "There is no question at all as to the readiness of the troops. They are well trained, fit and impatient to get the job started and completed."

PERSONAL COMMENTS

The readiness of the troops was complemented by the readiness of the commanders, including Eisenhower. The tone of his comments to Marshall show his increasing self-confidence. Where his letters from London in 1942 had been fulsome and those from the Mediterranean querulous and tense, those of this period are calm. His last letters before the invasion are on mundane matters and betray no great nervousness. His few personal comments to Marshall also illustrate this.

In his first letter, January 17, Eisenhower thanked Marshall, warmly but

[39] Winston S. Churchill, *The Second World War*, vol. V, *Closing the Ring*, pp. 465–78.

[40] This was done. See Craven and Cate, *Argument to V-E Day*, pp. 507–11; Butcher, *My Three Years*, p. 549.

[41] From February 1 to June 1 Eisenhower visited 26 divisions, 24 airfields, 5 ships, and numerous other installations. Eisenhower, *Crusade in Europe*, p. 238.

briefly, for arranging his visit to the U.S. Then, when on March 3 Eisenhower expressed surprise that one of his top subordinates had been promoted without his approval, Marshall promptly apologized.[42] Eisenhower also requested a personal favor. On March 15 he inquired whether Marshall could arrange for Eisenhower's son John, shortly to graduate from West Point, to visit him after graduation. Marshall agreed to arrange the visit.[43]

On March 21 Eisenhower awkwardly expressed the hope that Marshall was in good health and spirits, adding "When I think of all your problems as compared to those the rest of us have to solve, I wonder how you do it." Eisenhower's outburst was prompted in part by gratitude and an attempt to assuage Marshall's feelings, for this expression came immediately after Marshall's breaking of the ANVIL deadlock by his acknowledgment that the operation would have to be postponed.

On April 17, in referring to Marshall's advice about setting up a single head of replacement problems, he assured Marshall, "You may be sure that no objections on the part of subordinate commanders or staffs will deter me from setting up any system that appears to me to be the most efficient." But he also noted the advantage of planning for a single operation, unlike the situation in 1942, when he "had a warning from the very highest levels" on considering abandonment of Casablanca. This was also a reminder to Marshall, who had insisted on the Casablanca attack. In the same letter he said that the entire command was "approaching the task with determination and confidence," a sentiment he repeated on May 6 along with the observation that most were staying in good health.

On April 29 and again on May 21 he referred to Marshall's expressed desire to visit the European theater and assured Marshall of his welcome. This assurance was sincere and made clear that their relationship was still a good one. It had not been weakened by a period during which personal communications had fallen off sharply. Eisenhower had not sent Marshall a personal letter from late September, 1943, until the middle of December when he was preparing to leave the theater. Although the two men had seen each other in the Mediterranean in the latter part of that period, both must have been a little uneasy over the popularly manufactured rivalry between them over the OVERLORD command. After arriving in England Eisenhower had become immediately involved in the ANVIL debate, in which he supported Marshall's plans to the British, but soon differed with his Chief. In the midst of this he had also turned down Marshall's great airborne scheme.

In these circumstances the two men would surely have had to have been supermen not to feel some strain. Yet each had sufficient respect

[42] E. to M., March 10, 1944, *EP*, p. 1767, n. 1.
[43] E. to M., March 15, 1944, *EP*, p. 1769, n. 1.

for the other to survive this period and reestablish a warm communication. This is noticeable as of March 21 when the ANVIL deadlock had been broken. Before then there had been virtually no comments by Eisenhower of a personal nature. Perhaps the resumption of easy contact dates from Eisenhower's request for Marshall to arrange John's visit on the 15th. From then on, every time that Eisenhower wrote a letter on other than a single subject he included some personal reference to Marshall. Thus if there had been a temporary uneasiness it had been overcome. In the process, perhaps an even stronger link was forged.

Eisenhower's more maturing relationship with Marshall reflected his approach to the problems he encountered during this period. He had met the threat to his command of the Air Force with resolution, hardly mentioning it at all. Instead, his comments in this area had been mainly directed toward filling his organization with reliable personnel. Yet he knew that the threat to his authority always existed.

His role in the allocation of resources had grown as well. In 1942 he had been viewed as Marshall's staff man and had vacillated with Marshall and then backed down on his recommendations concerning the Mediterranean landings. In 1943 he had not participated in grand strategy-making, but in the carrying out of strategy he had progressed, aided by disagreements among others, to making the decision as to how and where to conduct operations against Italy. Now in 1944, he had participated as an equal in the great debate over ANVIL, had told Marshall of his disagreement with him, and had supervised the revision and overall planning of the OVERLORD assault. This last endeavor constituted his most valuable practical experience in determining the allocation of resources. It would make him even more aware of logistic factors in active operations. He had also displayed the conservatism that marked his tactics. After ANVIL was abandoned he had insisted that resources for OVERLORD be increased. He was determined to insure that his men could get ashore and stay there. From the start he had widened the assault and insisted that air power and airborne forces be employed in close support of combat operations.

Indeed, in all these areas, Eisenhower knew that even though this preparation period had its own frustrations and problems, they would pale alongside the difficulties posed by the combat operations which would begin on June 6. And when these difficulties seemed particularly threatening, Eisenhower would write of them to Marshall.

Dear General Marshall: After an all-day train ride from Prestwick, I arrived in London late Saturday night, roughly forty-eight hours after leaving Washington. The Press Relations people had done a good job on confusing the issue as to my exact whereabouts and I think that the announcement of last evening, stating that it was now possible to announce my presence here and I would accordingly have my first press conference, was probably successful in creating the impression that I had been here for some days. Of course if the Washington newspaper men want to do a little sleuthing, the exact facts could be turned up without a great deal of difficulty. However, I think that this point will not be of enough interest to anyone to create a lot of curiosity.

It is obvious that strong and positive action is needed here in several directions. The location of various headquarters, the exact pattern of command, the tactics of the assault, and the strength in units and equipment, are all questions that have not yet been definitely settled. The most important of all these questions is that of increasing the strength of the initial assault wave in OVERLORD. In order to assure themselves of what is deemed the necessary strength, most people here, including Montgomery,[1] Smith[2] and a number of others, have definitely recommended a serious reduction in ANVIL. This seems to me to be justified only as a last resort. I clearly appreciate—in fact much more than do these people— that the coming venture is the decisive act of the War from the viewpoint of the British-American effort. I know that this attack *must* succeed. However, I think the question to be weighed is that of increasing our insurance in obtaining the first foot-hold on the beaches against the advantages that would accrue from a really successful ANVIL. In addition, there are two other points that seem to me to be most important. The first of these is that according to my understanding the British and American staffs at Teheran definitely assured the Russians that ANVIL would take place. Secondly, we have put into the French Army a very considerable investment. Since these troops, plus the Americans and the British, cannot profitably be used in decisive fashion in Italy, we must open a gateway for them into France or all of our French investment will have been wasted. Altogether there would be a great number of American and other forces locked up in the Mediterranean from whom we will be deriving no benefit.

It is with such reasons as these in mind that I am determined to uncover every single expedient for increasing the initial weight of the OVERLORD attack before I am willing to recommend any great weakening of the ANVIL project. Today I am seeing Admiral Cunningham[3] because I have been informed by General Handy[4] that the present British commitment in landing craft is based upon a 70 per cent operational estimate. We can do better than this I know, and if General Handy's understanding of the case is accurate I am sure we can obtain a few more of these craft.

Beyond this there would seem to be no possibilities except such as are involved in increased production (of which I know nothing) and in attacking toward the end of the month instead of the beginning, in order to have additional equipment.

All of these things are highly important and they must be settled without delay.

On the American administrative side I have already directed the consolidation of the Theater and the S.O.S. Headquarters, and I feel sure that economy and efficiency will both be enhanced. General Lee[5] seems to have a good grasp of his affairs and so far as I can determine is working well with the British organization.

I must thank you again for the great trouble you took in making my visit home a pleasant one. I really got a definite rest and although my wife complained that a brief visit, after almost two years, was almost worse than waiting until my return could be a permanent one, I know that she too really appreciated the opportunity. I am absolutely certain that she loved the White Sulphur Springs layout. *Sincerely*

[1] General Montgomery was the senior British ground commander for OVERLORD. In the initial stages of the campaign, the American forces under Bradley were a part of his command as there was only one Army group headquarters—the 21st—and Montgomery was its commander. In late July an American Army group headquarters—the 12th—was activated with Bradley in command, but this new Army group remained subordinate to Montgomery until September 1 when Eisenhower assumed direct control of the land battle. At that point Montgomery and Bradley were placed on the same command level, with Montgomery commanding the 21st Army Group throughout the remainder of the war.

[2] Lieutenant General W. B. Smith was Chief of Staff for both of Eisenhower's commands—Supreme Headquarters, Allied Expeditionary Force (SHAEF), and the European Theater of Operations, U.S. Army (ETOUSA).

[3] Admiral A. B. Cunningham was First Sea Lord.

[4] Handy was Chief of the Operations Division (OPD).

[5] Eisenhower had a dual role as Supreme Commander of the Allied Expeditionary Force (SCAEF) and as the U.S. theater commander. To simplify his command structure, he ordered the consolidation of his theater headquarters and the Services of Supply, which had been charged with fulfilling the supply requirements of the American forces. Eisenhower retained command of the consolidated headquarters (ETOUSA), but it was actually controlled by Major General J. C. H. Lee, who was named Deputy Theater Commander for Supply and Administration. Lee's tasks included command of the actual supply organization for the American forces, the Communications Zone (Com Z). Lee became a lieutenant general on February 21, 1944.

39 LONDON   *January 29, 1944*

Dear General: From my viewpoint you were truly inspired when you wrote your radio No. 30, because at the moment it arrived I was much concerned in the problem of assuring that our major organizations have the very best possible commanders when this attack shall start. Your message puts the case so clearly and provides so much flexibility that I feel we can give the Army Commanders the men they want.

I am a bit puzzled as to why Devers[1] has not stated the name of the Corps Commander he desires. His query is now more than a week old and I am quite ready to send a man along as quickly as he will name him. The reason I want to do it quickly is that I want Collins[2] to get into saddle as soon as he arrives.

When Bradley[3] and I originally went over our slate, we tagged Truscott[4] and Gerow[5] as the Commanders of the two assault Corps (under the revised plan). Since it looks more and more as if we are not to have Truscott I think that we will substitute Collins in his place. However, I don't want to make two or three changes in shifting Corps Commanders around so I am hopeful that Devers will hurry up. As I have told you before I hope that he will pick Crittenberger.[6] I understand, from what I am told here, that Devers considers Crittenberger a top-flighter. . . .

Other changes will have to wait until my Army Commanders make definite recommendations to me. However, in preliminary conversations, I find that all of us are so sure of Gillem's[7] ability that I can almost promise you now that I will ask for him as soon as we can determine which one of the Corps Commanders now here we will want to trade you.

Among the Armored Division Commanders you named there seems to be universal agreement that Newgarden[8] and Leonard[9] are outstanding. Bradley says he will be glad to take either of them and place him in charge of either an Armored or an Infantry Division, depending upon the vacancy. There is likewise almost universal approval of Paul[10] as an Infantry Division Commander. This happens to be one man that I don't know personally, but Bradley thinks he is tops. So does Smith.

I have given you the above names with the request that you simply tag them, for the moment, as possibilities in this Theater. My thought is that this will keep them from going somewhere else until we can determine whether or not we should place them all.

If by good fortune I should get Truscott, this would make an additional change. *Very sincerely*

[1] Lieutenant General Devers had been named to command the American forces in the Mediterranean as Deputy Supreme Allied Commander. In September he assumed command of the 6th Army Group, formed from the forces which invaded southern France in August. He was promoted to general on March 8, 1945.

[2] Major General Joseph Lawton Collins (USMA 1917) was named commander of the VII Corps, U.S. First Army, in March and led it throughout the war. He was promoted to lieutenant general on April 16, 1945.

[3] Lieutenant General Bradley was the senior American ground commander for OVERLORD. In late July, 1944, he assumed command of the first U.S. Army group to be activated—the 12th. He retained that position until the end of the war and was promoted to general on March 12, 1945.

[4] Major General Truscott was commanding the 3d Infantry Division in Italy. In February, 1944, he assumed command of VI Corps at Anzio. He was promoted to lieutenant general on September 2, 1944.

[5] Major General Gerow was commanding V Corps in Bradley's first Army. He was promoted to lieutenant general on January 1, 1945, and assumed command of Fifteenth Army on January 16.

[6] Major General Willis Dale Crittenberger (USMA 1913) did go to the Mediterranean, where he assumed command of the IV Corps.

[7] Major General Alvan Cullom Gillem, Jr., had been in command of the XII Corps since December, 1943, and later commanded this same corps throughout the campaign in Europe.

[8] Major General Paul W. Newgarden (USMA 1913) commanded the 10th Armored Division, then in training in the United States but scheduled for Europe. General Newgarden died in an air crash in Tennessee on July 14, 1944.

[9] Major General John William Leonard (USMA 1915) commanded the 9th Armored Division. His division held Bastogne during the Battle of the Bulge until the 101st Airborne Division entered the city. In March, 1945, his division rushed the Remagen bridge at the Rhine River and secured the eastern approaches.

[10] Major General Willard Stewart Paul commanded the 26th Infantry Division, then in training in the United States. He led it into combat in October.

40 LONDON   *February 9, 1944*

Dear General: Yesterday I sent you a long telegram in which I think that for the first time since I became a Theater Commander I went a bit on the defensive in explaining my views to you. The reason was that there seemed to be an implication in your telegram that I might, merely in the interests of local harmony, surrender my convictions as to operations. I hope I cleared up that point.

Within a day or so I will have a complete draft of our "Air Preparation" plan. This plan will not only lay out exactly what we have to do, with priorities, but will also fix our recommended dates for the passage of command over Strategical Air Forces to this Headquarters. Before I present it to the Combined Chiefs of Staff I am going to have a full Commanders-in-Chief meeting on it so that thereafter it becomes "doctrine", so far as this Headquarters is concerned.

Bradley recommended, and I agreed, this morning, to place Collins in charge of the Assault Corps that will attack the eastern coast of the Cotentin Peninsula. I preferred him to Woodruff[1] for several reasons, the principal one of which is that he has had actual combat experience. I am just a bit uneasy about our failure to get a greater leaven of combat experience among our formations. We brought back from the Mediterranean only four divisions and two of these were special, that is, one was airborne and one was armored. That left only two battle-tried infantry divisions, and of these, the First Division is commanded by an officer who has not led them in actual battle during this war. (Huebner)[2] Devers has constantly reported it impossible to let any of his people come up here. I realize clearly that because we organized the North African staff and tested and placed the field commanders, we are quite likely to feel an unjustified proprietary interest in them and therefore exhibit a natural tendency to think that we are entitled to anything for which we ask. This, of course, is wrong and I try to avoid placing impossible requests on anybody, but I do know that in both the line of communications and in the combat troops I would feel happier if a wider combat experience could be represented.

150

The stalemate in Italy is quite disappointing but I think I can account for the conditions that brought it about. I would wager that bad weather in the early days of the landing made it impossible to give the necessary mobility to strong armored detachments that could have safely pushed forward across the Appian Way and secured the high ground to the east thereof. That would have controlled the main supply line just to the eastward. The imposed delays in build-up unquestionably forced a period of inaction that was not anticipated. Moreover, people have forgotten that our risky Salerno operation was justified by a reasonable prospect of good weather that would permit continuous operations by our Air Force. I suggested to the Prime Minister when I was in Marrakech that a bad weather development would create a continued demand for landing craft which we could not afford, and would possibly place the landing forces in a precarious position. I told Handy the same when I was home. But I believe that continued pressure in the south is finally going to crack the German line. It is true our divisions have been too long in line, but with the inactivity on the 8th Army front, Alexander[3] is able to bring fresh formations into the critical fighting and I believe will shortly produce quite a formidable offensive. I understand that he is now getting the New Zealanders into line and possibly the 4th Indians. An immediate improvement of the situation should result.

Recently I visited an area where the British have constructed a defense area typical of one of the beaches in Northwestern France. There is first a field of under-water and land mines. This is backed up by strong belts of barbed wired with occasional pill boxes. Back of this comes another mine field, and next is a solid, monolithic, reinforced concrete wall running from about 12 to about 15 feet in height and about 12 feet thick at the base. Back of the wall is a complete strong point all wired in and with critical points held by reinforced concrete pill boxes. It is a formidable looking thing. The particular visit was for the purpose of inspecting special items of equipment that are designated to help us through that type of defensive organization.

We are still struggling to move out to Widewing[4] and I am now promised that the majority of the staff can go before the end of the month. The further I can get from London the better I will be pleased. My own battle Headquarters, which I will occupy well before D day, will be at Portsmouth. Subsequently I will probably spend most of my time at Air Headquarters where the layout for assembling, analyzing and displaying information is quite amazing. This country has been fighting so long in the air that a very efficient communication system has been developed.

Our situation in lift for airborne troops is much better than I had anticipated. Of course what I would like to do is to drop two divisions simultaneously, one in the Peninsula itself, and one near Caen.

I am quite sure that we will be able to drop at least a Division plus a Regimental Combat Team, and it now looks as if we could drop two Regimental Combat Teams in addition to the full American Division.

General Lee,[5] commanding one of our Airborne Divisions, suffered a severe heart attack yesterday and I sent you a telegram on the subject this morning. I would be perfectly content to make Taylor[6] the Commander but am willing to take one of your Airborne Division Commanders, if you would prefer that solution.

My message about presenting the African Campaign Ribbon to the King may have imposed upon you a bit of a problem. However I was helpless in the matter as the Prime Minister himself suggested it. Since the military position of the King is such that he actually wears a uniform as the titular head of the British Forces, I hope that the matter can be readily approved. *Very Sincerely*

[1] Major General Roscoe Barnett Woodruff (USMA 1915) commanded the VII Corps. After Collins replaced him in March, 1944, he returned to the United States to command the 84th Infantry Division.

[2] Major General Clarence Ralph Huebner had assumed command of the 1st Infantry Division in July, 1943, when the division went from Sicily to the United Kingdom to train for OVERLORD. He remained in command of this division until January, 1945, when he succeeded Gerow as commander of V Corps.

[3] General Alexander commanded the ground forces in Italy. In November he became Supreme Allied Commander of the Mediterranean theater.

[4] The code name for SHAEF headquarters at Bushy Park, near Kingston-on-Thames on the outskirts of London.

[5] Major General William C. Lee had been commander of the 101st Airborne Division from the time of its activation in August, 1942.

[6] Brigadier General Maxwell Davenport Taylor (USMA 1922) commanded the artillery of the 82d Airborne Division. On March 31 he took command of the 101st Division and on May 31 was promoted to major general.

41 LONDON   *February 15, 1944*

Dear General: I have seen one or two of the telegrams passing back and forth on the political level, concerning so-called British and American areas or spheres of occupation in Europe after the Axis has been defeated. Naturally I well understand that our President wants nothing whatsoever to do with the policing of France, and more particularly Italy and the Balkans. If we were compelled to police any area separately I would quite agree that North Europe is the preferable region for us. However, as you know, because of the existence of German Naval Bases in that region in which the British Navy will have a transcendent interest, and the natural tie-in between British, Belgian and Dutch Air Services, we would be compelled to make many concessions and detailed arrangements that would be quite irksome.

My proposition is this: refuse to take specific American responsibility for any area.

Instead of this, why should we not place ourselves on record as saying we will retain responsibility, particularly military and relief responsibility in Europe, only so long as the Allied principle of unity of Command is observed, with orders and policies issued through the Combined Chiefs of Staff? Whenever, or if ever, Great Britain should decide that she wanted to control any specific major portion of Europe strictly from London, then we should simply withdraw U.S. physical occupational facilities, that is, military forces and large stocks of supplies.

It seems to me this simple formula would do much to keep us out of unnecessary difficulties and would still give our President a major voice in the establishing of policy.

An added consideration is the fact that the United States will have to furnish a good proportion of the products needed for European relief, and as long as that condition obtains we should be strongly represented in the *whole* controlling system.[1] *Very sincerely*

[1] Eisenhower sent Marshall another letter pursuing this subject on May 27. See E. to Smith, May 20, 1944, *EP*, pp. 1872–76.

42 LONDON   *February 19, 1944*

Dear General: This is a long letter, in tentative answer to yours of 10 February on the subject of Airborne operations. General Evans[1] and Colonel Bidwell[2] have presented their plan to me and are now working with others, pending opportunity to hold a meeting to be attended by Montgomery. If you are pushed for time I suggest that you have the Operations Division brief the following for your convenience.

You will recall that more than a year ago in Algiers, you talked to me on the idea that in the proper development of airborne operations lies one field in which we have real opportunity and capability to get ahead of the enemy. Obviously, it is only by getting definitely ahead of him in some important method of operations that we can expect to accomplish his defeat. Since that time this has been one of my favorite subjects for contemplation.

My initial reaction to the specific proposal is that I agree thoroughly with the conception but disagree with the timing. Mass in vertical envelopments is sound—but since this kind of an enveloping force is *immobile on the ground*, the collaborating force must be strategically and tactically mobile. So the time for the mass vertical envelopment is *after* the beachhead has been gained and a striking force built up! The reason on which I base these conclusions are discussed below.

As I see it, the first requisite is for the Expeditionary Force to gain a firm and solid footing on the Continent and to secure at least one really good sheltered harbor. All of our anxiety concerning Mulberries, Gooseberries,[3] and other forms of artificial aids in landing supplies and troops for assault and build-up are merely an indication of the great concern that everyone feels toward this problem of establishing and maintaining

153

ground forces on the Continent. This means that the initial crisis of the Campaign will be the struggle to break through beach defenses, exploit quickly to include a port and be solidly based for further operations. To meet this *first tactical crisis* I intend to devote everything that can be profitably used, including airborne troops.

The second consideration that enters my thinking on this problem is expressed in the very first sentence of your letter, in the phrase "air power as regards its *combination* with ground troops."

Whatever the conditions in other Theaters of War, the one here that we must never forget is the enemy's highly efficient facilities for concentration of ground troops at any particular point. This is especially true in the whole of France and in the Low Countries. Our bombers will delay movement, but I cannot conceive of enough air power to prohibit movement on the network of roads throughout northwest France. For the past five days there has been good weather in Italy and our reports show an average of 1000 sorties per day. Yet with only two main roads and a railway on which to concentrate, our reports show a steady stream of enemy traffic by night to the south and southeast from Rome. We must arrange all our operations so that no significant part of our forces can be isolated and defeated in detail. There must exist either the definite capacity of both forces to combine *tactically*, or the probability that each force can operate independently without danger or defeat.

The German has shown time and again that he does not particularly fear what we used to refer to as a "strategic threat of envelopment". Any military man that might have been required to analyze, before this war, the situation that existed in Italy on about January 24, would have said that the only hope of the German was to begin the instant and rapid withdrawal of his troops in front of the Fifth Army. The situation was almost a model for the classical picture for initiating a battle of destruction. But the German decided that the thrust could not be immediately translated into *mobile tactical action*, and himself began attacking. The Nettuno landing, due to the incidence of bad weather, was really not much heavier in scale than an airborne landing would have been during those critical days when time was all-important. The force was immobile and could not carry out the promise that was implicit in the situation then existing. But from our standpoint the situation was saved by the fact that our complete command of the sea allowed us to continue to supply and maintain and reinforce the beachhead. I am convinced it will turn out all right in the end, but there will be *no* great destruction of German Divisions as a result thereof.

An airborne landing carried out at too great a distance from other forces which will also be immobile for some time, will result in a much worse situation.

The resistance to be expected by our landing forces at the beaches is far greater than anything we have yet encountered in the European War and I have felt that carefully planned airborne operations offer us an important means of increasing our chances in this regard. The American Division, which has first priority, dropping in the Cherbourg Peninsula, gives us a reasonable expectation of preventing reinforcement of that area and of seizing exits from the great flooded area that separates, in that region, our only practical landing beach from the interior of the Peninsula. Unless we throw a very strong force in this vicinity, the Division attempting to land there will be in a bad spot.

The British Airborne Forces have the Caen area to seize. Subsequent airborne operations are planned to be as bold and in as large a mass as resources and the air situation then existing will permit. I do not agree with Bidwell that large-scale, mass use of airborne troops will thereafter be impracticable.

To a certain extent the conduct of airborne operations must be planned in accordance with the technicians' ideas of feasibility. Even under the most favorable circumstances the air people anticipate quite large losses among troop carrier craft because of the high efficiency of hostile Radar coverage and the impossibility of preventing enemy fighters from getting into such formations. I hope soon to have here a man that Arnold[4] is sending me from Kenny's Command.[5] Possibly he can show us wherein we may have been too conservative.

All of the above factors tend to compel the visualization of airborne operations as an immediate tactical rather than a long-range strategical adjunct of landing operations.

If we were not depending so definitely upon the bombardment effect of our bombers to help us both tactically and strategically, there would be available a greatly increased force to support and maintain airborne operations, but present plans call for an all-out effort on the part of both day and night bombers for a very considerable period both preceding and following D-day.

I instinctively dislike ever to uphold the conservative as opposed to the bold. You may be sure that I will earnestly study the ideas presented by the two officers because on one point of your letter I am in almost fanatical agreement—I believe we can lick the Hun only by being ahead of him in ideas as well as in material resources. *Sincerely*

[1] Brigadier General Frederick William Evans was commanding general of the Troop Carrier Command.

[2] Colonel Bruce Woodward Bidwell (USMA 1924) was serving in the Intelligence Division of the General Staff and in addition was OPD airborne consultant.

[3] Code name for artificial harbors—MULBERRIES were the two large harbors planned and GOOSEBERRIES were small ones designed to shelter lighter craft.

[4] General Arnold was Chief of the Army Air Forces. In December, 1944, he was nominated for the new five star rank of General of the Army.

[5] Lieutenant General Kenny commanded the Allied Air Forces in the Southwest Pacific. He became a general on March 9, 1945.

Dear General:

. . .

As we always anticipated, the Air features of our plans have been difficult to get completely in line. It is now my impression that Tedder[1] will become at least the de facto Commander-in-Chief of Air with Spaatz',[2] Harris'[3] and Leigh-Mallory's[4] forces each coordinate bodies under Tedder.

The Prime Minister was quite violent in his objections to considering Leigh-Mallory as the overall Air Commander-in-Chief, although this was his definite assignment. His query was, "Why did we give you Tedder?" and my answer was merely, "Why?". I must say that the way it is now shaping up I am far happier than I was a week ago.

The Mediterranean situation does not seem to improve, but I think that a spell of good weather will help us a lot. We had an emergency meeting the other night at the Prime Minister's because of the desperate immediate need to hold some LST's in the Mediterranean so that another Division could be gotten into the beachhead. Admiral Ramsay[5] and I immediately suggested that if the 26 U.S. LST's could be sent directly here instead of to the Mediterranean and could arrive at an early enough date so that they could train intensively here for a short period, we would agree that the first 26 LST's to sail out of the Mediterranean for the U.K. would remain there. This suggestion was sent to the U.S. Chiefs of Staff and I suppose was acted on favorably because I have not heard anything from it. It becomes daily more apparent that a 2 Division ANVIL is out of the question.

Just recently I have had a big meeting of all Armored Force Commanders and senior staff men because of disturbing reports as to certain deficiencies in the new Armored Division. I think on the whole it is going to be satisfactory but I have agreed to provide to each of the new Divisions the small amounts of additional transportation of which I am convinced they are badly in need.

I notice in this new Armored Division a tendency to expand still further the idea of "separate battalion" and "ad hoc group" organization. I think someone is forgetting the tremendous value of regimental and divisional esprit in battle. It is perfectly true that the German makes great use of ad hoc organizations, but it is noticeable that the units making up these battle groups frequently bear permanent names. Beyond all doubt the names that we find in the British Army, such as the Hampshires, the Black Watch, the Wellingtons, the Grenadier Guards, and so on, have given these organizations a pride and esprit that pay big dividends on the battle field.

For my own purposes, and for this particular campaign at least, I am studying with my commanders the idea of giving a sort of family name to groups of battalions that will ordinarily serve together, since I have no slightest intention of trading battalions in and out of Division except in emergency. My present thought is to allow the Infantry battalions, for example, of an Armored Division to select a name for themselves. The list to them will include names of past battles of the American Army and deceased American military leaders. I believe it will have a good effect.

This morning I see in the papers that General Lee is to be promoted. When in Washington I told Somervell,[6] who was very insistent that one of his supply people be made a three-star general, that I fully intended to recommend Lee as soon as I had completely satisfied myself as to the efficiency of his machine. I had already told Lee the same thing; but this is the first time one of my chief subordinates has been advanced without consulting me.[7]

Last night was a quiet one here. The Germans are now using some very large types of bombs, from which the demolition and blast effect is very noticeable. *Sincerely*

[1] Air Chief Marshal Tedder became Eisenhower's Deputy Supreme Commander and exercised supervision over the air forces.

[2] Lieutenant General Spaatz commanded the U.S. Strategic Air Force in Europe. He was promoted to general on March 11, 1945.

[3] Air Chief Marshal Sir Arthur Travers Harris headed the British Bomber Command.

[4] Air Chief Marshal Sir Trafford Leigh-Mallory commanded the Allied Expeditionary Air Force which was Eisenhower's tactical air force. The command was abolished in October and its function absorbed by the operating British and American air units. Leigh-Mallory was killed in a plane crash in November on his way to a new position in India.

[5] Admiral Ramsay, Allied naval commander, Expeditionary Force, led the naval forces in OVERLORD.

[6] Lieutenant General Somervell headed the Army's supply forces, the Army Service Forces. He was promoted to general on March 6, 1945.

[7] Marshall apologized for the mixup in a message of March 9. See E. to M., March 10, 1944, *EP*, p. 1767, n. 1.

44   BUSHY PARK   *March 15, 1944*

Dear General: This is a purely personal letter, its subject being the possibility of my son coming over here for a short term of temporary duty, some time after the completion of his cadet course about June 6. Since he is to have, I understand, a month's graduation leave, I would ordinarily ask for nothing more than air passage for him to the U.K. and return within that period. The difficulty is that for some time to come he has to be very careful of high altitudes because of old trouble with an ear. Since it is always possible in the transoceanic journey that a plane might have to go above 10,000 feet, I would not want to invite him over unless he could come by fast ship—such as one of the Queens. It might be permanently damaging to him.

I would not, of course, attach him directly to my own headquarters, because of the example set. But I could send him to Bradley or some other commander sufficiently near my own headquarters so that I could see him often. While it should be good experience for him as a young officer, my real purpose would be merely an opportunity to become acquainted again with my son. I think, at times, I get a bit homesick, and the ordinary diversions of the theater and other public places are denied me. I'd send him home, say after 60 days here. He should not, for his own good, stay in my theater too long. Many other officers happen to have their sons here, but it wouldn't do in my case—no matter how well he did, he'd always be the teacher's pet.

While I've talked in a rather vague way to my son about this possibility, I do not want definitely to invite him unless you fully approve. Of course, if he should be slated for a school, or some other type of special service immediately upon completion of his leave, then I don't want him to come. I'm assuming that such a visit would merely keep him away from *normal* assignment for a short period.

Would you be kind enough to give me your reactions? *Very sincerely*[1]

[1] Marshall replied that he would arrange the visit, but that he thought it best that no one know until the last moment. E. to M., March 15, 1944, *EP*, p. 1769, n. 1.

45 BUSHY PARK   *April 17, 1944*

Dear General Marshall: As usual at this stage of preparation for an operation our problems are seemingly intricate and difficult beyond belief. Each day though, there is definite progress and I have not lost any of my confidence that we shall make a go of it.

Right now we have the Assistant Secretary as well as General McNarney,[1] General Lutes[2] and General Scowden,[3] all of the War Department, going over various phases of our organizations and activities to check up and to assist us in determining that things are as tidy as possible before the battle really starts.

The subject of manpower, which is McNarney's specialty, is one to which I have expended a lot of energy ever since you first told me of the impending difficulties, some time last June. Your latest suggestion, namely, that I set up a Commander with no other responsibilities than that of handling replacement procedure, is one that I have been contemplating. The real difficulty is to find exactly the right man because he must be tough but understanding, and broadly experienced but still full of energy. Moreover, he must be able to get along easily with people. Except for lack of this last qualification General Hughes[4] would be almost the ideal man for such a job. In fact I have already put him with McNarney because I had intended making him an Inspector devoted exclusively to this particular

158

activity. But as a Commander I am not so sure he will do. Though I have gone over a lot of names I cannot think of exactly the man I would want. Certainly I agree with you that the procedures we adopt should be perfected before the attack so that we can depend upon the greatest economy and efficiency in the use of manpower. Here we should have the advantage of planning only for a single operation. In Africa this was not so. You will recall that when I contemplated abandoning Casablanca I had a warning from the very highest levels. Later, with directives that involved the opening of a new L of C[5] it was necessary to hang on to service units at North African ports and in Sicily that could otherwise have been eliminated. You may be sure that no objections on the part of subordinate commanders or staffs will deter me from setting up any system that appears to me to be the most efficient. I hope that General Lee will be back here next Thursday with General McNarney. If so, I should be able to thresh this thing out once and for all and will report further.

The other day I had a long talk with General Alexander. He explained why it was taking such a long time to set up a full-dress attack in Italy but I must say that although this delay seems unavoidable, it is disappointing. Also I had a letter today from General Gruenther, Chief of Staff of the 5th Army, who says that all the American Divisions are up to full strength and will be ready to give a fine account of themselves.

I have just received your long cable giving the exchange of messages between you and the British concerning the ANVIL operation. I still will not give up hope that there may become available in the Mediterranean a sufficient lift to enable that Force to keep on the offensive no matter what happens. I had one or two rather rough sessions in insisting that planning and preparation for ANVIL was the best way to assure that something positive would be done as early as possible. Incidentally will you please read NAF[6] 676 from Wilson[7] to Combined Chiefs of Staff. That telegram indicates that actual preparations for ANVIL are progressing including the building up of larger forces of Service Troops.

I have been quite busy inspecting troops and preliminary training, planning and preparation are going forward as rapidly as possible. All the troops in both ground and air are in good heart.

All of us realize that tremendous stakes are heaped up on the outcome of the impending operation but I am sure that all, both British and American, are approaching the task with determination and confidence.
Sincerely

[1] Lieutenant General McNarney was Marshall's Deputy Chief of Staff. In October, 1944, he became Deputy Supreme Allied Commander in the Mediterranean and was promoted to general on March 7, 1945.

[2] Major General LeRoy Lutes was Director of Plans and Operations of the Army Service Forces.

[3] Major General Frank Floyd Scowden (USMA 1910) would shortly become Chief of the Supply and Economic Branch of the Civil Affairs Division of Supreme Headquarters.

[4] Major General E. S. Hughes had come from Algiers to serve until the end of the war as Eisenhower's personal representative in the field.

[5] Line of communication.

[6] Symbol designating cables covering all subjects from AFHQ to CCS.

[7] General Sir Henry Maitland Wilson had succeeded Eisenhower as Supreme Allied Commander, Mediterranean theater. In November, 1944, he became head of the British Joint Staff Mission and senior representative of the British Chiefs of Staff in Washington.

46 BUSHY PARK   *April 29, 1944*

Dear General Marshall: This morning I sent you a telegram about the Patton[1] case. Frankly I am exceedingly weary of his habit of getting everybody into hot water through the immature character of his public actions and statements. In this particular case investigation shows that this offense was not so serious as the newspapers would lead one to believe, and one that under the circumstances could have occurred to almost anybody. But the fact remains that he simply does not keep his mouth shut. I am waiting on an answer to my telegram to you before taking final action.

Incidentally the question of censorship in this country is quite difficult to handle. In the past few weeks I have done a great deal of inspecting and at every station, both British and American, I normally talk for two or three minutes to the officers and men. Again and again I have issued flat orders that nothing I say is ever to be quoted directly or indirectly and in fact I have gotten to the point where I will not even allow a newspaper man to be in the same locality when I am talking. Yet on three different occasions I have found my words quoted almost exactly in the papers. This rather shakes a man because the things that he wants to say to his own soldiers are considerably different from what he might want to say in public—if a public statement were necessary. Just what happens is more than I can fathom.

Night before last German E-Boats[2] sneaked into one of our harbors and sank three of our LST's. Apparently we lost a considerable number of men. I got the news just as I was finishing a long hard day and I must say it was not a restful thought to take home with me. We are stretched to the limit in the LST category, while the implications of the attack and the possibility of both raiders and bombers concentrating on some of our important ports make one scratch his head.

The British Government has been trying to induce me to change my bombing program against the transportation systems, so as to avoid the killing of any Frenchmen. I have stuck to my guns because there is no other way in which this tremendous air force can help us, during the preparatory period, to get ashore and stay there. The Prime Minister talked to me about bombing "bases, troop concentrations and dumps." The fact is that any large dumps are obviously located near marshalling yards while troop concentrations are by battalion in little villages. Any immediate attempt to bomb the German troop units throughout France would probably kill four Frenchmen for every German.

160

I have gone over in detail the arrangements for marshalling and embarking our forces. I suppose McNarney has told you about these. In any event I consider them most efficient and have no fears on this score. Lee and his assistants have done a good job.

I assume that you will be making us a visit some time within the reasonable future; at least you hinted at such a possibility when I last saw you. I do not need to assure you of your welcome. I will be more than delighted to have you with us. *Sincerely*[3]

[1] Lieutenant General Patton was temporarily commanding a fictitious army as part of a plan to make the Germans think that the main assault would come at the Calais-Dunkirk area. On August 1 the U.S. Third Army was activated in France and Patton led it throughout the war.

[2] The E-boat was a small German speedy type of surface torpedo boat.

[3] Eisenhower added a postscript: "I inclose a copy of a letter I wrote to Patton. You may be interested. Please destroy it." E. to M., April 29, 1944, *EP*, p. 1839, n. 5.

47 BUSHY PARK   *May 6, 1944*

Dear General: Yesterday Wilson, from the Mediterranean, dropped in to see me and we had quite a talk on the possibilities of operations in that Region. I find that there is very little difference between his opinions and mine as to what should and can be done and I hope that as a result of our conference Wilson will submit to the Combined Chiefs of Staff another and more definitely concrete proposal for his summer's operations. I dread the possibility of strong Allied Forces in the Mediterranean becoming immobile and useless at the very time when they should be fighting full out.

Our worst problems these days involve methods for removing underwater obstacles, production of Mulberries and all the other special equipment pertaining to artificial harbors, accuracy in weather predictions and perfection of methods for getting a completely coordinated assault—including airborne. The obstacle problem, entirely aside from the extensive undersea mine fields, is a most serious one. However, there is one thing about it—the present intensive effort the German is making along this line shows that he does not completely trust his mobile troops to make good his defense of the coast line. I do wish that our assault could get off tomorrow, and on even a broader front.

In the midst of all these great problems some of my most intense irritations are caused by things that need never to have arisen. For example, the Patton case and the Miller[1] case. Such things take hours of earnest study and anxious thought. Then, only day before yesterday I ran into some evidence that expenditures here for things we have obtained—many of which cannot possibly be classed as absolutely necessary—have been exorbitant. I am putting a good inspector on the whole thing at once and it is entirely possible that there is nothing to it at all. Of course I know that war-time prices are out-of-sight, particularly here, where taxes start on a general basis of 50 percent and go on up. I realize also that it is always better to purchase here on reverse lend-lease than to use shipping to bring the things across the Atlantic. On the other hand I never forget that it is up to us to be as economical as possible.

The Ambassador to Russia, Mr. Harriman,[2] has just visited here and he is convinced that the Russians are going to go full out in conjunction with our attack. That is cheering news.

All in all most of us are staying in very good health and I must say that a general spirit of optimism pervades the whole Force.

There is one thing that I rather doubt is completely understood at home concerning my own staff organization. This is that for all practical purposes the Naval and Air Commanders-in-Chief, with their staffs, are part of my own Headquarters. This subject is brought up to me often by visiting officers and after they thoroughly understand our methods I think they see that the system is not only necessary when you are putting two Allied nations together with Air and Naval Commanders-in-Chief prescribed by the Combined Chiefs of Staff, but is more economical in personnel than any other system would be. The Planning Staff is a completely amalgamated one and works in SHAEF.

With personal regard, *Sincerely*

[1] Major General Henry Jervis Friese Miller, a West Point classmate of Eisenhower's, was commander of the Ninth Air Force Service Command. He had declared in a public dining room that the invasion would take place before June 15, 1944. He was removed from his post, reduced to his permanent rank of colonel, and returned to the United States. E. to Miller, May 5, 1944, *EP*, pp. 1848–49.

[2] William Averell Harriman had been appointed Ambassador to Russia in October, 1943.

48   BUSHY PARK   *May 21, 1944*

Dear General: This morning there was brought to my attention a charge against a naval officer, involving the most serious breach of security of which I have yet heard. Admiral Stark[1] is getting on the job at once and necessary action will be taken. Sometimes I get so angry at the occurrence of such needless and additional hazards that I could cheerfully shoot the offender myself. This following so closely upon the Miller case is almost enough to give one the shakes.

I have read over the telegrams that General Smith sent you on the subjects of film coverage of the operation and the case of Colonel LeBel.[2] In both instances I think his explanations covered the field and there is no use my cluttering up the ether with anything additional.

Inspections these days are occupying a large portion of my time. All the men in the air, ground and navy have an understandable desire to see the people, at least once, that are ordinarily little more to the men in the ranks than names on a piece of paper. All these trips have to be sand-wiched in between important and inescapable appointments in the London region. Time and effort are required in order to meet the commitment.

There is no question at all as to the readiness of the troops. They are well trained, fit and impatient to get the job started and completed. Last Wednesday morning I went through the enormous air depot and repair place at Burtonwood. That afternoon I inspected the 5th Division. The following day I inspected the 8th Division. The next day I visited four U.S. ships of war. At every stop I found morale and general readiness at the highest pitch. I am quite satisfied with all my commanders down to include Corps; while I have my fingers crossed in the case of two or three Division commanders, I believe they ought to come through.

Right now I have got several people, including Bradley, studying the question of a probable future battle order of each field army, so that we do not ask for more Corps and Army Headquarters than can be profitably used. The six infantry division Army, with two armored divisions attached, is in my opinion too small when organized into three Corps. I believe that two extra infantry divisions should be attached, which will give the Army Commanders a chance to rotate two divisions through the normal six in the front line and so keep up the persistence of operations as well as always to have available fresh troops for particular attacks.

According to my information General Cook[3] is the next Corps Commander to come here. From the list I have seen I would place Generals Gillen[4] and J. B. Anderson[5] next in priority.

In forecasting future possibilities it is, of course, necessary that we seek ways and means to bring to bear those factors in which we enjoy a great superiority over the enemy. These are control of the sea, command of the air, including resources in airborne troops, and armor. I am trying to visualize an operation in which we would bring in behind the initial beachhead a great strength in armor and seek an opportunity to launch a big armored attack in conjunction with a deep and very heavy penetration by airborne troops. Such an operation might be accompanied also by an additional amphibious affair. I have already instructed the Staff to look into this possibility because I believe that in some such movement, promising surprise from three directions, and in great strength, we might accomplish a lot.

You have not yet indicated to me a definite intention to come over here soon, although you mentioned this definite possibility when I last saw you at Cairo. I do hope your schedule will permit you to come.[6] *Sincerely*

---

[1] Admiral Stark was Chief of the U.S. Naval Forces in Europe.

[2] Colonel Albert J. P. LeBel was a French liaison officer in Bradley's command.

[3] Major General Gilbert Richard Cook (USMA 1912) was commanding the XII Corps, which was on its way to the United Kingdom for employment in the European campaign.

[4] Major General Gille*m*.

[5] Major General John Benjamin Anderson (USMA 1914) was commanding XVI Corps, which arrived in the European theater in September, 1944.

[6] General Marshall, Admiral King, and General ˙Arnold arrived in England on June 9, 1944.

49 BUSHY PARK   *May 24, 1944*

Dear General: I have just approved a project for placing on the uniform of commanders of actual combat units, a distinctive marking. In this Theater we have encountered such a variety of staff activities, all of which are manned by commissioned officers, that it becomes exceedingly difficult to give any kind of recognition to the man that definitely leads troops in action. The form of the marking we are adopting is a narrow green band around the shoulder loop of the officer's uniform, and for the enlisted man a narrow green stripe just below his chevron. We intend this to be worn by every man who commands others in combat echelons, and no one higher than Army Commander will be allowed to wear it.

This matter has been under discussion between Bradley and me, along with a few others, for a long time and we have come to the definite conclusion that it is a very good thing. The second a man ceases to command a combat unit he takes off his marking.

I feel quite sure that the War Department could have no strong objection to the contemplated action as long as it is applied merely as a Theater matter and the distinctive marking is removed before any officer or enlisted man returns home. On the other hand, it occurred to me that you might like to consider the matter as having some desirable application to the whole Army.

The marking itself will be nothing but a small, inexpensive piece of green cloth.[1] *Sincerely*

[1] Marshall approved. E. to M., May 24, 1944, *EP*, p. 1888, n. 1.

CHAPTER 5

Commanding in Europe, June, 1944–May, 1945

Eisenhower now faced his final and greatest test—the destruction of the German forces on the Western front. Everything that he had learned and experienced had been but a preparation for the OVERLORD command. Everything the Allies had done before was but a preliminary to the great operation in Europe.

Eisenhower's thirty-seven letters to Marshall across this time span reveal that he met this challenge in a calm and confident manner. He did not make many personal references to Marshall. Usually he was direct and honest. For example, when the first great debate over command and tactics was at its peak, he told Marshall that he was working things out but urged him to come to Europe so they could discuss various problems. Marshall's visit marked a watershed in Eisenhower's references to command and even tactical arguments, as he provided Eisenhower with the necessary extra assurance he needed to plan for the final drive into Germany. After the visit Eisenhower rarely referred to command difficulties and made even less mention of disputes over tactics. In unfolding his plans, he was careful to retain maximum flexibility. He outlined these operations to Marshall with the assurance of a commander who felt that he was proceeding in the most correct manner.

Command Organization

As in the Mediterranean, Eisenhower wrote Marshall about organization only when he encountered a new command situation—when he was due to assume command of the forces that had landed in southern France; when his ideas were requested on a postwar command structure; when he assumed ground command; and when control of the air forces was taken from him. On the first two of these, Eisenhower commented only briefly in letters of August 31 and October 31.

He faced one continuing major and open challenge to his command—a challenge which erupted into two major controversies. Montgomery, Brooke, and Churchill argued that Eisenhower should appoint a single ground commander rather than having two army group commanders. Eisenhower has labeled Montgomery's idea as "fantastic."[1] He contended that operations in Europe were too immense for one man to have control over detailed planning and execution; it would be impossible for that person to direct overall allocation of resources, determination of theater tactics, shifting of boundaries, and coordination between vast groups of armies—the operational imperatives of the modern Supreme Commander.[2] He fully understood the implications in Montgomery's proposal: "The only effect of such a scheme would have been to place Montgomery in position to draw at will, in support of his own ideas, upon the strength of the entire command."[3] Montgomery's ideas included a plan for his army group to make a single thrust into Germany, a design which clashed with Eisenhower's own plan to advance into Germany on a broad front. As Supreme Commander of an Allied expedition, Eisenhower faced constant pressure from all persons to whom he was responsible.

The first command debate started in mid-August and became quickly intertwined with the tactical issue of whether or not Montgomery should be allowed to make the dash to Berlin. The controversy had begun in the press. In accordance with pre-invasion planning, on August 1 Eisenhower had activitated a second army group headquarters—the 12th Army Group—and named Bradley as its commander. London papers had interpreted this as a demotion for Montgomery, who, as commander of the sole army group—the 21st, had been Bradley's superior. Actually the command setup had not changed. Montgomery was to continue to give Bradley orders until Eisenhower himself assumed direct command in the field on September 1. The American press had in turn been upset by the furor in the British press. Marshall told Eisenhower to take direct command as soon as possible in order to end the public acrimony. He had responded to Marshall and then to the Combined Chiefs that he was still unable to specify the exact date he could take charge because necessary signal communications had not been completed.[4] When, on August 23, as the Allies rapidly approached the Seine, Eisenhower visited Montgomery, the latter man raised both the issues of sole command and the single

---

[1] Eisenhower, *Crusade in Europe*, pp. 284–85.

[2] For one Eisenhower statement on this, see E. to Montgomery, October 13, 1944, *EP*, pp. 2221–25.

[3] Eisenhower, *Crusade in Europe*, p. 285.

[4] E. to M., August 19, 1944, *EP*, pp. 2074–77; and E. to CCS, August 22, 1944, *EP*, pp. 2087–89.

thrust to Berlin. Montgomery told Eisenhower that it was a mistake for the Supreme Commander to lead directly the land battle, that instead he should remain aloof to objectively view all the various problems of the war. The land battle should be left in the hands of Montgomery or Bradley.[5]

Montgomery's outburst galvanized Eisenhower into action. He wrote Marshall the next day that despite the fact that he would "not have even minimum communications" at his headquarters, he would assume direct command. On August 31 he told Marshall that he was holding a press conference to explain ". . . the complete development of this operation, including the command arrangements for it." Although the argument over command continued, Eisenhower made no further mention of it. Marshall came to visit Eisenhower in early October in response to Eisenhower's request of September 18 that he come over to discuss ". . . present and future problems." The problems no doubt included Montgomery's questioning of Eisenhower's command structure and battle tactics. During this visit, Eisenhower temporarily settled the argument over a single ground commander by a firm letter of the 13th to Montgomery—drafted by Whiteley and Smith and reviewed by Eisenhower and Marshall.[6] Yet Eisenhower did write again about the dispute over battle tactics. Although he might not be absolutely certain (as indeed no one could be) that a direct push toward Berlin was ill advised, he was quite certain of the necessity for unity of command.

The British press depicted Montgomery as having saved the Americans from confusion and disarray during the German counteroffensive in mid-December. The situation had arisen because Eisenhower had decided to give Montgomery temporary control of two of Bradley's armies after Bradley's communications had been disrupted. Montgomery then told Eisenhower that he wanted to be sole ground commander as he was anxious to prevent "another failure."[7] Eisenhower later told Marshall in a letter of February 9 that Bradley had been particularly upset by the publicity over the move. Even though Montgomery's attack was coupled with one by the British Chiefs of Staff on Eisenhower's tactical planning, Eisenhower, strongly backed by Marshall, did not waver in his insistence on retaining unity of command. Having just received a message from Marshall saying that it would be unacceptable to give a British general command of any substantial American forces,[8] he immediately told Montgomery, "In the matter of command I do not agree that one Army Group

[5] E. to Montgomery, August 24, 1944, *EP*, pp. 2091–92, n. 1. Montgomery explains his position in his *Memoirs*, pp. 238–57.
[6] E. to Montgomery, October 13, 1944, *EP*, pp. 2221–25.
[7] E. to Montgomery, December 31, 1944, *EP*, p. 2387, n. 2.
[8] *Ibid.*

Commander should fight his own battle and give orders to another Army Group Commander."[9] Although Eisenhower did indicate on January 10, 1945, that he would not object to a proposal to bring Alexander in as his Deputy Supreme Commander to replace Tedder, he made it clear that Alexander's position would not in any way be that of a ground Commander in Chief.[10] When Marshall visited Eisenhower on January 28 on his way to the Malta Conference, he said that he would resign his post if a ground Commander in Chief were named by the Combined Chiefs.[11] Marshall had also objected to Eisenhower's naming of Alexander as his deputy, for he feared that the latter would be under the influence of Churchill.[12] Eisenhower wrote Brooke on February 16 to make clear that Alexander would be no more than his deputy if the transfer were effected.[13] He sent Marshall a copy of the letter, and talked of the incident on the 20th: "The matter is unimportant, except from its Public Relations aspect, but since Public Relations often cause me my biggest headaches, I wanted to make sure that the C.I.G.S. clearly understood what might occur." He said Montgomery had told him that he believed in the "efficacy of our command organization," whereupon Eisenhower had asked him to relay the same message to Churchill. Shortly afterward Churchill dropped the proposal.[14]

Eisenhower's handling of the dispute clearly indicated that he would not tolerate disruption of the line of command. Marshall had also said that it was unacceptable to allow Montgomery to command substantial U.S. forces.[15] However, Eisenhower left under Montgomery's control one of the two armies he had given him during the December emergency and did not restore the army to Bradley until the following spring. By this time Eisenhower had no doubt of the need for unity of command and so did not write very much about it. He had realized that Montgomery would not subordinate himself in the face of an official directive to the contrary, as Alexander had been willing to do in the Mediterranean. He was determined therefore to maintain legal authority as an essential to maintaining real authority.

Eisenhower also had to cope with the problem of retaining clear control of the heavy bomber air forces. The command settlement in April, 1944, had specified that the Allied tactical air force, the U.S. Strategic Air Force under Spaatz, and the British Bomber Command, each would report in-

[9] E. to Montgomery, December 31, 1944, *EP*, pp. 2386–87.

[10] E. to M., January 10, 1945, *EP*, pp. 2415–20; and E. to M., January 12, 1945, *EP*, pp. 2422–23.

[11] Conference Notes, January 28, 1945, *EP*, pp. 2460–61.

[12] E. to M., January 10, 1945, *EP*, p. 2423, n. 1.

[13] E. to Brooke, February 16, 1945, *EP*, pp. 2480–83.

[14] E. to Churchill, February 25, 1945, *EP*, p. 2495, n. 3.

[15] E. to M., January 1, 1945, *EP*, p. 2391, n. 1. The controversy over command led to Eisenhower's only major dispute with Bradley. Bradley, *Soldier's Story*, pp. 483–92.

dependently to Eisenhower, who used his deputy Tedder to coordinate their activities.[16] Meeting at Quebec on September 14, the CCS removed the strategic bombers of both countries from Eisenhower's control.[17] Although they instructed the bomber commanders to direct their atttacks against targets set by Eisenhower, the commanders were empowered by the CCS to put any necessary changes into effect.[18] It was the opinion of the British that Eisenhower would have difficulty in directing the attacks of the England-based bombers from his headquarters in France. Eisenhower complained in letters of the 18th and 25th, but he decided to proceed as he had in the Mediterranean—namely, to ignore it. He had been able to do so when he received the January, 1943, directive diluting his power over subordinate commanders, largely because his ground commander Alexander was willing to serve under Eisenhower. The official historians of the U.S. Air Force have paid tribute to Eisenhower and his subordinates for their ability to make the best of a defective command structure.[19]

These two command disagreements showed Eisenhower at his best. With Montgomery, he realized that he had to have legal control. With the air forces, while he obviously advocated explicit control, he knew that he could achieve maximum cooperation without it, and acted accordingly.

All these difficulties reinforced Eisenhower's awareness of the need for selecting the right people for his organization. He wrote about his visits to subordinate commanders, about the current performance of his subordinates, and about present and future needs, all the while maintaining close contact with his top commanders. At times he mentioned these visits to Marshall, although he did not usually couch his resultant reports on operations in terms of a specific visit.

On June 19, Eisenhower told Marshall that he had sent some promotion recommendations for "battle-field leadership." In contrast to the situation in the Mediterranean, Eisenhower mentioned no other promotions below the rank of general. This no doubt reflected the fact that he now relied more on Smith and Bradley for promotion reviews. He commented on the performance of division commanders in several letters, but his remarks were more frequently devoted to higher commanders—that is, to the corps, army, and army group level. Particularly significant among these was a letter of July 12, which was devoted entirely to the rumor that Lieutenant General Devers, slated to head the ANVIL forces when they became a part of Eisenhower's jurisdiction, felt that the Supreme Commander did not

---

[16] E. to CCS, August 22, 1944, *EP*, pp. 2087–89.

[17] Eisenhower had tried to retain the existing arrangements. See E. to M., September 2, 1944, *EP*, pp. 2111–12, and E. to M., September 18, 1944, *EP*, pp. 2159–60, n. 1.

[18] Eisenhower, *Crusade in Europe*, pp. 307–8.

[19] Craven and Cate, eds., *Argument to V–E Day*, p. 622.

want him to assume command. Eisenhower told Marshall that he did not have anything against Devers and that he realized that the selection of the commander of those forces was not yet his business. "However, I am writing it [this letter] in pursuance of my regular policy of trying to keep you personally informed as to my reactions concerning any point that arises affecting Americans in this part of the world." This remark is an excellent explanation of the dominance of references to U.S. rather than Allied personnel in his letters. Marshall was mainly interested in the performance of American commanders. In any event he would have been faced with an extremely sensitive situation if Eisenhower sought his help in relieving a British officer. This was yet another of the limitations of coalition command.

Eisenhower referred to Bradley more, by far, than to any other individual. In addition to pressing most strongly for Bradley's promotion to full general, Eisenhower cited Bradley's agreement to certain tactical moves and rating of officers. On March 26, when he had obtained the Rhine, he told Marshall that the campaign had been planned by Bradley and himself. On April 15 he acknowledged: "Bradley, of course, remains the one whose tactical and strategical judgment I consider most unimpeachable." In his last letter of the war in Europe to Marshall, Eisenhower balked at giving Bradley a command in the Pacific which Eisenhower feared would have the effect of diminishing Bradley's postwar stature. He pointed out that names such as Bradley, Spaatz, and Patton had become symbols to the troops in his theater. "In the reputations of those men the mass sees its own deeds appreciated, even glorified."

Eisenhower was also concerned with Marshall's future needs for officers in the Pacific. He wrote to his Chief as early as September 25, "I assume that at an appropriate time you will communicate to me something of your ideas as to the forces and commanders for which you will have immediate need in the Japanese War after we have finished this job." Eisenhower offered his opinion on the qualifications of the senior officers in his theater. On February 9 he told Marshall that he had made up a list of thirty to forty outstanding general officers with the advice of Smith and Bradley.[20] In his letter of the 26th about the postwar adjustment in grades and assignment of general officers, he expressed concern that staff officers, because their role was necessarily less manifest than that of active commanders, might be overlooked.

Eisenhower was indeed pleased with the officers in his command and felt that he now knew which ones were capable of satisfactory performance. In his April 15 letter, he aptly expressed views on the command organization he had built: "This sounds like I am completely and wholly

[20] The list is Memorandum, February 1, 1945, *EP*, pp. 2466–69.

satisfied with everything that I see. This is far from the case, but the point is that higher commanders have learned to handle the important things and we have gradually developed an organization that keeps nagging details in the hands of people that can give their whole attention to them."

STRATEGY AND TACTICS

Eisenhower's operational directive from the Combined Chiefs was a model of simplicity: "You will enter the continent of Europe and, in conjunction with the other Allied Nations, undertake operations aimed at the heart of Germany and the destruction of her Armed Forces."[21] In response, Eisenhower approved a general plan of operations that was equally broad. His plan was to land on the Normandy coast, fight decisive early battles in the Normandy-Brittany region, and break out across France. He would then pursue the enemy on a broad front with two army groups, emphasizing the northern (or left) attack led by Montgomery to gain necessary ports, reach the boundaries of Germany, and threaten the Ruhr. At the same time, the right attack led by Bradley would link up with the force that was to invade France from the south. The forces then would gain strength by securing ports in Belgium and Brittany as well as in the Mediterranean, while continuing the offensive to the extent possible. The final attack would be launched as a double envelopment of the Ruhr, again stressing Montgomery's assault. This would be followed "by an immediate thrust through Germany, with the specific direction to be determined at the time."[22] Then the Allies would subdue the rest of Germany. Eisenhower maintained, "This general plan, carefully outlined at staff meetings before D-day, was never abandoned, even momentarily, throughout the campaign."[23]

Of course Eisenhower is quite right, but the statement may well have seemed of dubious value to the members of the Combined Chiefs of Staff, to Churchill, even to Bradley and above all to Montgomery. For example, although his detailed plan called for a halt and regrouping at the Seine, he did not stop at that point. Moreover, operating under a directive affording him great freedom of choice, Eisenhower had drawn up a broad plan that would continue to assure him that latitude and flexibility. In the course of executing it he would at various times infuriate nearly everyone. But by capitalizing on the very ambiguities of his plan, he was able until nearly the end of the war to retain enough pliability—in the form of emphasizing one or another attack and of holding out the hope

[21] Eisenhower, *Crusade in Europe*, p. 225.
[22] *Ibid.*, p. 229.
[23] *Ibid.*

of an increased role for one or another force—to prevent the coalition command from dissolving into intransigence.

An analysis of Eisenhower's correspondence to Marshall is one of the best ways to shed light on some of the more controversial issues of World War II in Europe. The Americans did get their way on the issue of the broad front and the final drive to Berlin. It seems valid, therefore, to examine at length the correspondence of the two most important Americans involved in the making and carrying out of these decisions. The letters of this period were dominated by discussions of operations and reflected Eisenhower's method of controlling overall theater tactics. He was above all else flexible, never committing himself far in advance of a specific attack. Remembering the failure of the rush to Tunis, he was cautious, insisting on the broad front attack while carefully omitting to mention to Montgomery that he would never allow the single thrust to Berlin. Eisenhower's operational directives repeatedly reflected both his elasticity and his careful evasion of the problem of the single thrust until he could no longer avoid it. He continually divided future operations into phases, with the final assault on Europe never being spelled out until late March.[24]

He outlined only general theater plans, leaving detailed implementation to Montgomery and Bradley,[25] but retained overall control by deciding which force received which men and materials. His general plans always included an awareness of the crucial importance of ports, for he remembered both the incredible supply problems he had faced in the Mediterranean and the consequences of the German stronghold in Tunis, which had enabled the enemy to pour men and material into North Africa. Finally, he took into account that he was dealing with Montgomery and not Alexander. He tried to overcome this difficulty in the same way he handled other problems—by always stressing the areas in which he agreed with Montgomery. Only as the campaign wore on did he become firmer with Montgomery. This method usually worked well to solve the problem of the moment in Eisenhower's favor. What Montgomery and others finally discovered was that the final comprehensive plan did in fact emerge as the sum of its component parts. Eisenhower's absorption in accomplishing this extraordinary task of asserting his own will without completely alienating all who disagreed with him forms the real theme of this group of letters.

[24] See, for example, E. to Commanders, October 28, 1944, *EP*, pp. 2257–60.
[25] See, for example, E. to Bradley, December 31, 1944, *EP*, p. 2389, in which he tells Bradley, "As you can see, the only mission I give the forces under your command is to drive forward on the line Prum-Bonn. Naturally you will have hundreds of tactical problems on the way up, but I want you to drive First and Third Armies on that general line."

Eisenhower's comments included reports on the current battle, his moves in response, future plans, and concern for supply and logistics. His frequent writing was due in part to Marshall's insistence that he be kept informed about operations. Eisenhower's letters showed the Chief that he was maintaining a tight control over tactics. He first wrote on June 19 at the beginning of a four-day storm that was to wreak havoc with supply facilities.[26] By July 5, when Eisenhower next wrote Marshall, Bradley had taken Cherbourg, but Montgomery had been stalled at Caen, the gateway to the Seine and the point at which the Allies had hoped to break out of the beachhead.[27]

The failure to take Caen "was the greatest single disappointment of the invasion."[28] It forced Eisenhower, Montgomery, and Bradley to alter their plans, for they could no longer count on outflanking the Cotentin's hedgerows. Their new plan called for Montgomery to draw the bulk of the German forces to his position at Caen while Bradley made the breakthrough on the Cotentin Peninsula toward the Seine (and Paris), and Patton's Third Army moved on Brittany.[29] By July 26, as Eisenhower wrote Marshall, the breakout had begun and the stage was set for the opening of the dispute over the conduct of the campaign. "We are staging major offensives in both armies . . . If either show goes on with reasonable success, we will be in a much improved position."[30]

After the breakout, Eisenhower wrote even more frequently concerning

[26] For the story of the storm, see Samuel E. Morison, *The Invasion of France and Germany, 1944–1945*, History of the United States Naval Operations in World War II, vol. XI (Boston, 1964), pp. 176–80.

[27] For an account of Montgomery's battle for Caen, June 25–29, see Major L. F. Ellis, *Victory in the West*, vol. I (London, 1962), pp. 274–86; for his earlier attacks, see Martin Blumenson, *Breakout and Pursuit*, U.S. Army in World War II, ed. Stetson Conn (Washington, 1961), pp. 3–16. For the entire campaign, see Esposito, ed., *West Point Atlas*, II, maps 50 and 51.

[28] Blumenson, *Breakout and Pursuit*, pp. 13–14.

[29] There are continuing arguments as to exactly what Montgomery intended to do. Many at SHAEF felt that he had promised to break through himself, while Eisenhower, Montgomery, and Bradley all agreed that Montgomery's attack, which preceded Bradley's, was designed to support the breakout by Bradley. The official narrator of the campaign, Blumenson, in his *Breakout and Pursuit,* has an objective analysis of the various positions on pp. 194–96; the extreme anti-Montgomery position is given in Tedder, *With Prejudice*, pp. 565–67; Chester Wilmot, *The Struggle for Europe* (London, 1957), pp. 338–62, has a useful analysis of SHAEF's views; Ellis, *Victory in the West*, vol. I, pp. 325–46, gives his position; Eisenhower himself supports Montgomery in his *Crusade in Europe*, pp. 266–67.

[30] The breakout was first made by the VII Corps of First Army just west of St. Lô, with Coutances as the objective. Other elements quickly followed. E. to Montgomery, July 10, 1944, *EP*, p. 1990, n. 1; E. to Montgomery, July 13, 1944, *EP*, pp. 2002–3, n. 1; E. to Montgomery, July 21, 1944, *EP*, 2020, 2021, n. 2 and n. 6; E. to Montgomery, July 26, 1944, *EP*, p. 2029, n. 1; E. to Bradley, July 26, 1944, *EP*, p. 2029, n. 1; and Esposito, ed., *West Point Atlas*, II, map 53. The British shortly attacked at Caumont toward Vire. See E. to Montgomery, July 28, 1944, *EP*, pp. 2041–42, n. 4 and n. 5; and E. to Montgomery, July 31, 1944, *EP*, p. 2046, n. 1.

the campaign, for reasons that follow. First of all, Marshall had complained that Eisenhower was not keeping him fully abreast of current and future operations.[31] Then, in the last week of August Eisenhower decided not to have troops stop to regroup at the Seine, as had been scheduled in OVERLORD planning. Finally, Montgomery and Bradley, having reached the Seine, had raised the issue of whether to advance into Germany on a broad front or by a single thrust. Eisenhower considered both of these decisions his prerogative because they involved overall theater objectives. By contrast, he had let Montgomery and Bradley do the planning for the breakout because it involved only an immediate tactical situation.

Eisenhower decided to push on beyond the Seine all the way to the Rhine if possible.[32] He rightly felt that the only thing hampering his advance would be the shortage of supplies caused by lack of port facilities. His decision, in addition to complicating the distance and scale of operations that supply facilities would have to face, precipitated the beginning of the argument over the means to be employed in exploiting the success. The debate over theater strategy, necessarily intertwined with Montgomery's continuing demand for control of ground operations, involved Eisenhower in a confrontation not only with his subordinate commanders Bradley and, especially, Montgomery, but ultimately with Churchill and the British Chiefs of Staff. The central fact about the controversy, however, is that the decisions were made by Eisenhower and remained within the framework of his own general plan.

Eisenhower outlined the dilemma in his letter of August 24. He had just returned from Montgomery's headquarters where the latter proposed a thrust along the northern coast led by his 21st Army Group, expanded to include the U.S. First Army and the First Allied Airborne Army. He would clear the coast as far as and including the vital port of Antwerp, establish his air force in Belgium, and strike into the Ruhr. Eisenhower had pointed out the disadvantages of this plan to Montgomery—namely, that it was risky and exposed his right flank to counterattack. In order to give Montgomery all of the supplies and gasoline he asked for, Eisenhower would have had to immobilize Patton's Third Army. This would have been dangerous tactically and disastrous politically in the United States.[33]

[31] Eisenhower promised to have the staff draw up a weekly appreciation for the Combined Chiefs of Staff. See E. to M. and CCS, August 2, 1944, *EP*, pp. 2048–51.

[32] For a discussion, see Blumenson, *Breakout and Pursuit*, pp. 631–33, 657, and Roland G. Ruppenthal, *Logistical Support of the Armies*, vol. II, *September, 1944–May, 1945*, U.S. Army in World War II, ed. Kent Roberts Greenfield (Washington, 1959), pp. 3–8.

[33] For accounts of the meeting and the reactions of those involved, see Ellis, *Victory in the West*, vol. I, pp. 461–64; Montgomery, *Memoirs*, pp. 239–43; Bradley, *Soldier's Story*, pp. 398–401, 410–12; and Blumenson, *Breakout and Pursuit*, pp. 657–60, 684–88. E. to Montgomery, August 24, 1944, *EP*, pp. 2091–92, n. 1.

So Eisenhower compromised. Ultimately, he gave Montgomery preference in supplies and one corps from the U.S. First Army because he considered Antwerp and the Ruhr the key objectives. But he also permitted Bradley's 12th Army Group to continue to move east and northeast from Paris. He was able to enforce this decision because he had control over the allocation of resources. In the face of this control, Montgomery and Bradley were virtually powerless.

Eisenhower made his intentions perfectly clear to Marshall. He said that "obviously" the first priority was Montgomery's drive northeast to destroy the greatest number of enemy forces and seize the German rocket sites, airfields, and Antwerp. But Montgomery would have to detach forces to capture the Le Havre Peninsula and Bradley would have to complete the conquest of Brittany. "In addition to all the above, I want Bradley to build up quickly, from incoming divisions, a force in the area just east of Paris so as to be ready to advance straight eastward to Metz." After outlining the specific plans of the army groups, he emphasized to Marshall that, although he had decided to concentrate for the moment on Montgomery's drive, he had no intention of having Bradley play a minor role. Eisenhower hoped that the forces which had landed in southern France would move quickly up the Rhone Valley to combine with the OVERLORD forces, thereby giving him control of those operations as well. He also wrote about the forces driving north from Italy, the only other strategic area of operations which concerned him in 1944. He felt that German resistance was "rapidly weakening" there and was afraid of the possibility of lingering guerilla warfare in the mountainous regions. This fear of a guerilla redoubt, expressed so early by Eisenhower, was to loom ever larger as a consideration in his already conservative tactical thinking.

Yet the prospect of success intensified other problems. Success made it less costly for the Allies to act selfishly and Eisenhower was already beginning to feel pressure from Montgomery. He told Marshall that ". . . as signs of victory appear in the air, I note little instances that seem to indicate that Allies cannot hang together so effectively in prosperity as they can in adversity." Eisenhower's fears were soon realized. In his operational directive of August 29 he had outlined the principal mission of the Central Group of Armies (Bradley's group) as assisting the Northern Group of Armies (Montgomery's group). He had authorized Bradley's Group to then ". . . advance rapidly across the Somme, prepared to continue the advance to the northeast."[34] But on the 4th of September he ended the "preparation" or immobilized stage of Patton's army by assigning Bradley's forces the additional assignment "to occupy the sector of the Sieg-

[34] E. to Commanders, August 29, 1944, *EP*, pp. 2100–2102.

fried Line covering the Saar and then to seize Frankfurt."[35] Whatever difficulties Patton had caused Eisenhower had not dimmed Eisenhower's faith in the commander's ability to mount a combat offensive. Eisenhower was not about to entrust his "bold" (in Eisenhower's view) plan of crushing the retreating Germans solely to the cautious Montgomery.[36] Predictably, Montgomery was enraged at Eisenhower's decision to bring all the forces up the Rhine instead of allowing Montgomery to have all supplies and the additional army which he felt would allow him to penetrate to Berlin.

Eisenhower handled the controversy in typical fashion by emphasizing one thing to Montgomery, another to the Combined Chiefs of Staff, and another in his private letters to Marshall. He told Montgomery "While agreeing with your conception of a powerful and full blooded thrust toward Berlin, I do not repeat not agree that it should be initiated at this moment to the exclusion of all other maneuver. . . . No re-allocation of our present resources would be adequate to sustain a thrust to Berlin."[37] With the Combined Chiefs he adhered to his policy of dividing the campaign into phases, the final phase of which he refused to firmly define. He told them that "The possibilities for further advance, depending on the situation at the time, are: (a) The Ruhr via Hanover or Hamburg or Berlin. (b) Frankfurt via Leipzig or Magdeburg or Berlin. (c) A combination of both." He specifically added, "I wish to retain freedom of action to strike in any direction so far as the logistical situation permits." The Combined Chiefs should have read this more carefully than they did, for it represented Eisenhower's frankest expression to them of his future plans. Usually he said that he would not discuss the final phase of the campaign at all and coupled this with an implication that the northern thrust would probably enjoy the final priority. But Brooke chose to view this report rather casually. The Combined Chiefs reminded Eisenhower of the advantages of the northern thrust and they commented, ". . . you appear to be of the same mind."[38] Such self-delusion ultimately fitted in perfectly with Eisenhower's approach, enabling him to assert his will every time even though each episode would serve to increase the intensity of shock for the British over his final decisions.

Eisenhower addressed Marshall more directly. On September 14, in a long letter about the campaign, he wrote that the Allied advance was

[35] For the order of September 4, see E. to Commanders, September 4, 1944, *EP*, pp. 2115–18.

[36] Memorandum, September 5, 1944, *EP*, pp. 2121–22.

[37] E. to Montgomery, September 5, 1944, *EP*, pp. 2120–21. For the best discussion as to whether or not Montgomery could have succeeded, see Roland G. Ruppenthal, "Logistics and the Broad-Front Strategy," *Command Decisions* (Washington, 1960), pp. 419–28.

[38] E. to CCS, September 9, 1944, *EP*, p. 2128, n. 4.

beginning to slow down to a halt scarcely 50 miles west of the Rhine because "the fact is that we are stretched to the absolute limit in maintenance both as to intake and as to distribution after supplies are landed."[39] He then discussed Montgomery's plan of rapidly pushing on to Berlin and concluded that it was impossible. He had two reasons, both the results of earlier lessons. The first deterrent was the lack of proper port capacity— Eisenhower had witnessed the chaos wrought by a devastating storm in the early days of OVERLORD. It had caused him to fight for port facilities in any planned operation and was a key factor in his insistence on the landing in southern France.

Eisenhower's second reason was also a product of experience: "The attack would be on such a narrow front that flanking threats would be particularly effective and no other troops in the whole region would be capable of going to its support." He had long alluded to difficulties in North Africa which threatened to destroy isolated units. It had been one of the considerations in his decision to make a concentrated landing in Sicily. He had then observed the near-annihilation of the Salerno beachhead. All of this had caused him to insist from the first on a strengthened OVERLORD assault. He had no intention of disregarding these hard lessons. In fact, Eisenhower took pains to register his astonishment at Montgomery's folly.

Eisenhower then gave Marshall an idea of the final shape of the campaign, by stressing its lack of rigidity. He said that he intended to ". . . hustle all our forces up against the Rhine, . . . build up our maintenance facilities and our reserves as rapidly as possible and then put on one sustained and unremitting advance against the heart of the enemy country. Supporting this great attack will probably be subsidiary operations against the German ports on the left and against his southern industrial areas on the right." Eisenhower did not say so, but Montgomery, whatever else he would be doing, would have to be responsible for the ports on the left (north). The Southern Group of Armies under Devers would be in part responsible for the south. This left the great advance for the center. Eisenhower did not mention Berlin by name but wrote that he was going

[39] Eisenhower's concern with the proper supply arrangements was also the theme of a letter to Marshall of August 21 (*EP*, pp. 2080–81) in which he supported a plan to simplify the arrangements for insuring a proper supply of vital petroleum. The basic problem with the supply situation was the rapidity of the Allied advance. Planning had called for twelve U.S. divisions to be at the Seine on D plus 90 (September 4) and pause there for thirty days. Yet by September 4, sixteen divisions were already 150 miles beyond the Seine, and eight days later U.S. First Army had elements near Aachen, 200 miles beyond Paris. The U.S. supply troops simply could not keep up with this advance. In addition, the logistic capacity had to be increased by the addition of a major port if all the forces were to be maintained. Ruppenthal, *Logistical Support of the Armies*, vol. II, pp. 3–21; Pogue, *Supreme Command*, pp. 256–59.

into the heart of the country. Although again there might be a dispute as to what indeed constituted the heart of Germany,[40] the way Eisenhower phrased his letter indicated that he did not intend to commit himself to a thrust to Berlin. His next comment seemed to underscore this point. "I have sacrificed a lot to give Montgomery the strength he needs to reach the Rhine in the north and to threaten the Ruhr. That is, after all, our main effort for the moment." Eisenhower did give first priority to Montgomery's drive up to and across the Rhine. But ". . . thereafter it is absolutely imperative that he quickly capture the approaches to Antwerp so that we may use that port."

But in maintaining control with this policy of "something for everyone," Eisenhower assented to an operation which was to prove a great tactical mistake.[41] He approved an attack he described in his letter of September 14 to Marshall as a "great Airborne attack." This may have pleased Marshall, who had been urging greater use of airborne operations. Operation MARKET-GARDEN was designed to support Montgomery's efforts to cross the Rhine. Eisenhower felt that the operation was a limited one, designed only to effect a linkup with ground troops across the Rhine. Operation MARKET planned to drop airborne troops into a narrow corridor extending some eighty miles into Holland from Eindhoven north to Arnhem. They would secure bridges across the Maas, Waal, and lower Rhine. At the same time, Operation GARDEN, involving the British Second Army, would rush along the corridor and push out from Arnhem to the Zuider Zee. If successful, the entire operation would cut off the exit of the enemy troops in western Holland and outflank the German West Wall, the line of heavy Germany fortifications misnamed the Siegfried Line by the Allies. Montgomery's 21st Army Group would then be able to drive into Germany along the northern plain.[42]

The Supreme Commander was overly optimistic about the success of this operation and about operations in general. He told Marshall in the September 14 letter that he thought he would have to fight only one more major battle in the theater. In a memo to himself on September 5 he had noted that "The defeat of the German armies is complete, and the only thing now needed to realize the whole conception is speed. Our rapidity of movement will depend on maintenance, in which we are now stretched

[40] E. to Commanders, September 9, 1944, *EP*, p. 2117, n. 4; Pogue, *Supreme Command*, pp. 249–50.

[41] The arguments concerning this operation are summed up in Charles B. MacDonald, "The Decision to Launch Operation Market-Garden," *Command Decisions,* ed. Kent Roberts Greenfield (Washington, 1960), pp. 429–42.

[42] For the course of the campaign, see Charles B. MacDonald, *The Siegfried Line Campaign*, U.S. Army in World War II, ed. Stetson Conn (Washington, 1963), pp. 119–39.

to the limit."[43] Eisenhower's overconfidence led to a misstep on his part in talking about future operations with Montgomery. Obviously assuming the success of MARKET-GARDEN, due to start in two days, Eisenhower wrote Montgomery on the 15th about operations after control of the Ruhr, Saar, and Frankfurt areas had been assured. He wrote, "Clearly, Berlin is the main prize, and the prize in defense of which the enemy is likely to concentrate the bulk of his forces. There is no doubt, whatsoever, in my mind, that we should concentrate all our energies and resources on a rapid thrust to Berlin." In this statement Eisenhower was on safe and familiar ground (but one clearly does not have to wonder why Montgomery got the idea that Eisenhower would let him go to Berlin). Eisenhower then told him that "Our strategy, however, will have to be coordinated with that of the Russians, so we must consider alternative objectives." He outlined them and added: "Simply stated, it is my desire to move on Berlin by the most direct and expeditious route, with combined U.S.-British forces supported by other available forces moving through key centers and occupying strategic areas on the flanks, all in one coordinated, concerted operation."[44] Montgomery reacted predictably by replying on the 18th that Eisenhower should decide on a single thrust to Berlin either by Montgomery through the north or by Bradley through Frankfurt and central Germany.[45] Montgomery realized that as long as Eisenhower allowed other offensive operations to develop, the commanders involved, especially Patton, would get themselves into precarious positions that would demand reinforcement to prevent disaster.[46]

On the same day that Montgomery was sending off his strong protest to Eisenhower, Eisenhower wrote to Marshall that "This team is working well. Without exception all concerned have now fully accepted my conception of our problem and are carrying it out intelligently and with energy." He had to resolve the dispute with Montgomery, and on the 20th he wrote Montgomery that there were really no great differences between them. Furthermore, "Never at any time have I implied that I was considering an advance into Germany with all armies moving abreast." And more: "Specifically I agree with you in the following: My choice of routes for making the all-out offensive into Germany is from the Ruhr to Berlin." He did veto any suggestion of the other forces being immobilized by stripping them of needed supplies, but reiterated, "I merely want to make sure that when you start leading your Army Group in its thrust onto Berlin and Bradley starts driving with his left to support you, our other forces are in

[43] Office Memorandum, September 5, 1944, *EP,* pp. 2121–22.
[44] E. to Montgomery, September 15, 1944, *EP,* pp. 2148–49.
[45] *Ibid.,* p. 2149, n. 4.
[46] Pogue, *Supreme Command,* pp. 292–93.

position to assure the success of that drive."[47] Montgomery replied the next day that he and Eisenhower were not in agreement. He maintained that Eisenhower had to stop the right flank of Bradley's 12th Army Group and put everything into the attack in the north, warning, "It is my opinion that if this is not done you will not get the Ruhr."[48]

Eisenhower seized upon Montgomery's warning and used it to ease the dispute. He told him on September 22 that he had been acting under the assumption that Montgomery was basing his recommendations on the views which Montgomery had expressed on the 4th—that is, that this was the time to go to Berlin. "With that statement I did not repeat not agree but I do agree emphatically with what you have to say about attaining our immediate objective, the Ruhr."[49] In other words, Eisenhower chose to stress the fact that he and Montgomery agreed that the northern attack on the Ruhr would enjoy priority at the present time. At the same time he called for a meeting of the commanders on the 22d to have priorities delineated.

Eisenhower gave Marshall a preview of what he was going to say at the meeting by writing on September 21 that the key to the campaign was to capture the approaches to Antwerp. He might have added that his remembrance of one of the lessons of Tunisia had been temporarily obscured by his vision of a cheap and rapid crossing of the Rhine. Operation MARKET-GARDEN was shortly to be a complete failure because of increasingly severe weather problems and powerful German counterattacks. Moreover, it had drained resources away from the attack on Antwerp. Eisenhower's letters to Marshall as well as his operational directives indicate that he failed to give Antwerp clear priority over all other operations until October 9.[50]

At the meeting on September 22 Eisenhower asked for general acceptance of the fact that possession of a deep-water port in the north was indispensable for the final attack on Germany. He insisted on a distinction between logistical requirements for the drive to the West Wall and the drive to Berlin. The main operations at the moment were to be Montgomery's freeing of Antwerp and attack on the Ruhr from the north. Bradley would take over part of Montgomery's sector in support while continuing his own offensive to the extent possible toward Cologne and Bonn. Patton's Third Army would take no aggressive action for the present.[51] Bradley was annoyed because Hodges' First Army had to take over part

[47] E. to Montgomery, September 20, 1944, *EP*, pp. 2164–66.
[48] *Ibid.*, p. 2165, n. 3.
[49] E. to Montgomery, September 22, 1944, *EP*, pp. 2175–76.
[50] E. to Montgomery, September 13, 1944, *EP*, p. 2135, n. 5; E. to Commanders, September 13, 1944, *EP*, pp. 2136–38; E. to Montgomery, October 9, 1944, *EP*, pp. 2215–16; Pogue, *Supreme Command*, p. 296.
[51] *Ibid.* p. 294.

of Montgomery's sector, and Montgomery was displeased that he had not received the control over First Army that he wanted—instead, he only received permission to communicate directly with Hodges.[52] Yet the crisis over tactics had been calmed for the moment—the first encounter over the wide versus the narrow approach had been resolved.

On September 25 Eisenhower acknowledged the approaching autumn stalemate to Marshall.[53] He said that Bradley was forcing his left flank even further to the north so that Montgomery could concentrate greater troop strength to cross the Rhine. Although he did not mention it to Marshall, he had written Montgomery the day before of his fear that with Bradley's expanded front, ". . . we are getting fearfully stretched south of Aachen and may get a nasty little 'Kasserine' if the enemy chooses at any place to concentrate a bit of strength."[54]

Eisenhower discussed all these problems with Marshall when the Chief arrived for a week's visit on October 6. Significantly, during this period Eisenhower not only sent his firmest letter to Montgomery on the subject of command but also sent him a cable which for the first time specifically ordered the capture of Antwerp as the first priority.[55] Marshall's visit obviously served Eisenhower well, for in future debates over tactics, he did not mention disagreements nearly so often to Marshall, and he seemed quite certain of the correctness of his plans. The letter on command included a lecture to Montgomery on the tactical function of the overall commander.

The autumn campaigns continued to occupy Eisenhower's attention. On October 15, he informed Marshall that "We are having a sticky time in the North but Montgomery has at last seen the light and is concentrating toward his west, left, flank in order to clear up the Antwerp situation." This move meant that the U.S. Ninth and First Armies would lead the drive to the Rhine.[56] On October 28 Eisenhower set the objectives (after clearing the estuary at Antwerp) of Montgomery's, Bradley's, and Devers' army groups as being to obtain and cross the Rhine. He did not specify his plans beyond that.[57] On November 2, on the eve of the clearing of Antwerp, Eisenhower set the starting dates for the offensives in the north and center. These two operations would be coordinated with each other. Bradley's forces south of the Ardennes would continue to occupy the Saar and approach the Rhine in support of the main effort in the north.

---

[52] Bradley, *Soldier's Story*, pp. 422–23.

[53] Hodges' First Army came to a sudden halt at the West Wall and did not reach Cologne until March, 1945. Pogue, *Supreme Command*, pp. 256 and 453.

[54] E. to Montgomery, September 24, 1944, *EP*, pp. 2185–86.

[55] The letter on command is E. to Montgomery, October 13, 1944, *EP*, pp. 2221–25; the cable on operations is E. to Montgomery, October 9, 1944, *EP*, pp. 2215–16.

[56] See E. to Montgomery, October 15, 1944, *EP*, p. 2228, n. 1.

[57] E. to Commanders, October 28, 1944, *EP*, pp. 2257–60.

On November 11 Eisenhower commented at length to Marshall on the offensives but was not optimistic because of the weather. On the 27th Eisenhower still complained about the weather but operations in the interim had met with somewhat more success. Patton had closed to the West Wall and the Ninth and First Armies were in the act of overcoming it and reaching the Roer River.[58] Eisenhower was most pleased with operations in the south, even though they had encountered only weak resistance. He reported that Seventh Army had broken through the Vosges and was getting ready to attack the Siegfried Line.[59]

While Eisenhower was fairly satisfied with the progress of the offensive, Montgomery was not. His 21st Army Group had been forced to assume an almost defensive role. The two men had a meeting on November 28 and Montgomery reopened the debate over theater strategy and command responsibility. On the 30th he asked for a conference and concluded, "I suggest that we want no one else at the meeting, except Chiefs of Staff: who must not speak."[60] Montgomery could scarcely have infuriated Eisenhower more than by this combined assault on Eisenhower's concept of command and tactics and the insult to his trusted Chief of Staff Bedell Smith. During the first debate over tactics, Eisenhower had suffered a similar insult to Smith and this made him resent the offense even more.[61] In his reply of December 1, he did not equivocate. He rejected Montgomery's characterization of the campaign as a failure, did not commit himself as to where the theater should be divided between Bradley and Montgomery, said that Smith would indeed be at the conference and, "I will not by any means insult him by telling him that he should remain mute at any conference he and I both attend." He said that he had no intention of stopping other operations as long as they were useful. He reminded Montgomery that in the battle around the Mareth Line in 1943, the latter had abandoned his main attack because of heavy resistance and employed a successful flanking maneuver.[62] Montgomery then backed down somewhat, saying that he had only meant that the Allies had failed to close to and cross the Rhine.[63] Montgomery's attack did cause Eisenhower to send a long justification of the campaign to the Combined Chiefs on December 3 and to defend himself to Marshall on the 5th.

But Eisenhower's frank approach to Montgomery did not end the debate.

[58] For an account of the campaign, see MacDonald, *Siegfried Line Campaign*, pp. 390–578.

[59] The German counteroffensive of mid-December forced the abandonment of this plan. E. to M., November 27, 1944, *EP*, p. 2321, n. 2.

[60] E. to Montgomery, December 1, 1944, *EP*, p. 2325, n. 2 and n. 4.

[61] Montgomery had insisted on talking to Eisenhower alone on August 23 even though Smith had accompanied Eisenhower to the meeting. Eisenhower to Montgomery, August 24, 1944, *EP*, pp. 2091–92, n. 1.

[62] E. to Montgomery, December 1, 1944, *EP*, pp. 2323–25.

[63] E. to Montgomery, December 2, 1944, *EP*, p. 2326, n. 1.

The meeting with Montgomery on December 7 failed to clear the air, so Eisenhower decided to present the issue before Churchill and the British Chiefs of Staff. He did so at a meeting on December 12.[64] There the chasm between Eisenhower and Brooke, who supported Montgomery's advocacy of the single thrust, was revealed. So Eisenhower, who had troubled Marshall less and less with this sort of problem as the war went on, turned to his superior. That he did so is a strong indication of how intensely constrained he felt. He asked Marshall once again for help in easing the pressure on him to change his tactics. He had done the same thing in the dispute over tactics in September. This time he made no effort to gloss over the disagreement. He wrote Marshall on the 13th, recounting the meeting. He did feel that he had succeeded in getting Brooke "to understand the situation better than he had before," and made it clear that he was going to advance broadly to the Rhine and clear the Germans west of the river. The only change that Eisenhower made was to specify that all incoming replacements would go to the northernmost of American armies, the First and Ninth.[65] This was hardly against Eisenhower's will, since he had pointed out to Marshall in his letter of the 5th that their attacks were particularly feared by the Germans.

A German counterattack complicated the debate over tactics and dictated Eisenhower's next moves. On December 16 the German forces attacked the American front in the Ardennes,[66] which split Bradley's command and left him in effective communication only with the forces in the south of the Ardennes. For this reason Eisenhower's first response was to assign the northern part of Bradley's army group, the First and Ninth Armies, to Montgomery's command.[67] Marshall told Eisenhower that he had directed that no one in the War Department bother Eisenhower while he gave full attention to the fighting, and at the same time expressed his "complete confidence" in Eisenhower.[68] The seriousness of the German counterattack did provide the British with an opportunity to reopen the issue of command and tactics. On January 8, when the battle crisis was over, Marshall forwarded to Eisenhower the familiar British arguments and told him that the British Chiefs wished to review theater plans at the forthcoming Malta and Yalta Conferences in January, with the object

[64] E. to Marshall, December 5, 1944, *EP*, p. 2336, n. 7.
[65] E. to Marshall, December 13, 1944, *EP*, p. 2342, n. 1; Memorandum, December 23, 1944, *EP*, pp. 2371–76.
[66] For the official history of the campaign, see Hugh M. Cole, *The Ardennes: Battle of the Bulge*, U.S. Army in World War II, ed. Stetson Conn (Washington, 1965). See also Esposito, ed., *West Point Atlas*, II, maps 59–64. For a complete account by a combat historian, see S. L. A. Marshall's *Bastogne: The First Eight Days* (Washington, 1946).
[67] E. to CCS, December 20, 1944, *EP*, p. 2363; Memorandum, December 23, 1944, *EP*, pp. 2371–76.
[68] Pogue, *Supreme Command*, p. 381.

of strengthening the northern attack. Eisenhower emphasized that area in his response and came very close to committing himself to it by promising that there would not be two main attacks in the final drive. However, he said that the final phase was still "indefinable."[69] In a message of the 20th he retreated from his stand by pointing out that the main effort might have to take place elsewhere, specifically stating, "Depending on the degree of enemy resistance it may be necessary to use either or both of these two avenues."[70] Yet Eisenhower did not write Marshall about the new controversy until February 9, when it had ended. The failure of MARKET-GARDEN had conclusively demonstrated to Eisenhower the unfeasibility of a single thrust and Marshall's visit in October had bolstered his view. He had told Marshall his battle plans. Moreover, he and Marshall were to meet on January 28 at Marseilles on the Chief's way to the conference at Malta.

Instead, Eisenhower's principal concern in his letter to Marshall of January 12 was the current military problem caused by the French. He told Marshall that "When Devers turned his complete Seventh Army northward, he was badly mistaken in the ability of the French Army to finish off the Colmar pocket."[71] The Germans had launched a minor offensive on January 1 north of Strasbourg toward the Saverne Gap and the interior of Lorraine. Instead of forcing Eisenhower to shift troops from the crucial Ardennes area, this action resulted in his tightening his position there and withdrawing from Strasbourg.[72] Eisenhower said that De Gaulle had then convinced him that the blow to French public opinion would be such that De Gaulle would lose control of the situation in France. Eisenhower had decided that he could not tolerate the ensuing danger to his rear and line of communications and therefore rescinded his orders.[73]

After the German attack had been stopped all along the line, Eisenhower returned First Army to Bradley's control but left Ninth Army under Montgomery for the drive to the Rhine.[74] This had not mollified Montgomery, who wanted an even stronger commitment from Eisenhower in building up his attack.[75] Montgomery also held that his northeast attack by the U.S. Ninth Army to link up with the Canadians on the Rhine as they moved southeast could not be launched until other operations in the Ardennes had come to a halt. Eisenhower soon came to agree with

[69] E. to M., January 10, 1945, *EP*, pp. 2415–20.

[70] E. to CCS, January 20, 1945, *EP*, p. 2450–54.

[71] The pocket was not pinched off until February 9. See Pogue, *Supreme Command*, p. 318; Cole, *Ardennes*, p. 51; Esposito, ed. *West Point Atlas*, II, map 64a; E. to Bradley and Devers, p. 2357, n. 3.

[72] E. to De Gaulle, January 2, 1945, *EP*, p. 2392, n. 1.

[73] E. to De Gaulle, January 5, 1945, *EP*, pp. 2396–97; and E. to M., January 6, 1945, *EP*, pp. 2399–2401.

[74] Pogue, *Supreme Command*, p. 395.

[75] E. to Commanders, January 18, 1945, *EP*, p. 2441, n. 4.

this point of view[76] but insisted on his plan to eliminate the forces west of the Rhine before crossing that river in force, which Marshall endorsed during his visit.[77] As Eisenhower's representative at Malta, Smith managed to get out of the conference with Eisenhower's plans sufficiently flexible, a fact which frustrated Brooke.[78]

The offensives went well. Eisenhower wrote Marshall on February 9 about his decision to leave the U.S. Ninth Army with Montgomery to spearhead the drive. On the 20th he ordered Bradley to plan immediate resumption of offensive operations to clear the enemy from the west of the Rhine north of the Moselle.[79] Eisenhower wrote Marshall the same day and made it clear that he considered weather the only obstacle to a broad advance. Although the Germans had flooded the Roer River, he hoped that Simpson's Ninth Army attack, scheduled on the 23d, would succeed in getting across the river. Eisenhower's optimism proved to be well-founded. On the extreme northern flank, the British Second and Canadian First Armies were closing to the Rhine. Simpson's attack did succeed and he broke loose from the bridgehead on the Roer River on February 28. In the center, Hodges' First Army launched a successful offensive on the 23d which was to bring it in force to the Rhine by March 10, thereby closing the Rhine from the Moselle north. Elements of First Army seized an intact bridge at Remagen on the 7th and Eisenhower immediately approved his subordinate commanders' decisions to take advantage of the windfall by establishing a firm bridgehead across the Rhine.[80] In the south, immediately to Hodges' right, Patton's Third Army was racing to the Moselle River and toward the Saar. The U.S. Seventh Army under Patch, on Patton's right, was preparing to attack through the Saar to the Rhine. In the extreme south, the French First Army was maintaining its defensive position at the Rhine.

The attack in the south occupied Eisenhower's attention. On March 12 he gave Marshall an accurate prediction of the timing and course of the attack. On the 18th Eisenhower confessed that he found it incomprehensible that the Germans elected to fight along the entire western side of the Rhine instead of pulling back and using the river as a defensive barrier.[81]

[76] Ibid.; E. to Montgomery, January 21, 1945, EP, pp. 2455–56; E. to Bradley and Montgomery, February 1, 1945, EP, pp. 2465–66; E. to Bradley, February 20, 1945, EP, pp. 2489–90.

[77] Conference notes, January 28, 1945, EP, pp. 2460–61.

[78] Arthur Bryant, Triumph in the West (New York, 1959), pp. 300–301; E. to Smith, January 31, 1945, EP, p. 2464, n. 3.

[79] E. to Bradley, February 20, 1945, EP, pp. 2489–90; and E. to Bradley, March 3, 1945, EP, pp. 2504–5.

[80] Bradley, Soldier's Story, pp. 510–11; Eisenhower, Crusade in Europe, pp. 378–80; E. to CCS and BCOS, March 8, 1945, EP, pp. 2510–11.

[81] See E. to M., March 12, 1945, EP, p. 2523, n. 6; and E. to M. March 18, 1945, p. 2533, n. 4.

This action made Eisenhower's decision to fight the major battle west of the Rhine even more meaningful.

By March 26, when Eisenhower next wrote Marshall, the Allies were crossing all along the Rhine. He reported on the success of Simpson's Ninth Army. In the north, the Canadian First, British Second, and U.S. Ninth had all crossed on the 23d and 24th. Hodges' First Army had continued to exploit their beachhead at Remagen in the center. Below Frankfurt, Patton's Third Army had begun crossing at Oppenheim on the 22d. South of Patton, the U.S. Seventh Army would cross at Mannheim on the 26th and the French First at Phillipsburg on April 1.[82]

Eisenhower was immensely pleased and congratulated himself as well as Bradley. He told Marshall that Brooke now expressed the view that Eisenhower had been right all along.[83] He ended his pat on the back with "I hope this does not sound boastful, but I must admit to a great satisfaction that the things that Bradley and I have believed in from the beginning and have carried out in the face of some opposition both from within and without, have matured so splendidly."

But the war was not yet over and Eisenhower faced a third and final dispute over his operational plans with the British, who were not nearly so pleased with developments. The first two arguments had found Eisenhower defending the broad front attack against the British advocacy of a single thrust in the north. The argument now took an ironic twist, for Eisenhower at last had determined where to make the final push to join the Russians. He had already told the Combined Chiefs on March 24 and Montgomery, Bradley, and Devers on the 25th, that he intended to make a double envelopment of the Ruhr, the industrial area which he considered the key to Germany. He based this decision on the fact that the entire German front was vulnerable and that the attack in the north had all the strength that could be effectively deployed. He had ordered Montgomery and Bradley to advance and squeeze the Ruhr between them, effecting a junction in the general area of Kassel-Paderborn.[84]

Then on March 28 Eisenhower at last revealed his plans for the final assault in a message to Stalin with copies for the Combined Chiefs. Eisenhower wrote that, after Montgomery and Bradley had completed the encirclement of the Ruhr, the next task would be to split the German forces in two by joining the Russians. He intended to have Bradley do this in the center at Erfurt-Leipzig-Dresden. As soon as possible, he would also mount

---

[82] For the crossings of the Rhine, see Esposito, ed. *West Point Atlas*, II, map 68.

[83] See also Eisenhower, *Crusade in Europe*, p. 372. Brooke later denied this. Bryant, *Triumph in the West*, p. 333.

[84] E. to CCS, March 24, 1945, *EP*, pp. 2539–40; and E. to Bradley and Devers, March 25, 1945, *EP*, pp. 2541–42.

a secondary advance to also link up in the Regensburg-Linz area in order to prevent the formation of a German redoubt in the south. In a separate message he told Montgomery that the mission of his army group during this period would be "to protect Bradley's northern flank. . . ." The U.S. Ninth Army would therefore revert to Bradley. Eisenhower did tell Montgomery that he might later return the Ninth Army to Montgomery to aid the British in crossing the Elbe.[85]

Several things about Eisenhower's decision are worth noting. First of all, by managing to avoid commitment until he could avoid it no longer, he had retained the flexibility to take advantage of the current situation—namely, that the Russians, numbering a million men in strength, were within forty miles of Berlin while he was still two hundred miles away. Since his directive had called for the destruction of the enemy forces, he could point out that the line from Kassel to Dresden offered the shortest line to the liaison with the Russians and, hence, fulfillment of the objective. That route avoided the northern waterways, left him with the option of turning south or north if later necessary, and led directly to the Silesian Basin, Germany's second greatest industrial area.[86] This situation forced the British to resort to political arguments and Eisenhower had learned throughout the war that among the Allies this was the most frequent area of disagreement. In the resulting morass he could and did say he was acting on military considerations alone.

Another factor to consider is whether Eisenhower ever really had decided to try for Berlin. This is not to say that he did not consider it, but only that he never decided to do it. He never hinted in his letters to Marshall that he was going to do it, and it is reasonable to assume from the subject matter of his letters that he would have told his Chief. He had told Montgomery as early as September 15 that operations would have to be coordinated with the Russians.[87] Moreover, he had several times specifically prevented Montgomery from pushing through to Berlin even though he continued to dangle the prize before him.

It would have been a reversal of Eisenhower's entire tactical approach to have gone to Berlin even at this time, for Eisenhower believed that his decisions were based primarily on military necessity. He at times did in fact make political decisions, but the only instance he ever really admitted was his insistence on a continuing role for American forces in the Tunisian campaign. Certainly the element of nationalism was also present here, but Eisenhower had justified the decision in Tunisia in terms of the

[85] E. to Deane and Archer, March 28, 1945, EP, p. 2551; and E. to Montgomery, March 28, 1945, EP, p. 2552.

[86] E. to M., March 30, 1945, EP, p. 2559, n. 1. Pogue, Supreme Command, pp. 434–35, analyzes the decision. A complete account is in Stephen E. Ambrose, Eisenhower and Berlin, 1945 (New York, 1967).

[87] E. to Montgomery, September 15, 1944, EP, pp. 2148–49.

exacerbating effect of a contrary policy on American troops and public opinion already at a terrible low ebb.

The situation by the spring of 1945 had changed considerably. The United States now had a galaxy of leaders and victories. Although the war with Japan still had to be won, Eisenhower could not deceive himself in terms of a political decision. And from a military point of view the decision was in perfect accord with his basic conservatism. He chose the plan that seemed most reasonable and certain of success.

There was another difference between Tunisia and Europe. Eisenhower was often dissatisfied with Montgomery but had come to rely more and more on Bradley. In his letters to Marshall he frequently mentioned Bradley in connection with overall theater plans, even citing him as co-author of the overall tactical scheme in his letter of March 26. Of course, this was in part due to personality clash, in part to the fact that Bradley had been Eisenhower's classmate. But Eisenhower also felt that he could depend on Bradley's military decisions and was skeptical of Montgomery. He would naturally have regarded with some professional disfavor a man whose ideas on command and tactics consistently disagreed with his own.

There was one final factor. Eisenhower himself had grown in self-confidence as a commander. He had clung doggedly to his plan and gloated that it had succeeded. He displayed this sureness dramatically in the way he handled his statement of plans for the final offensive. He communicated directly with Stalin and thereby aroused the annoyance of the British Chiefs and Churchill. Eisenhower reacted angrily in print to the British Chiefs of Staff and to Montgomery, strongly resisting attempts to persuade him to push on to Berlin.[88] He was certain of success.

Eisenhower recounted the unfolding of that final success in several letters in the last month of the campaign. On April 6 he reported to Marshall: "As you can see from the reports, our plans have been developing almost in exact accordance with original conceptions." With the objectives of the Ruhr offensives completed, Eisenhower wrote Marshall on April 15 of his final battle dispositions. On April 23 and 27 he expressed anger over the lack of German cooperation to ease starvation in Holland.[89] In these letters, Eisenhower addressed himself to some of the problems of reallocation raised in his theater by redeployment, but he had one last battle

[88] E. to M., March 30, 1945, *EP*, pp. 2560–62; E. to Churchill, March 30, 1945, *EP*, pp. 2562–63; E. to Montgomery, March 31, 1945, *EP*, pp. 2567–68; E. to CCS, March 31, 1945, *EP*, pp. 2568–71; E. to Churchill, April 1, 1945, *EP*, pp. 2572–74; E. to M., April 7, 1945, *EP*, pp. 2592–93; E. to Montgomery, April 8, 1945, *EP*, pp. 2593–95.

[89] The Germans did cooperate. Pogue, *Supreme Command*, pp. 457–59.

concern and, fittingly enough, it involved Montgomery. He complained of Montgomery's slowness in taking Lübeck and said he hoped that Montgomery would soon reach the port. Montgomery did on May 2, and the war ended a few days later.

In these letters describing the course of the war, Eisenhower demonstrated that he never lost control of operations in his theater. He had allowed his subordinate commanders latitude but within the framework of an overall design set by him. He had also resisted attempts from above to interfere with his campaign by skillfully unveiling his plans only as the situation demanded. Remembering experiences in Tunisia and Salerno, he had pursued a sure and steady campaign. When the time came for his final battlefield decision, he made it and communicated it to the Russians without clearing it with anyone. Charged with preparing and executing the campaign in Europe, Eisenhower had played a vital role in deciding where and in what strength to land and where supporting operations would take place. His experiences, especially those in Tunisia, had shown him that decisions on where to commit resources initially played a large role in determining the course of the entire campaign.

But then in August, Marshall had admonished him to keep him more closely informed, and in the same month the argument over tactics had shifted to an examination of overall theater planning. Thereafter Eisenhower was careful to apprise Marshall of his broad front attack and to reassure him that he was in full control of the battle. He had written frequently during the first debate, but the abortive attempt in September of a single thrust across the Rhine had convinced him that the broad front plan was the safest and most reasonable one. Marshall's visits had also helped. Eisenhower therefore did not write nearly so much about the debate in late 1944 and early 1945. On his third and final great tactical decision, he acted before he wrote. There was no panic in Eisenhower's letters at that time. He reacted more in anger than in uncertainty to the arguments raised against his tactics.

DIPLOMACY

During this period, to a certain extent, Eisenhower was forced to disregard Marshall's early injunction not to write about diplomatic matters. The references to such matters were still infrequent, however, and most of them concerned difficulties either with Churchill or the French. In addition, he made some comments on postwar matters.

He wrote on August 11 concerning Churchill's continuing uneasiness over the decision to attack in southern France. By the 24th Eisenhower reported that Churchill had completely reversed his opinion. Yet a month later, on September 21, Eisenhower said that he shortly expected a visit from Churchill and added that Churchill had again condemmed the ANVIL operation. This exchange provides a glimpse of the difficulties Eisenhower faced in the art of putting policies into practice and the variety of pressures with which he had to contend.

Eisenhower also complained to Marshall on February 20 about the "back door" communicating among the British and told Marshall that he was going to point out the harmful effects when Churchill visited him. Near the end of the war, on April 15 and 23, he complained about Churchill's attempt "to intermingle political and military considerations" in establishing a procedure for the conduct of the various forces when the junction with the Russians had been effected.[90]

Yet for all his complaints about the Prime Minister, Eisenhower was plagued more by troubles with the French. With particular frustration, he told Marshall on February 20 that he would place the French second only to the weather in causing him difficulty: "They even rank above landing craft." This indeed was quite an accolade. "As usual we will work out something that will cause us as little damage as possible." He reported to Marshall on August 31 that it had been necessary for him to go into Paris upon its liberation. On September 25 he noted that De Gaulle wanted two divisions pulled out of the line to maintain law and order. On January 12, during the German counteroffensive, Eisenhower reported that the French insisted that Eisenhower not abandon Strasbourg, and Eisenhower had at last consented, justifying his decision to himself as a military necessity.

Problems continued, some in connection with postwar occupation. On September 25 Eisenhower referred to the decision made at Quebec in August, 1944, to accept the planners' original recommendation to divide Germany into three parts, one each to be ruled by the U.S., Great Britain, and Russia,[91] and told his Chief that the French would probably demand a section of Germany for occupational purposes. Eisenhower said that he had recommended previously that the Allied headquarters be maintained with responsibility for administration of the entire Allied area, that ". . . on our side of the Western boundary of the Russian area we should use the same system in the control of military forces that had brought about victory."

[90] See E. to CCS, April 5, 1945, *EP*, pp. 2583–84; E. to M., April 15, 1945, *EP*, pp. 2612–13; E. to Deane and Archer, April 22, 1945, *EP*, pp. 2634–36. The Russians and the U.S. met at the Elbe on the 25th. *Ibid.*, p. 2634, n. 2.

[91] Maurice Matloff, *Strategic Planning for Coalition Warfare, 1943–1944*, US. Army in World War II, ed. Kent Roberts Greenfield (Washington, 1959), p. 511.

VISITS TO THE TROOPS

Eisenhower wrote more frequently during this period about his visits to troops and was concerned about the attitude of the troops preparing to go home.

Although Eisenhower had written Marshall short letters on August 15 and September 28 about proper indoctrination and possible psychiatric disorders, he did not comment on the condition of troops at the front until November 11. He told Marshall in a letter of October 31 that he would sample enlisted opinion concerning treatment in the rear areas. On the 11th he reported that "Within the last three days Bradley and I have visited every division of the First and Ninth Armies. Morale is surprisingly high . . .", an observation he echoed on the 27th. He did not comment again until the following February when, after a brief reference on February 20, he wrote a long letter on the 25th dealing with the recurring complaint of poor treatment of enlisted men in the rear.

In the last two months of the war, Eisenhower's references to troop visits increased. On March 12 he was concerned about the difficulty of obtaining proper publicity for them; on the 18th and 26th he worried about their criticism of various items of equipment and clothing. With troops pouring across the last barrier, the Rhine, he commented on the 26th, "I have noted so many unusual and outstanding incidents in the forward areas that it would almost weary you to tell you of the fine performances of American and other troops." On April 15, inspired by a visit to the front, he devoted most of his letter to praise of his troops and commanders. In his last letter he summed up the morale of the troops: "But it is certain that the mass feeling of the 3,000,000 American soldiers here is that they have done a remarkable job."

PERSONAL COMMENTS

Eisenhower's letters show that he thought he had also done a good job. His personal comments to Marshall—which had been fulsome in 1942, complaining in 1943, and confident in the first six months of 1944—reveal that he met his final and greatest test without losing that confidence which education in combat had instilled in him. His chief concern with the staff in Washington was that they become more aware of the seriousness of such problems as ammunition, a reversal of his earlier concern with their understanding.

Eisenhower's first significant personal comment to Marshall did not come until September 18. It was honest and direct: "I suppose there is no use suggesting to you the possibility of your making us a visit. I should very much like to see you to talk over present and future problems and we are now in position to give you a rather quick survey of the front most conveniently." There is little doubt as to what prompted this clear call for help from Eisenhower. The breakout had been made—the plan for defeating Germany could now be plotted. The great debate on command and tactics had erupted and Eisenhower clearly wanted to discuss these matters with Marshall.[92] On September 25 he commented on past rather than future operations—his stay in Washington with Marshall at the beginning of the war. He caustically recommended to Marshall a book written by one of General MacArthur's admirers which purported to show that neither Marshall nor any of his assistants in the War Department in 1941–42 had had any real concern for the forces in the Philippines. The irritated Eisenhower closed with, "I admit that the book practically gave me indigestion, something you should know before considering this suggestion further." On November 11, while bemoaning the weather, Eisenhower assured Marshall that "no one is discouraged."

On November 27 Eisenhower felt he had to mollify Marshall about the continuing ammunition argument. As early as July 5 he had told Marshall in the strongest terms that "We cannot wait for further experimentation" by the War Department to get effective ammunition.[93] Ammunition shortage had led to recurring friction with the War Department.[94] Eisenhower told Marshall that he was sending a group of staff officers to Washington to present ETO's view of the situation. "I have tried, all through this war, to avoid presenting any problems in such a way as to appear to be whining or weeping, thus adding needlessly to your own burdens. The purpose of this Staff mission is merely to make certain that the War Department clearly understands our situation and you may be sure that we will carry on in the most effective way that we can design with whatever can be made available to us." Whether or not Eisenhower's effort to ease the friction helped, the resulting conference did produce some agreement on ETO's ammunition problems.[95]

In December the fight over command and tactics resumed and was not completely settled until the end of February. On December 5 he told Marshall everyone was "in surprisingly good heart and condition." On the 23d he warmly acknowledged Marshall's Christmas letter. On January 12

[92] Marshall did pay Eisenhower a visit in October, which Eisenhower acknowledged in his letter of October 15.

[93] Marshall had replied on July 13 that deliveries of a more powerful gun carriage would be speeded up. E. to M., July 5, 1944, *EP*, pp. 1973–74, n. 3.

[94] See E. to M., November 20, 1944, *EP*, pp. 2310–11; and Ruppenthal, *Logistical Support of the Armies*, II, pp. 247–75.

[95] E. to M., November 20, 1944, *EP*, p. 2311, n. 2.

he again assured Marshall that everyone was "in good heart," and on February 20 noted his own optimism.

In the last months of the war, with victory only a matter of time, Eisenhower's comments to Marshall, like his comments on command and tactics and on the troops, became almost reminiscent in tone. On March 12, with the bridgehead over the Rhine at Remagen established, he commiserated with Marshall over the problems Marshall had described to him. "Sometimes when I get tired of trying to arrange the blankets smoothly over several prima donnas in the same bed I think no one person in the world can have so many illogical problems." But, upon reading about some of Marshall's problems, he "went right back to work with a grin." By April 15 resistance in the Ruhr had largely ended, and Eisenhower wrote Marshall that he wished he could visit ETO while offensive operations were still underway. "You would be proud of the Army you have produced." In his final letter of the war, he closed with, "Yesterday I saw Duke Shoop, a reporter on the Kansas City Star. He brought me lots of gossip, and says that you are looking as young as when the war started, and generally in fine health. I don't know how you do it, but I am mighty glad of it."

It was singularly appropriate that Eisenhower's last comment to Marshall was an acknowledgment of his Chief's importance to Eisenhower's evolution as a commander. Throughout the war he had written to and relied on Marshall in his tense moments. Early in the war, Marshall had told him that a man had to accept responsibility, had to be able to grow. Eisenhower's letters show that he applied practical lessons from the battlefield to the basic education in command he had learned from Marshall and others, and emerged as Supreme Commander in fact as well as in name.

Dear General: Today I sent you our recommendations for promotion of Colonels to Brigadier Generals for battle-field leadership. While one of the men concerned was a Divisional Chief of Staff at the operation his case is an unusual one and we have a definite vacancy in sight for him.

The pilotless aircraft, of which you and General Arnold saw the remains, must have had something freakish about it because most of them create much heavier damage than that described by you. One of them, for example, knocked down twelve houses. They have been very much of a nuisance the last few days. The worst of it is that the whole eastern coast of the Channel is tied up in the worst weather we have had yet. If we can only get twenty-four hours of really good weather we shall devastate that area. All our big bombers, both night and day, are prepared to do two sorties each in the first twenty-four hour stretch of good weather we get. That should help a lot.

After many difficulties our unloading at the beaches is sorting itself out very well. I am going to see Bradley again tomorrow, the 20th, after which I will probably not go back to the beaches for five or six days. Bradley is doing extremely well in the Peninsula and our hope is that the defenses there will be too disorganized to make a firm stand in the Fortress of Cherbourg.

The attack of our left flank has had to be put off from day to day but it is now set up for tomorrow morning and I hope it will get things started. The plan of battle of that flank remains almost identical with that explained to you when you were here. I am very hopeful it will actually break up the German formations on that front.

At this moment our chief trouble is bad weather (the usual complaint), and some shortages in MT ships[1] and LCT's.[2] We are having a big conference this afternoon on this latter subject to see whether we can loosen up some log jams. If not, we may have to ask for a little more.

It was grand to see you looking so well. I wish you could have stayed longer. I truly enjoyed seeing and talking to you. *Sincerely*

[1] Motor transport.
[2] Landing craft, tank.

Dear General: When I returned today from the Continent I found your letter of the 1st awaiting me. I have previously discussed with General Lee the necessity for using up the accumulated supplies in this country, that is, down to a minimum theater level in reserves that we will always have to hold. I will give the matter my special attention.

I spent four days in the beachhead. We began attacking southward with the VIII Corps on the 3rd and the VII Corps joined in with one Division on July 4th. I was particularly anxious to visit these Corps and their Divisions during actual operations. The going is extremely tough, with three main causes responsible. The first of these, as always, is the fighting quality of the German soldier. The second is the nature of the country. Our whole attack has to fight its way out of very narrow bottlenecks flanked by marshes and against an enemy who has a double hedgerow and an intervening ditch almost every fifty yards as ready-made strong points. The third cause is the weather. Our air has been unable to operate at maximum efficiency and on top of this the rain and mud were so bad during my visit that I was reminded of Tunisian wintertime. It was almost impossible to locate artillery targets although we have plenty of guns available. Even with clear weather it is extraordinarily difficult to point out a target that is an appropriate one for either air or artillery.

The nature of the country is playing such an important part that I took a quick flight over it yesterday, carefully escorted by a half-dozen fighters. I rode in a modified fighter myself and was up only about twenty or thirty minutes. Unfortunately, I hear that the newspapers, as usual, have gotten hold of the incident and I am afraid they will try to make something of it. Actually it was pure business (1) to see the country, and (2) a gesture to our pursuit pilots who are doing yeoman work in attempting to find and plaster targets.

Our Corps Commanders are all doing splendidly. I think Middleton[1] does not display the enthusiasm in his leadership that do the others but he is tactically sound and a very fine, straightforward workman. Among the Division Commanders we still have a few doubts. Strangely enough, all of us, (Bradley, Hodges[2] and myself) are much concerned about Landrum.[3] I sincerely hope he makes good because we have been counting on him very much. Nevertheless, he seems quite negative. One point to remember, however, is that he is commanding the 90th Division. Collins and our other Commanders agree that this unit is less well prepared for battle than almost any other Division they have seen. I do not know who its original Commander was, but our seniors are quite sure that the Division was not well brought up. To some extent these same observations apply to the 83rd, although the Commanders believe that Macon,[4] the present Commander, will do a good job. On the showing to date I would rate the 1st and 9th Divisions as tops; the 4th, 29th, 2nd and 79th as good, and the others largely untested.

My latest reports on Cherbourg are more hopeful than they were at first. I personally visited the city and while I do not know how long it will take us to get rid of the mine hazard, I must say that otherwise the place is not demolished like some of the other ports we have been forced to use in the past.

Allow me once again to thank you most earnestly for your kindness in permitting my son to come over here for a visit. It meant much to me to have a member of my family with me, even for such a brief period. He joins with me in expressing to you our very deep appreciation. *Sincerely*

¹ Major General Middleton commanded the American VII Corps.

² Lieutenant General Hodges was acting as Bradley's deputy at First Army and would assume command of First Army on August 1 when Bradley moved up to command of the 12th Army Group. He was promoted to general on April 15, 1945.

³ Major General Eugene M. Landrum had commanded the 87th Infantry Division before assuming command of the 90th Infantry Division on June 12, 1944.

⁴ Major General Robert C. Macon commanded the 83d Infantry Division from January, 1944, through the duration of the war. The division went into combat on June 27, 1944, and remained almost constantly on the battlefield until the end of the war.

52 BUSHY PARK   *July 12, 1944*

Dear General: Yesterday I received a round-about, vague message from the Mediterranean, brought to me by Spaatz who has just returned from that area. It is to the general effect that Devers would like very much to command the ANVIL operation in person but apparently felt that, looking forward to the time those forces would come under my jurisdiction, he might not be acceptable to me. I think the message came without any knowledge on Devers' part.

I well know that such things are not my business, but I do want to make clear that I have nothing in the world against General Devers. Every report that I have had about his activities in the Mediterranean leads me to believe that he is doing a very fine job, and I must say tends to eliminate the uneasy feeling I once held with respect to him. I have never known him well—and any doubts I had about his ability were based completely upon impressions and, to some extent, upon vague references in this Theater. They have never had any basis in positive information.

I understand that Devers has been on the battle front a lot and that he has demonstrated a happy faculty of inspiring troops. That is enough for me, and if you want to arrange the American affairs in the Mediterranean so that he can be free to command ANVIL while someone else takes over the administrative burden, I would accept the decision cheerfully and willingly.

This letter is, of course, extremely confidential as I do not like to express even a casual opinion about something that is none of my present business. However, I am writing it in pursuance of my regular policy of trying to keep you personally informed as to my reactions concerning any point that arises affecting Americans in this part of the world. *Very sincerely*

Dear General: You can imagine what a pall of sadness has been cast over me and the others here that knew General McNair.[1] I warned him time and time again about unnecessary risk. I don't know any of the details as yet but am very much afraid that he may have been hit by one of our own bombs that fell short while preparing the attack.

I directed Smith to send you a telegram today saying that we would release news of his death as quickly as possible. Our Security people feel that they cannot do this before day after tomorrow, in the afternoon. This will give opportunity for the continued working of the security plan.

We are staging major offensives in both Armies. On the British side we are trying to break out into suitable tank country, while in the American sector we are attempting to cut off a sizeable chunk of the enemy's forces. If either show goes on with reasonable success, we will be in a much improved position.

The weather would try my patience if there was anything a person could do about it. I get so weary looking for even one minute of sun that I am thinking of living in a dark room where I will know nothing at all about the outside conditions.

I am grateful for your news about Clark[2] and his possible future availability; when the time comes I will communicate with you further on the matter.

I hope that we will have some very definitely good news for you in a short time. *Sincerely*

[1] Lieutenant General McNair had arrived in the European theater as Chief of the Army Ground Forces, in mid-July, 1944, to replace Patton as commander of the fictitious army group which, under the cover plan, threatened an attack at Calais. He was supposed to stay three months but was killed by a bomb that fell short into a forward observation post.
[2] Lieutenant General Clark remained in command of the Fifth Army in Italy until November when he assumed command of 15th Army Group in that theater. He became a general on March 10, 1945.

Dear General: My entire pre-occupation these days is to secure the destruction of a substantial portion of the enemy forces facing us. Patton, on the marching wing of our forces, is closing in as rapidly as possible—his deployment through the bottle-neck near Avranches was exceedingly difficult but we have now got the strength on that wing to proceed definitely about our business. We have detached only one corps for the conquest of the Brittany Peninsula so as to have the maximum force for the main battle. Within a week there should be real developments on the present front.

I came back from France night before last to inspect both our Airborne Divisions. That evening I had a long conference with the Prime Minister and I must say his obvious reactions to latest decisions in the Mediterranean disturb me greatly. He seems to feel that United States is taking the attitude of a big, strong, and dominating partner rather than attempting to understand the viewpoint that he represents. His real distress comes about from our seeming indifference toward the Italian campaign, in which he feels there are tremendous potentialities. As you know, he has gone down to the Mediterranean to confer with Alexander. His personal hope seems to be that they can keep in Italy all the forces now operating there and with these he still has a strong hope of reaching Trieste before Fall. So far as I can determine he attaches so much importance to the matter that failure in achieving this objective would represent a practical failure of his whole administration. I am not quite able to figure out why he attaches so much importance to this particular movement, but one thing is certain—I have never seen him so obviously stirred, upset, and even despondent.

All this is for your confidential information only. I would feel guilty of eavesdropping and tale-bearing if it should go further. As I have told you, I am extremely hopeful about the outcome of our current operations. If we can destroy a good portion of the enemy's army now in front of us we will have a greater freedom of movement in northern France, and I would expect things to move very rapidly.

I suspect you will have been to Honolulu with the President, although press despatches do not say so.

I am going back to France within an hour but plan to come back here for about one day per week.

With best wishes for your good health. *Sincerely*

55 TOURNIÈRES   *August 24, 1944*

Dear General: Only recently I sent you a long telegram outlining my intentions both with respect to command and to future operations. I followed this up with a report to the Combined Chiefs of Staff.

The decision as to exactly what to do at this moment has taken a lot of anxious thought because of the fact that we do not have sufficient strength and supply possibilities to do *everything* that we should like to do simultaneously. Obviously we must drive hard to the northeast to complete the destruction of the principal concentration of enemy force now in this region, seize the CROSSBOW[1] sites in the Pas de Calais area and the airfields in Western Belgium and then push on to secure a permanent and adequate base at Antwerp.

While we are doing this Montgomery will have to detach forces to capture the Le Havre Peninsula, as well as the city and fortress. Bradley must rapidly complete the conquest of Brittany so as to provide for necessary maintenance and the accelerated flow of divisions into this theater. We must also provide protection in the general area of Paris because you will note that the U.S. supply lines coming down out of the Cherbourg Peninsula make an enormous curve from the south to the northeast. They would be particularly sensitive even to a shallow thrust from the Paris region on the part of the enemy. In addition to all the above, I want Bradley to build up quickly, from incoming divisions, a force in the area just east of Paris so as to be ready to advance straight eastward to Metz.

For a very considerable time I was of the belief that we could carry out the operation to the northeast simultaneously with a thrust eastward, but later have concluded that due to the tremendous importance of the objectives in the northeast we must first concentrate on that movement. The general distribution of troops will be as follows: The Army Group of the north will operate toward the northeast generally westward of the line Amiens-Lille with its principal missions as given in an earlier part of this letter. Bradley will be directed to clean up the Brittany Peninsula, protect our right rear and to thrust forward with the bulk of his offensive units along the right boundary of the 21st Army Group so as to assist in the rapid accomplishment of the missions in that area. At the same time he will be directed to begin the accumulation of forces east of Paris to take up the eastward advance south of the Ardennes. You will be interested to know that the British have already been compelled to cannibalize one division, the 69th, and will have to break up another before the end of the month. Their replacement situation is tight.

We hope to use the entire Airborne Army in its first concentrated operation in the Pas de Calais area.

In spite of all of the effort I could put behind the matter, I will not have even minimum communications at my headquarters on the Continent by my target date. Nevertheless I am going to effect the reorganization of which you are already aware. This will cause some outcry and some uneasiness but I am sure that, all things considered, it is absolutely sound. The principal argument that will be advanced against it is that we are trifling with a winning combination but the actual fact is that Bradley has operated with a considerable degree of independence for a long time. He and I are in constant touch and the change is really more obvious than real. Montgomery will necessarily have the right to effect tactical coordination between his own forces and the extreme left wing of Bradley's Army Group so that there will be no chance of any lack of cooperation in the day by day battling in that particular corridor.

I cannot tell you how anxious I am to get the forces accumulated for starting the thrust eastward from Paris. I have no slightest doubt that we can quickly get to the former French-German boundary but there is no point in getting there until we are in position to do something about it.

Very soon we will have a double-track to Chartres. This will ease our situation immeasurably. Right now we are operating on the basis of having today's supplies only with each division, and are accumulating no fat.

Recently I had a telegram from the Prime Minister in which he seemed to be most enthusiastic about ANVIL. When I think of all the fighting and mental anguish I went through in order to preserve that operation, I don't know whether to sit down and laugh or to cry. In any event, I sent him a wire and told him that since he had now apparently adopted the newborn child it would grow quickly and lustily.

As you know, I am not yet in control of that operation. I saw a dispatch yesterday from Devers in which he said he was sending two of the American divisions toward Grenoble to cut off escaping Germans. I do not know the factors involved but I hope he comes quickly up the Rhone Valley, unless such a move can not be properly protected on the flanks.

This morning's radio says that Rumania has quit and that Marseilles is captured. I told the Prime Minister we would get that city in 16 to 20 days after landing even though the Mediterranean plans had allowed 60 days for the job. They are finding conditions in that area exactly as we predicted—namely, that there was nothing there but a shell and that they would quickly overrun the whole area, once they got ashore. Even the beach defenses were apparently rather futile. *Sincerely*

---

[1] Allied code word covering German preparations for, and Allied measures against, attacks by rockets and pilotless aircraft in 1943–44.

56 BUSHY PARK   *August 31, 1944*

Dear General Marshall: Some of the rumors that have come to my ears concerning the command set-up in DRAGOON[1] have left me very much puzzled and I have sent a request to Devers to come up to see me in order that I may understand exactly what is planned.

I have had discussions with Spaatz concerning the types and amount of Air Forces that should accompany the 7th Army up the Rhone Valley. Already in this Theater we have two administrative headquarters for Air, that is, the 8th and the 9th. Also, we have all the bomber strength that will likely prove necessary in direct support of all three groups of Armies. Because of this Spaatz believes that only fighters, fighter bombers and a small contingent of light bombers, should come up the Rhone with the 7th Army. This unit would be called the 12th Tactical Air Command, and would be joined up with the 9th Air Force for administrative purposes. This, he says, is very easy to do and would be quite simple. Through Spaatz, I, of course, retain operational direction over the 15th Air Force.

As signs begin to add up that the German resistance both on the battle front and possibly even in the interior is rapidly weakening there has developed in my mind some suspicion that the fanatics of that country may attempt to carry on a long and bitter guerilla warfare. Such a prospect is a dark one and I think we should do everything possible to prevent its occurrence.

From this angle the Italian campaign assumes added importance. For the present, of course, it is fighting and killing Germans and forcing the enemy to extend himself while he tries to meet the requirements of the main battle fronts in Russia and in France. But if any kind of RANKIN[2] conditions should develop the rapid thrusting of Alexander's Forces into Vienna and into the mountains around there, would help to defeat any hope the German fanatics might have for making that country one of guerilla action. For this reason I believe that the Italian Forces should be kept at sufficient strength to operate effectively against anything they are likely to meet.

Bradley and I had planned to have four Armies going in through our own ports to be commanded by Hodges, Patton, Simpson[3] and probably Gerow. If, however, Patch's[4] U.S. Force of three Divisions is to be separated from the French, then it may be possible, by switching his American Corps to the left flank of the DRAGOON operation we can add, later, a few American Divisions to him and thus he would have the fourth U.S. Army to be established in this Region. All this should be cleared up through a conference with Devers.

If we put off the formation of an additional Army, Bradley may want to step up one of our Corps Commanders ahead of Simpson. Please understand that none of us has any objection to Simpson. We are merely getting to the point where we believe that some of our Corps Commanders (notably Gerow and Corlett[5]), who have done so well and actually demonstrated capacity for leadership and for handling large formations, are better bets for taking over a new Army Command than is a man who has not actually demonstrated this capacity.

We have had some little trouble with DeGaulle[6] and LeClerc[7] in Paris but Gerow handled it firmly and I rushed in there Sunday morning for an hour to back him up. I guess we should not blame the French for growing a bit hysterical under the conditions, and I must say that they seem now to be settling down in good order.

I had to come back here to London for a series of conferences yesterday and today, but am leaving this afternoon for my Continental Headquarters. Among other things I am holding a press conference this morning and am going to explain to correspondents, on the record, the complete development of this operation, including the command arrangements for it. These matters have finally become of such interest to the press that I think the best thing to do is to give a full and honest explanation of the whole works, then they can say what they please.

I understand that the President and the Prime Minister are soon to meet. I hope that much good will come out of the conference because as signs of victory appear in the air, I note little instances that seem to indicate that Allies cannot hang together so effectively in prosperity as they can in adversity. Any backward step in the progress we have made along this line would be a pity.

With best wishes for your continued health, *Sincerely*

¹ New name for ANVIL, the 1944 invasion of southern France.

² Initially the code name for a return to the Continent in the event of a deterioration of the German position or an internal upheaval. After the attempt on Hitler's life, the code name used to denote any sudden deterioration in the general German position followed by a swift Allied advance into the country for occupation purposes.

³ Lieutenant General William Hood Simpson (USMA 1909) commanded the U.S. Ninth Army, which became operational on September 5, 1944.

⁴ Lieutenant General Alexander McCarrell Patch, Jr. (USMA 1913) had assumed command of the U.S. Seventh Army in March, 1944. The Seventh had landed in southern France in August, 1944.

⁵ Major General Charles Harrison Corlett (USMA 1913) commanded the XIX Corps until December when ill health forced him to return to the United States.

⁶ General de Gaulle headed the French Committee of National Liberation which he had proclaimed as the Provisional Government of the French Republic on August 30, 1944. The United States, Great Britain, and Russia recognized the government on October 23, 1944.

⁷ Major General Jacques-Philippe LeClerc commanded the French 2d Armored Division which began to move into Paris on August 23–24, 1944.

57 GRANVILLE   *September 14, 1944*

Dear General: I think that by forwarding to the Combined Chiefs of Staff periodic appreciations as well as copies of principal directives you are kept fairly well acquainted with our situation. The fact is that we are stretched to the absolute limit in maintenance both as to intake and as to distribution after supplies are landed.

From the start we have always known that we would have to choose, after breaking out of the original bridgehead, some line which would mark a relative slackening in offensive operations while we improved maintenance facilities and prepared for an offensive operation that could be sustained for another indefinite period. At first it seemed to me that the German would try to use some one of the number of lines available to him in France on which to make a rather determined stand, but due to the decisiveness of our victory below the Seine I determined to go all out in effort and in risk to continue the drive beyond the German border, up to and including the Rhine before we began the process of regrouping and re-fitting.

While this was going on Montgomery suddenly became obsessed with the idea that his Army Group could rush right on into Berlin provided we gave him all the maintenance that was in the theater—that is, immobilize all other divisions and give their transport and supplies to his Army Group, with some to Hodges. Examination of this scheme exposes it as a fantastic idea. First of all, it would have to be done with the ports we now have, supplemented possibly by Calais and Ostend. The attack would be on such a narrow front that flanking threats would be particularly effective and no other troops in the whole region would be capable of going to its support. Actually I doubt that the idea was proposed in any conviction that it could be carried through to completion; it was based merely on wishful thinking, and in an effort to induce me to give to 21st Army Group and to Bradley's left every ounce of maintenance there is in the theater.

As opposed to this the only profitable plan is to hustle all our forces up against the Rhine, including Devers' forces, build up our maintenance facilities and our reserves as rapidly as possible and then put on one sustained and unremitting advance against the heart of the enemy country. Supporting this great attack will probably be subsidiary operations against the German ports on the left and against his southern industrial areas on the right.

I have sacrificed a lot to give Montgomery the strength he needs to reach the Rhine in the north and to threaten the Ruhr. That is, after all, our main effort for the moment. The great Airborne attack which will go in support of this operation will be Sunday the 17th, unless weather prevents. It should be successful in carrying Montgomery up to and across the Rhine; thereafter it is absolutely imperative that he quickly capture the approaches to Antwerp so that we may use that port. The port facilities themselves are practically undamaged and we have there ample storage for bulk oil, something that we critically need.

Le Havre will be developed for utilization by U.S. forces.

During the early and middle summer, I was always ready to defer capture of ports in favor of bolder and more rapid movement to the front. But now approaches the season of the year when we can no longer afford this, especially in view of the resistance the German is ready to offer in Fortress defense, as demonstrated both at St. Malo and at Brest. Every day I thank my stars that I held out for ANVIL in the face of almost overwhelming pressure. Marseilles may yet be a Godsend to us.

My own belief is that, assuming continuation of the Russian pressure at its present scale, we will have to fight one more major battle in the West. This will be to break through the German defenses on the border and to get started on the invasion. Thereafter the advance into Germany will not be as rapid as it was in France, because we won't have the F.F.I.[1] in the German rear, but I doubt that there will be another full-dress battle involved. The big crash to start that move may prove to be a rather tough affair.

Recently Spaatz received a message from Arnold suggesting the desirability of moving a lot of our heavy bombers to France immediately. This is simply beyond the realm of feasibility at the moment. Big bombers can still operate effectively from England and we need every ton of space and every bit of port capacity to get in the things that the ground troops and their shorter range air support units require. This will continue to be true for an indefinite period. *Sincerely*

---

[1] French Forces of the Interior.

Dear General: The arrival of the Chiefs of Staff directive removing all Strategic Air Forces, including the American, from the control of Shaef threw consternation into the Headquarters. The most disturbed individual was Spaatz. However, I have calmed down everybody and I assure you that I can make the system work.

One cause of the bewilderment was that all of us thought we were in exact accord with the U.S. Chiefs of Staff attitude on the matter and felt so sure of the correctness of the system we had been using that it was difficult at first to find any logical reason for the change. It was apparent to me that considerations somewhat outside of my own scope of responsibility were involved, and since I am absolutely certain of the good will of the key individuals involved, principally Harris and Spaatz, I have no qualms about the matter.

As I have told you before, I believe we have one more major battle to fight and during that phase I think it extremely important that every single atom of strength be available for the job. The terminology of the directive clearly indicates that the Chiefs of Staff want me to have that assistance during the critical period.

I cannot tell you how much I appreciate your actions in getting Bradley made a Major General on the regular list. It may not be easy for him to communicate with you immediately, but I can tell you also that there is nothing that would have pleased him more.

This team is working well. Without exception all concerned have now fully accepted my conception of our problem and are carrying it out intelligently and with energy. Yesterday we started the greatest airborne operations we have yet attempted. Although preliminary reports are rather sketchy, it would seem that, so far, we have succeeded even beyond our best expectations. We know already that of 1800 transport aircraft employed only 30 have been lost, although the concentration of enemy anti-aircraft guns in the area was the heaviest we have yet encountered. According to Brereton and from our own observations, this seems to prove rather conclusively that even very heavy flak concentrations can be temporarily neutralized by the intelligent application of overwhelming bombing strength. By evening today, if nothing unforeseen happens, we will have the combat elements of three and a half Divisions on the ground and with their help I believe we can establish a firm bridgehead over the Rhine at Arnhem. Thereafter, on that flank, we simply must get a major port working to support the left flank on the final drive into Germany.

Meantime Hodges is going well. His operations are coordinated with those of Montgomery. Hodges is driving straight on to Cologne and Bonn for the eventual purpose of attacking the Ruhr from the south as Montgomery swings into it from the north.

Similarly, the plan calls for pushing Patton toward the left to support Hodges while Simpson coming up on Patton's right, will be the connecting link between the main body of the 12th Army Group and the 6th Army Group whose left boundary will cross the Rhine just north of Mannheim. An interesting estimate received this morning from G–2 is that we have about 225,000 Germans of all categories cut off in various pockets in France and the low countries. Many of these groups are trying their best to surrender now. Incidentally, the care of our mass of prisoners constitutes quite a problem.

I quite agree with your idea that it is important to get Patch's Army up to a decent strength quickly. I have already given orders that we will begin to strengthen him from this flank as quickly as Brest has fallen, and with a couple of Divisions coming in through Marseilles, it should not be long before he has a very respectable force. I put this project above the building up of Simpson's Army.

It is about time that Gerow has to come home for that investigation. I hate it terribly because his Corps is an important part of Hodges' attack and Gerow is doing beautifully. Since the formation of another Army has now been deferred, I may give that Corps a temporary commander waiting Gerow's return. I may even spare Bull[1] for this purpose. It would be a good thing for Bull to get a couple weeks of actual field service, and I have a very fine deputy in his Section.

I suppose there is no use suggesting to you the possibility of your making us a visit. I should very much like to see you to talk over present and future problems and we are now in position to give you a rather quick survey of the front most conveniently. You and Admiral King[2] would receive a most warm welcome if you could come even for two or three days.

Both via Smith and General de Witt[3] I sent you messages to the effect that if you wanted, either in your own name or in mine, to invite key members of the House and Senate to make us a visit, we could take care of two groups, say of six each. Quite a number of Congressmen have been coming to England on invitation of the British Government, and I cannot tell how many will do so in the future. I have declined to allow them to come over here as individuals, because eventually there would be no end to the thing and we could be harrassed by important visitors, but if the thing could be done logically—that is, through you—I could take care of the matter very easily.

From what I can read in the paper, your Quebec Conference went off very nicely, but I suppose, as is usual, there was a lot under the surface that was not reported.

With best personal regards, *Sincerely*[4]

---

[1] Major General Harold Roe Bull was G–3 of SHAEF.

[2] Admiral King was Chief of Naval Operations. In December he was nominated to the new rank of fleet admiral of the U.S. Navy, comparable to the five star general of the army.

[3] Lieutenant General John Lesesne DeWitt had been commandant of the Army and Navy Staff College since September, 1943. In August, 1944, he had been sent to replace McNair as commander of the fictitious army group in the cover plan. He was now returning to his post at the Army and Navy Staff College.

⁴ Eisenhower added the following postscript: "Just have a group message from 9 Congressmen visiting in England. They give me 2 pages of reasons why they must come over. I told Lee [Ernest R. Lee, Eisenhower's aide] he could have the PRO take them around in a *body*—not as individuals, however."

59 VERSAILLES   *September 25, 1944*

Dear General: Recently General Anderson¹ came back from Washington giving me two of the major decisions of the Quebec Conference, namely, that Strategic Air Forces were no longer under my command, and that future occupation of Germany would be on strictly nationalistic lines with Allied headquarters abolished.

The first of these decisions I already knew about, since it was placed into effect immediately the decision was taken. As I wrote you then, we can make the scheme work because of the saving clauses in the Directive regarding support for OVERLORD and because of the good will of the individuals involved. You might be interested to know, in view of earlier expressed fears that Air Chief Marshal Harris would not willingly devote his command to the support of ground operations, that he actually proved to be one of the most effective and cooperative members of this team. Not only did he meet every request I ever made upon him, but he actually took the lead in discovering new ways and means for his particular types of planes to be of use in the battle field. I am quite sure he was genuinely disappointed to lose his status as an integral part of this organization. However, he keeps his representative right here at my headquarters and it is because of the perfection of our past associations that I have no real fears for the future. When the great battle occurs for the real entry into Germany, he will be on the job.

With respect to the decision to divide Germany on nationalistic lines, I had known for a long time the way political thought was leaning and I was not astonished. Naturally, I always knew that decisions between Governments would have to be taken on a tripartite basis, and the suggestions I advanced had no implication of making Great Britain and the United States political partners vis-a-vis the third member of the triumvirate. My thoughts were restricted to the military problem; that is, the use of armed forces for carrying out the decisions of the Governments. I felt that on our side of the Western boundary of the Russian area we should use the same system in the control of military forces that had brought about victory. All this had been presented many times to my superiors and since they have decided otherwise, this is the last time that my own ideas on the subject will be expressed.

I assume that at an appropriate time you will communicate to me something of your ideas as to the forces and commanders for which you will have immediate need in the Japanese War after we have finished this job. I will be prepared to give you, whenever you may desire, my opinions as to the qualifications of the senior officers that will be available and for which you may have need as division, corps, army and even group commanders. This will likewise apply on the Air side.

I must confess that post-armistice matters do not occupy any great share of my thoughts. We still have a long ways to go here because of the intention of the enemy, which I think is becoming obvious, to continue the most bitter kind of resistance up to the point of practical extermination of the last of his armed forces. Thereafter, we may be faced with some kind of guerrilla problem.

I have not yet received this morning's reports on the progress of the battle in the North. It is heavy going. Bradley is thrusting his left flank still further to the North in order to permit Montgomery to concentrate more strongly against the Germans on the left of his present corridor and to thrust forward more rapidly across the Rhine. Until we get Antwerp, however, we are always going to be operating on a shoestring. In the meantime, I am trying to send to Devers everything that I possibly can because he can maintain them through Marseilles and continue aggressive fighting without additional drain upon our lines of communication.

The general French situation is not too happy in some of its important aspects. DeGaulle has made request on me to get two French divisions out of the battle lines so as to ensure law and order in certain disaffected sections. I cannot spare these divisions at this moment, and won't, but my own reports show that DeGaulle's fears have some foundation in fact. Incidentally, I am quite sure that the French are going to demand some particular section of Germany for occupational purposes, a contingency that I had hoped to avoid under my proposed solution to the problem. Now it will become a problem for the heads of the Governments and further demands of his along this line will be merely referred to the Combined Chiefs of Staff.

Possibly, to end up this long letter, you might not mind a personal suggestion. It is that you take for your "bedtime reading" a little book written by Frazier Hunt called "MacArthur and the War Against Japan." You will be quite astonished to learn that back in the Winter of '41/42, you and your assistants in the War Department had no real concern for the Philippines and for the forces fighting there—indeed, you will be astonished to learn lots of things that this book publishes as fact. I admit that the book practically gave me indigestion, something you should know before considering this suggestion further. *Sincerely*

---

[1] Major General Frederick L. Anderson, Jr. (USMA 1928) was deputy commander for operations, Strategic Air Forces.

Dear General: On the day you left I went forward to see Bradley and discussed the proposition of getting up Infantry for relief purposes. He is starting immediately on what we have on hand and he, my Staff, and Somervell, are going to try to coordinate in expanding the idea to apply the same principle with respect to some Divisions not yet afloat or embarking.

The disappointment you had on your trip with respect to our failure to provide some senior commanders for you to decorate was all the more useless in view of the fact that Bradley had his list entirely made out with citations, ready to give you on the day you and he went to visit Montgomery. He had expected to discuss the matter with you on the way back from Montgomery's headquarters, and when you got separated the subject later slipped his mind. I am really sorry about this.

We are having a sticky time in the North but Montgomery has at last seen the light and is concentrating toward his west, left, flank in order to clear up the Antwerp situation.

My luncheon yesterday with the King went off very well and the King took advantage of the opportunity to present the KCB[1] to Bradley. He met quite a number of our senior officers and was highly pleased with his visit. He asked me to tell you again how sorry he was to have missed you, and hopes that the next time you come this way he may have a chat with you.

Today, the 15th, is probably the most miserable one we have had during this entire operation. It is raining the proverbial cats and dogs. I am at my Forward Camp in the hope of flying down to see Devers tomorrow morning, but the prospects look dim, to say the least.

All of us enjoyed having you here and trust that soon you will find an opportunity to repeat the trip. *Sincerely*

[1] Knight Commander of the Bath.

Dear General: Thank you for your letter giving me the information gathered from returning enlisted men. There is no question of the necessity of doing something at once and I am going to do it on a little bit broader basis than you suggested.

I am going to find a very good colonel or brigadier general and give him a staff of two officers and three or four non-commissioned officers. His entire staff must be made up from wounded men who are now limited Service. I will give them a couple of small automobiles and start them on this job through the rear areas, including England. I have worried about this subject considerably but I did not know that the attitude of men returning from here reflected so much complaint and discontent. God knows we have tried but it is obvious we must do something more.

This week is rather crowded with appointments but I intend to spend the entire week beginning next Sunday, the 5th, along the front. So far as I possibly can, I am going to do a little sampling of enlisted opinion myself.

The Special Board developing a plan for reorganization of the defense service is to be here tomorrow. I wish that I had made specific notes of your ideas because there was one point concerning which my memory is a little hazy. I think that you stated there should be no over-all Chief of Staff. Moreover, you limited the functions of the Joint Chiefs of Staff, in time of peace, to submission of the yearly estimates directly to the President. I will largely limit my own comments to higher organization in the field.

My reports this morning from all the Supply people show a little bit brighter picture. I think we can get going soon again. General Clay[1] arrived and has already gone up to take charge of Cherbourg. *Sincerely*

---

[1] Major General Lucius DuBignon Clay (USMA 1918) was Director of Material for the Army Service Forces. He assumed temporary command of the Normandy Base Section of the European Theater of Operations (ETO), where he was in charge of the port of Cherbourg until November 26 when he returned to Washington.

62 LUXEMBOURG   *November 11, 1944*

Dear General: I am getting exceedingly tired of weather. Every day we have some report of weather that has broken records existing anywhere from twenty-five to fifty years. The latest case is that of the floods in Patton's area. His attack got off exactly as planned and with an extraordinarily fine example of cooperation between the Eighth Air Force and the ground troops. Then the floods came down the river and not only washed out two fixed bridges, but destroyed his principal floating bridge and made others almost unusable. It was so bad that in one case where we had installed a fixed bridge, the approaches to it were under three feet of water. At one point the Moselle is more than one mile wide, with a current of from seven to ten feet a second. Nevertheless, the peak of the flood should be passed in a day or so—provided rain in that basin is not too great—and Patton will get ahead all along his front.

The attack of the First and Ninth Armies was scheduled anywhere between the 11th and the 16th, depending upon the weather necessary to get the desired air support. The jump-off had to be postponed this morning even after a rather favorable prediction yesterday. The predictions now give us a sorry outlook, and it appears that we will have to go, eventually, without the planned air support. The weather is apt to prevent even our fighter-bombers from rendering the help that they otherwise could.

Within the last three days Bradley and I have visited every division of the First and Ninth Armies. Morale is surprisingly high and the men have succeeded in making themselves rather comfortable. There are no signs of exhaustion and the sick rate is not nearly as high as we would have a reasonable right to expect.

All of us keep hoping that some little spell will come along in which we can have a bit of relief from mud, rain, and fog so that tanks and infantry can operate more easily on the offensive and so that we can use our great air asset. In spite of difficulties, no one is discouraged and we will yet make the German wish that he had gone completely back of the Rhine at the end of his great retreat across France.

Yesterday afternoon Bradley and I came south through the Ardennes Hills. Snow covered the fields to a depth of about six inches. In the lower country to the north and to the south of the Ardennes there were traces of snow, but it melted rather rapidly.

I am writing this from General Bradley's Headquarters and he joins me in best wishes to yourself. *Sincerely*

63 VERSAILLES   *December 5, 1944*

Dear General: Much now depends on the date and scale of the anticipated winter offensive of the Russians. I say "anticipated" although we have nothing except conjecture on which to base our ideas as to Russia's intentions. At present we have newly formed Divisions arriving on our front, and have attracted several Divisions directly from Hungary and East Prussia. In spite of all this, the enemy is badly stretched on this front and is constantly shifting units up and down the line to reinforce his most threatened points. G–2 studies show that he is more frightened of our operations in the First and Ninth Armies than anywhere else. He is assisted in that area, however, by the flooded condition of the Roer River and the capability he has of producing a sudden rush of water by blowing the dams near Schmidt. Bradley has about come to the conclusion that we must take that area by a very difficult attack from the west and southwest.

There can be no question of the value of our present operations. The German is throwing in the line some Divisions with only six weeks' training, a fact that contributes materially to his high casualty rate. As explained in my most recent appreciation to the Combined Chiefs of Staff, our problem is to continue our attacks as long as the results achieved are so much in our favor, while at the same time preparing for a full-out, heavy offensive when weather conditions become favorable, assuming the enemy holds out. Unless some trouble develops from within Germany, a possibility of which there is now no real evidence, he should be able to maintain a strong defensive front for some time, assisted by weather, floods and muddy ground.

Today I sent Truscott to the Mediterranean area. I regretted to have him go because I have always had such tremendous confidence in him as a fighting leader and because he so obviously wanted to stay a member of this team. From the over-all picture it looked to me to be the best thing to do.

I enlisted Handy's help in the question of checking up on Division Commanders that I send home for a rest. It is always possible that one or two of them will not completely recover. Both Stroh and O'Daniel[1] have lost only sons in this war, and this shock and distress, coupled with the abnormal strains always borne by an active Division Commander, are really more than any one man should be called upon to bear. But with anything like a recovery to their usual spirits and vigor, I hope to get all these men back, (I have already told Handy he can send Corlett to the Pacific if he so desires), because each is an outstanding leader. Corps, Army and Army Group Commanders stand up well. They are in that more fortunate middle area where their problems involve tactics and local maintenance, without on the one hand having to burden themselves with politics, priorities, shipping and Maquis, while they are also spared the more direct battle strains of a Division Commander.

Everybody is in surprisingly good heart and condition. *Sincerely*

[1] Major General Donald Armpriester Stroh commanded the 8th Infantry Division. General Stroh returned to ETO in February as commander of the 106th Infantry Division. Major General O'Daniel commanded the 3d Infantry Division.

64 LONDON   *December 13, 1944*

Dear General Marshall: I have just had a conference with the Prime Minister and three British Chiefs of Staff.

Field-Marshal Brooke seemed disturbed by what he calls our "dispersion" of the past weeks of this campaign. When I explained to him that up until the moment that the flooded conditions in the lower Rhine Valley prevented any further offensive action in that region, we had supported our Northern thrust with everything we could possibly maintain, he seemed to understand the situation better than he had before. Moreover, I explained to him that in the later attack toward Bonn and Cologne, Bradley had used all the Divisions he thought he could possibly employ on that narrow front. That attack is held up for the moment, not by lack of strength but by conditions on the Roer River which is at flood level and has three dams a short ways up the River. Bradley is now engaged in a subsidiary operation to capture the dams; we have failed to destroy them by bombing.

All the new strength, now coming in, is being directed to the left flank of the Twelfth Army Group. I regard it as a matter of first importance that we get on to the Rhine from Bonn northward. Secondary to that, but still most vitally important when the time comes that conditions will permit a crossing of the River, we should be on the Rhine at Frankfurt. Bradley is confident that he will achieve both of these objects.

When Admiral Byrd[1] was here he hinted that he was representing the President, yourself, and others in a number of important projects. He seemed vague to me. *Sincerely*

[1] Admiral Richard Evelyn Byrd (USNA 1912), the famous explorer, served at Headquarters, Commander in Chief, U.S. Fleet.

65 VERSAILLES   *December 23, 1944*

Dear General Marshall: Receipt of your Christmas letter to me was the brightest spot in my existence since we reached the Siegfried Line.[1] Short of a major defeat inflicted upon the enemy, I could not have had a better personal present.

For my part, I pray that the coming year will see all of your great efforts and plans well on the road to fulfillment and, for the United States, my most fervent hope is that your health and strength will be preserved to carry your great burdens until victory has been achieved.

With warm personal regard, and with the request that you pay my respects to Mrs. Marshall. *Sincerely*

[1] In his letter, Marshall told Eisenhower, "You have my complete confidence." E. to M., December 23, 1944, *EP*, p. 2378, n. 1.

66 VERSAILLES   *January 12, 1945*

Dear General Marshall: While it seems to me that within the past two weeks I have sent to you on various subjects telegraphic words that in their total would fill a good sized volume, I have not recently written you a personal, confidential letter.

At the moment our most worrisome area is the south. While there is nothing vital in that region that we should not be able to cover easily if we could solve all of our problems from the purely tactical viewpoint, the great danger is that Devers will be caught out of position and some of his troops manhandled. The French were so completely upset over my plan to pull out of the Alsace Plain, that obviously the problem became, in its larger sense, a military one. I could not have the weakened French forces trying to fight a battle by themselves and, more serious than this, I could not have the French government getting in extremely bad position with its population, a consequence which it was apparent de Gaulle thought would follow upon a voluntary evacuation of Alsace.

When Devers turned his complete Seventh Army northward, he was badly mistaken in the ability of the French Army to finish off the Colmar pocket. At that time he had been directed to turn part of the 15th Corps northward, west of the Vosges, in order to support Patton's right but it was expected that his first concern east of the mountains would be to clean up his own rear. I must say that he can scarcely be blamed for making a miscalculation with respect to the French, because the forces opposing them in the pocket were at that time estimated at not over 12,000 to 14,000 fighting men. Nevertheless, it is a very bad thorn in our side today.

Tomorrow morning the attacks on the northerly side of the Ardennes salient are being extended. Ridgway's[1] 18th Corps will come in, attacking in the direction of St. Vith. As our lines shorten in the salient I will be able to get a reserve out of refitting divisions, and these will be so stationed as to support our right.

I am going to visit Bradley tomorrow. I hope that if he can only make some significant penetration from his side of the salient, particularly one that might result in the destruction or capture of considerable enemy forces, you will consider him at once for four star promotion. I think it would have a fine general effect. For many reasons I should like to have Spaatz promoted also.

The weather is abominable. It seems to me that I have fought weather for two years and a half. Right now, at my base headquarters, a foot of snow is on the ground. Flying conditions in the battle zone have been almost impossible for several days. A week of good weather would be nothing less than a godsend.

Gasser[2] came in today and I have given him sweeping authority.

Everybody is in good heart. You need have no fear that we will eventually solve our problems. *Sincerely*

---

[1] Major General Matthew Bunker Ridgway (USMA 1917) had taken command of the XVIII Airborne Corps in August, 1944.

[2] Major General Lorenzo Dow Gasser was president of the War Manpower Board in Washington. He was sent on temporary duty to ETO to help in the most efficient utilization of manpower in the theater.

67 VERSAILLES   *February 9, 1945*

Dear General: Although you are still on your trip to Yalta, I have time this morning to write to you an account of our latest doings.

I was glad to have a talk with you at Marseilles. I understand your embarrassment about the four star promotions; but I feel that, considering the Navy's liberality in the past, you could nominate a minimum list of two in Washington, two or three here, two in the Mediterranean and one or two in the Pacific without having to apologize to anyone. I hear that the Navy, aside from its five star people, has thirteen in the four star category. Looking at the matter from a comparative viewpoint, you could make every Army Group and fighting Army Commander you have and be perfectly within the bounds of reason. This list could also contain commanders of all important Air Forces. I figure such a list would not be over 15 or 16.

Locally, my position is that Bradley and Spaatz should, by all means, immediately be made. These promotions would be most helpful to me.

With respect to future operations, I sent word to Smith at Malta that I had decided to abandon temporarily the general attack in the Ardennes (which decision was opposed by Bradley) and throw our entire weight into a rapid closing of the Rhine below Dusseldorf. I am certain I am right and it turned out that based on *purely military* considerations, Bradley agreed with me. The unfortunate burst of publicity that came out in the British papers in late December about Monty's temporary command of the First and Ninth Armies is still rankling in Bradley's mind, and I must say that I cannot blame him much. As soon as the Prime Minister comes back I am going to enlist his help to see whether such things cannot be avoided in the future. On Monday, the 6th, I had a conference with Bradley and Montgomery and I warned the Field-Marshal that he must use his entire influence to prevent this type of thing from starting again. There is nothing to indicate that he had, personally, anything to do with the former incident. To the contrary, his statements were eminently correct.

Montgomery's attack has gotten off to a good start and the Colmar pocket seems cleared up.

Lear[1] seems to be bucking into his new job in good style. It is a little difficult for him to understand that I want him to use the *existing* organization and to devote himself to a single but highly important group of functions. He has been in a different status at home and consequently it is not too easy for him to adjust himself. But he is getting it. Right now he is pressing on re-training of troops as riflemen, and is getting some of our *sour* camps straightened out. Because of lack of time and facilities to train specialists, it appears that I'll have to use negro volunteers by platoons. Patton has done this and it apparently works. I'd prefer to make them independent battalions, and as time goes on perhaps we can accumulate them into such formations.

I have made up, and constantly revised during the past many weeks, a list of some thirty to forty of our outstanding General Officers arranged roughly in accordance with my ideas of the value of the services they have rendered in this war. In doing so I got similar lists from Smith and Bradley and have attempted to make the final one a reflection of our composite judgment. I do not know whether such a thing would have any value to you at all, but if you should like to have it, I will be glad to send you a copy. *Sincerely*

¹ Lieutenant General Ben Lear had been named by Eisenhower as deputy theater commander to handle manpower problems.

68 VERSAILLES   *February 20, 1945*

Dear General: Because of your personal concern in the steps we have been taking in the matter of the lost truck of the 28th Division, I am enclosing a cable received from General Devers.

I believe that General Hull¹ brought back with him a copy of a letter I sent to the C.I.G.S.² outlining the implications, from my viewpoint, of the appointment of Alexander. The matter is unimportant, except from its Public Relations aspect, but since Public Relations often cause me my biggest headaches, I wanted to make sure that the C.I.G.S. clearly understood what might occur.

The Germans handled the Roer dams in the one way that was most detrimental to us. Rather than blow out the dams completely, they jammed the flood gates in such a way as to create flood conditions throughout the length of the Roer river and to prolong the flood period to the greatest possible extent. We have already reported that we believe we can attack on the 23rd. I sincerely hope that we will not be longer delayed. Hull will have told you that all our preparations are made, the troops are in fine fettle and there is no question in my mind that if we get off to a good start over the river, the operations will be a complete success.

Throughout the front the German has thinned out very much indeed. If we had only a few extra divisions we could put on a very worthwhile attack anywhere between Karlsruhe and the Ardennes.

The French continue to be difficult. I must say that next to the weather I think they have caused me more trouble in this war than any other single factor. They even rank above landing craft. Right now they want three divisions released from the line to assist in the development of new divisions and to exhibit armed might throughout the countryside. Of course there is some merit in their contentions but I suspect also that they are showing a bit of pique at what they consider the slight that General de Gaulle suffered in not being invited to Crimea. As usual we will work out something that will cause us as little damage as possible, but the most popular note in the French press these days is expression of dissatisfaction with the Allies, including this Command, for failing to bring in more foodstuffs and rolling stock for the French, and lack of political deference to their government.

Hull has probably given you the sequence of our projected operations. If the weather improves with the advancing spring I feel that matters will work out almost exactly as projected. I get terribly impatient during periods such as we are now forced to undergo, but I never forget the situation of the German and consequently never lose my basic optimism.

I am not sure that the Prime Minister has yet returned to England. I assume that shortly after he gets back he will probably want to pay us a visit. I am certainly going to take the occasion to point out clearly to him what "back door" communications can do toward creating uncertainty.

I have had two conferences with Montgomery since he returned from leave somewhere around the 3rd or 4th of February. In both instances he has been emphatic in his statement that everything is developing soundly, and he has been especially vehement in protesting his complete loyalty and his belief in the efficacy of our command system. I took occasion to tell him that if he believed these things then he should talk that way to the Prime Minister so as to avoid the creation of uneasiness among our military superiors. Actually, of course, the vague rumors and statements that tend to create such uneasiness are largely froth—the fundamental soundness of this organization and readiness of all components to carry out my orders have been remarkable from the beginning. The trouble often is that to gain a particular end, people, even in high places, are sometimes not above using gossip and misinterpretation. All these things I ignore as long as they have no important effect upon this Command. *Sincerely*

¹ Major General John Edwin Hull had succeeded General Handy as the head of the Operations Division on October 22, 1944.
² Chief of the Imperial General Staff.

69 REIMS   *March 12, 1945*

Dear General: Today I sent you a long telegram in answer to your letter of March 6th because I felt that some of the subjects demanded a quick reply. One thing that I did not tell you in my radio was the pleasant feeling of "misery loves company" I got out of reading of a few of your troubles. Sometimes when I get tired of trying to arrange the blankets smoothly over several prima donnas in the same bed I think no one person in the world can have so many illogical problems. I read about your struggles concerning the eighteen year old men in combat, and about the criticism of our equipment, and went right back to work with a grin.

Enclosed you will find a memorandum I have written to Bradley and Devers. This subject has been often discussed among us but I wrote this memorandum in an effort to furnish commanders something that they could pass on to their public relations officers, if they so desired, but which could still stand the test of criticism in the event that it should inadvertently fall into the hands of a reporter. I agree with you that our technique in this publicity business is not good. As I pointed out in my telegram to you, one of our troubles is our size. The Army here has

216

fifty divisions on a battle front; the Marine Corps normally has one or two in an island battle. This makes it easy for the Marines to publicize units and personalities. However, I think that we might exploit this very fact of size a bit more. I believe the War Department P.R.O.[1] might emphasize the number of divisions the Army has deployed and fighting all over the world—I think I will try something along the same line here.

I am delighted that Mr. McCloy[2] is coming. I hope he can stay because I have already told you something of our troubles in this business of getting the proper set-up to control Germany.

We will go full tilt into the matter of using the L–5 for night interdiction work. Incidentally, I have just ordered one of our best men to go home to present our requirements in these light liaison planes. It is one matter in which I have never been able to stir up much enthusiasm in the Air Force. More than two years ago I begged for a consignment of a couple hundred of exactly the same type of ship that the Stinson Company made for the British in the desert. In spite of all our so-called development that is still the best plane for liaison purposes that I have seen in the war. Possibly they have an improvement by this time, but I have not seen it.

I share your puzzlement about this four star promotion business, but I adhere to my former presentation of my own particular problem. I can see why Patton's color and publicity appeal so mightily to the Secretary of War, but as long as I have absorbed Devers and he is doing his job satisfactorily, the appointments should be made in the order I have already given. Both Bradley and I believe that our successful Army commanders should eventually be promoted to four star rank, but I would consider it unwise at this time to imply a comparison to the discredit of Hodges, Patch and Simpson by making Patton on a separate list ahead of them.

Tomorrow morning the 20th Corps of Patton's Army begins a local attack in the Trier area as a preliminary to the general attack by Seventh Army on the 15th. So far as we can determine there is not a single reserve division in this whole area. If we can get a quick breakthrough, the advance should go very rapidly and success in the region will multiply the advantage we have secured in the bridgehead at Remagen. It will probably be a nasty business breaking through the fortified lines, but once this is accomplished losses should not be great and we should capture another big bag of prisoners. I have given Seventh Army fourteen divisions for their part of the job, and 20th Corps jumps off with four. Patton will throw in another subsidiary effort from north to south across the Moselle with about four to five divisions. If it goes as I think it will I am going to take one day's vacation—although I don't know where I'll go. *Sincerely*

---

[1] Public relations officer.

[2] John Jay McCloy, a New York lawyer, had come to Washington at the request of the Secretary of War in December, 1940, as a special assistant. The following April he became Assistant Secretary of War.

Dear General: Only receipt of recent letters and telegrams from you has warned me that the criticism at home against our equipment is of a really serious nature. Yesterday I visited Patton and have asked him to make an appropriate statement himself on the matter and then to interest a few good reporters in going further down to seek stories from officers and enlisted men who will make statements in favor of our equipment to counteract adverse ones. A sergeant's statement seems to mean more to the average person than does one from a higher officer. Very recently I ran into a sergeant in a tank who said something to this effect:

> "These big old Panthers are poison when you run square into them. The big thing is to prevent them catching you by surprise. This Platoon has learned how to handle them and we have knocked off a lot more than we have lost."

I looked at Third Army totals yesterday. Patton has lost about 800 tanks, and has knocked out about 820 German tanks. For myself, I am tentatively planning to have a large press conference shortly after we have cleared up the Saar Basin. This will mark the end of one task, on which we have been working for a long time, and will give me a good excuse for a general talk with the press. In that conference I will take up the whole matter of equipment. I should guess that I could do it about the 26th or 27th.

I have likewise spoken to Bradley about the matter and he will try to give us some help.

There are, of course, certain points in which honest complaints could be registered. Shipments of winter clothing to this Theater were subject to the same interruptions and difficulties last summer and fall as were those of every other kind of supplies. As a result we could not always get up to the front lines winter clothing at the moment it was first needed. Overshoes were difficult to obtain, particularly in the large sizes, and certain other items were not only in short supply but their delivery was difficult. All in all, however, our men have been well taken care of. Early in the summer, when I told all of my senior commanders that I was determined to fight on through the winter, I always insisted that it was their responsibility to see that their men were more warmly clad, and better equipped to withstand the rigors of a winter campaign, than was the enemy. Incidentally, one of our big troubles has always been the tendency of the American soldier to discard any cumbersome clothing or piece of equipment for which he does not have an instantaneous need. During the fall we lost thousands of overcoats and overshoes because of this tendency.

I have not yet found out the cause of the death of the German prisoners, recently reported to me, nor do I know who is responsible. It is irritating to have such things occur because I certainly loathe having to apologize to the Germans. It looks as if this time I have no other recourse.

I am puzzled by the enemy's actions in the Saar. It seems to me that he has misread our intentions very seriously. I am extremely hopeful that we will succeed in eliminating many enemy troops that would otherwise be available to oppose our Rhine crossings. *Sincerely*

71 REIMS   *March 26, 1945*

Dear General: Enclosed are copies of two letters relating to comparisons between our equipment and that of the German. You will note that Rose,[1] one of our finest Division Commanders, as well as junior officers and enlisted men serving within his Division, are all dissatisfied with the performance of the present Sherman tank. Their criticisms, of course, relate primarily to direct duel between the Sherman and the Panther or Tiger. We have always known that the Sherman, particularly with the 75 gun, was very badly handicapped in this specific set of circumstances. As long ago as last June we had correspondence with the War Department on the matter and my own armored force officer was sent home to confer with the Ordnance Department about it.

There is the general agreement that the new T–26, particularly when it gets the newest high-velocity gun, will be a match for the Tiger and Panther even in single combat. Nevertheless you will note that one or two of the tank commanders would like to have even more armor, particularly in front. The fact is that when a man is actually on the front line engaging a gun or a tank, he could not have, in his own estimation, a big enough gun or enough armor. While this would result in nothing but a steel pill box, it is clear that the Ordnance Department should do everything it can to speed up production of the T–26 with the very high-velocity gun.

In other items of equipment I think that only the German's bazooka can be considered superior to a similar item of our own. I have heard some unfavorable comment with respect to our mortars but our 4.2 is a great favorite with the men on the battlefield.

I have just finished a rapid tour of the battle front. Yesterday and the day before I was with the 9th Army to witness its jumpoff and the early stages of the Rhine crossing. Simpson performed in his usual outstanding style. Our losses in killed, during the crossing, were 15 in one assault division and 16 in the other. I stayed up most of one night to witness the preliminary bombardment by 1250 guns. It was an especially interesting sight because of the fact that all the guns were spread out on a plain so that the flashes from one end of the line to the other were all plainly visible. It was a real drum-fire.

I have noted so many unusual and outstanding incidents in the forward areas that it would almost weary you to tell you of the fine performances of American and other troops. For example, the Engineer of the 7th Corps (his name is Colonel Mason Young[2]) laid a Treadway bridge across the Rhine in ten hours and eleven minutes. While not actually under fire, this job was done under battlefield conditions with all the necessary precautions taken to prevent unusual damage by a sudden concentration of enemy artillery fire. It was a brilliant performance. This officer has carried out every mission since D-day in the same fashion.

Naturally I am immensely pleased that the campaign west of the Rhine that Bradley and I planned last summer and insisted upon as a necessary preliminary to a deep penetration east of the Rhine, has been carried out so closely in accordance with conception. You possibly know that at one time the C.I.G.S. thought I was wrong in what I was trying to do and argued heatedly upon the matter. Yesterday I saw him on the banks of the Rhine and he was gracious enough to say that I was right, and that my current plans and operations are well calculated to meet the current situation. The point is that the great defeats, in some cases almost complete destruction, inflicted on the German forces west of the Rhine, have left him with very badly depleted strength to man that formidable obstacle. It was those victories that made possible the bold and relatively easy advances that both First and Third Armies are now making toward Kassel. I hope this does not sound boastful, but I must admit to a great satisfaction that the things that Bradley and I have believed in from the beginning and have carried out in the face of some opposition both from within and without, have matured so splendidly.

Bradley and Patton were extraordinarily proud of the messages you sent them. In this connection I am sending to the Adjutant General copies of short personal commendations I have sent each of the four Army Commanders. Patton is a particularly warm friend of mine and has been so over a period of 25 years. Moreover, I think I can claim almost a proprietary interest in him because of the stand I took in several instances, well known to you, in this war. In certain situations he has no equal, but by and large, it would be difficult indeed to choose between him, Hodges and Simpson for Army command, while Patch is little, if any, behind the others.

Today I visited two corps headquarters of the First Army east of the Rhine. They were advancing rapidly and before you get this letter it is my belief that Frankfurt will be in our hands and we will be well on the way toward Kassel.

With best wishes for your continued health. *Sincerely*

[1] Major General Maurice Rose, the 3d Armored Division commander, was killed in action on March 31, 1945.
[2] Colonel Mason James Young was a classmate of Eisenhower's at West Point.

Dear General: As you can see from the reports, our plans have been developing almost in exact accordance with original conceptions. You must expect, now, a period in which the lines on your map will not advance as rapidly as they did during the past several weeks because we must pause to digest the big mouthful that we have swallowed in the Ruhr area. It should not take too long and, of course, in the meantime, maintenance will be pushed to the limit to support our next main thrust. My G–2 figures that there may be 150,000 German soldiers left in the Ruhr but a number of these will change into civilian clothes before we liquidate the whole thing. He is confident, however, that we will capture at least 100,000. The enemy has been making efforts to break out of the area but our persistent policy of knocking out his communications to the eastward, and his lack of mobility within the pocket, both make it very difficult for him to launch a really concerted attack. I am confident that he can do nothing about it.

Yesterday I saw Patch at his headquarters near Frankfurt and today I am to see Montgomery in the North. Arnold was visiting Patch's headquarters. He looks to me as if he needs a real rest.

You have already been informed that Ninth Army has passed back to Bradley's control and will remain with him at least until the Ruhr is cleared up and we have achieved the purposes of our central drive. The situation on the right flank seems to be straightening up very well and once Patch is in proper position he should be able to collect a small reserve which will be most valuable.

This morning I received a very nice telegram from Field-Marshal Brooke on Army Day. In it he took occasion to make most flattering references to my leadership throughout this campaign. This was especially pleasing because of the past arguments we have had and to my mind shows that there is a bigness about him that I have found lacking in a few people I have run into on this side of the water.

Smith is again in very fine shape after suffering for some time with a bad infection of his jaw.

Do you think there is any use of my sending in to you my four fighting Army Commanders for promotion? *Sincerely*

Dear General: Today I forwarded to the Combined Chiefs of Staff the essentials of my future plans. In a word, what I am going to do now that the western enemy is split into two parts, is to take up a defensive line in the center (along a geographical feature that will tend to separate our forces physically from the advancing Russians) and clean up the important jobs on our flanks. A mere glance at the map shows that one of these is to get Lubeck and then clear up all the areas west and north of there. The other job is the so-called "redoubt". I deem both of these to be vastly more important than the capture of Berlin—anyway, to plan for making an immediate effort against Berlin would be foolish in view of the relative situation of the Russians and ourselves at this moment. We'd get all coiled up for something that in all probability would never come off. While true that we have seized a small bridgehead over the Elbe, it must be remembered that only our spearheads are up to that river; our center of gravity is well back of there.

Montgomery anticipates that he will need no help from the Americans other than that involved in an extension of Simpson's left. However, I rather think that he will want possibly an American Airborne Division and maybe an Armored Division. I will have enough in reserve to give him this much if he needs it. But assuming that he needs no American help, that job will be performed by the 17 divisions of the 21st Army Group.

In the center, extending all the way from Newhouse on the Elbe down to the vicinity of Selb on the border of Czechoslovakia, will be the Ninth and First Armies, probably with about 23 to 24 divisions, including their own reserves. This will be enough to push on to Berlin if resistance is light, and the Russians do not advance in that sector. Bradley's main offensive effort will be the thrust along the line Wurzburg–Nuremberg–Linz, carried out by the Third Army with about 12 divisions. Devers, with another 12 U.S. divisions and 6 French divisions, will capture Munich and all of the German territory lying within his zone of advance.

About 8 divisions at that time will be on strictly occupational duties, largely under Fifteenth Army. This will leave about 5 divisions, including Airborne, in my Reserve.

The intervention of the British Chiefs of Staff in my military dealings with the Soviet has thrown quite a monkey-wrench into our speed of communication. If you will note from Antonov's[1] reply to the telegram that we finally sent (as revised on recommendations of the BCOS) the point he immediately raised is whether our message implies an attempt, under the guise of military operations, to change the occupational boundaries already agreed upon by our three governments. Frankly, if I should have forces *in the Russian occupational zone* and be faced with an order or "request" to retire so that they may advance to the points they choose, I see no recourse except to comply. To do otherwise would probably provoke an incident, with the logic of the situation all on the side of the Soviets. I cannot see exactly what the British have in mind for me to do, under such circumstances. It is a bridge that I will have to cross when I come to it but I must say that I feel a bit lost in trying to give sensible instructions to my various commanders in the field.

On a recent tour of the forward areas in First and Third Armies, I stopped momentarily at the salt mines to take a look at the German treasure. There is a lot of it. But the most interesting—although horrible—sight that I encountered during the trip was a visit to a German internment camp near Gotha. The things I saw beggar description. While I was touring the camp I encountered three men who had been inmates and by one ruse or another had made their escape. I interviewed them through an interpreter. The visual evidence and the verbal testimony of starvation, cruelty and bestiality were so overpowering as to leave me a bit sick. In one room, where they [there] were piled up twenty or thirty naked men, killed by starvation, George Patton would not even enter. He said he would get sick if he did so. I made the visit deliberately, in order to be in position to give *first-hand* evidence of these things if ever, in the future, there develops a tendency to charge these allegations merely to "propaganda."

If you could see your way clear to do it, I think you should make a visit here at the earliest possible moment, while we are still conducting a general offensive. You would be proud of the Army you have produced. In the first place, the U.S. ground and air forces are a unit; they both participate in the same battle all the way down the line from me to the lowest private. I can find no evidence whatsoever of any mutual jealousy, suspicion or lack of understanding. In fact, I know of one or two Major Generals in the Air Force that one of my Army Commanders would accept as Division Commanders today.

Next, you would be struck by the "veteran" quality of the whole organization. Commanders, staffs, and troops, both air and ground, go about their business in a perfectly calm and sure manner that gets results. I am quite certain that no organization has ever existed that can re-shuffle and re-group on a large scale and continue offensives without a single pause, better than can Bradley and his staff.

Another thing that would strike you is the high average of ability in our higher command team. In recent telegrams to you I explained something of the quality of our Corps Commanders. Inadvertently I left out the name of Ridgway, one of the finest soldiers this war has produced. If ever we get to the point that I can recommend to you additional Corps Commanders for promotion, he will certainly have to be one.

In Army command, there is no weakness except for the one feature of Patton's unpredictability so far as his judgment (usually in small things) is concerned. These Army Commanders, with Bradley, make up a team that could scarcely be improved upon. Bradley, of course, remains the one whose tactical and strategical judgment I consider almost unimpeachable. Only once have we had a real difference of opinion on a major question. He is big, sound, and has the complete confidence of those above and below him.

Patton's latest crackpot actions may possibly get some publicity. One involved the arbitrary relief of a censor (over whom he had no authority whatsoever) for what Patton considered to be an error in judgment. All the censor did was to allow the printing of a story saying we had captured some of the German monetary reserves. Three or four newspapers have written very bitter articles about Patton, on this incident, and to my disgust they call it another example of "Army Blundering". I took Patton's hide off, but there is nothing else to do about it. Then again, he sent off a little expedition on a wild goose chase in an effort to liberate some American prisoners. The upshot was that he got 25 prisoners back and lost a full company of medium tanks and a platoon of light tanks. Foolishly, he then imposed censorship on the movement, meaning to lift it later, which he forgot to do. The story has now been released and I hope the newspapers do not make too much of it. One bad, though Patton says accidental, feature of the affair was that his own son-in-law was one of the 25 released. Patton is a problem child, but he is a great fighting leader in pursuit and exploitation.

This developed into quite a long story, all to convince you that in a short visit here you could see, in visible form, the fruits of much of your work over the past five years. In a matter of three or four days I am sure you would see things that would be of great satisfaction to you from now on. This sounds like I am completely and wholly satisfied with everything that I see. This is far from the case, but the point is that higher commanders have learned to handle the important things and we have gradually developed an organization that keeps the nagging details in the hands of people that can give their whole attention to them.

With best wishes, *Sincerely*

[1] General Alexei Antonov was acting Chief of Staff of the Russian Army.

74 REIMS   *April 23, 1945*

Dear General: Operations continue to follow the pattern we have laid down, except for some slowness on the North where I am most anxious to get a flank anchored firmly at Lubeck.

The problems and eventualities that are bothering me most are the Holland affair and the lack of an agreed procedure with the Russians when we meet on the front.

The Holland situation has deteriorated steadily but I am in no position to carry out a strong attack in that area. Even if I could, the further destruction due to the fighting and to additional flooding would be deplorable. As you know, there has been some talk of establishing a state of quasi-neutrality, with the Germans cooperating in the distribution of such food as we might be able to bring into the country. Any such agreement can come about of course, only with the full concurrence of Russia and of our own political heads. Even so, the German would then probably try to hold out for concessions that we would be unwilling to give.

My personal solution would be the simple one of laying down orders to the German commander which he would be compelled to obey under

224

the penalty of having himself and his entire command classed as violators of the laws of war or as war criminals. I have asked the Combined Chiefs of Staff to give me authority to move on this basis if the present negotiations fail. The weakness of my suggestion is that if it did not work, the people that would suffer would be the Dutch.

I do not quite understand why the Prime Minister has been so determined to intermingle political and military considerations in attempting to establish a procedure for the conduct of our own and Russian troops when a meeting takes place. My original recommendation, submitted to the CC/S, was a simple one and I thought provided a very sensible arrangement. One of my concerns in making that proposal was the possibility that the Russians might arrive in the Danish peninsula before we could fight our way across the Elbe and I wanted a formula that would take them out of that region on my request. The only area in which we will be in the Russian occupational zone is that now held by American troops. I really do not anticipate that the Russians will be arbitrary in demanding an instant withdrawal from this region (although I would save troops for the campaigns on the flanks if they should do so), but if they should take an arbitrary stand and serve notice that they intend to push directly ahead to the limits of their occupational zone, the American forces are going to be badly embarrassed. As I say, I think this fear will never be realized— but my hope was to protect my subordinate commanders from uncertainties and worry.

We are working very hard on the redeployment business and on all our plans for the occupation of the American zone in Germany.

I telegraphed to you my recommendations on the zone to be allotted to the French. Smith had a conference with Juin[1] and it develops that the French are not particularly concerned about giving up the areas we require. They are rather upset, though, about the British refusal to allow them to occupy the Rhineland as far North as Cologne. I suspect there is some underlying political struggle on this point, of which I am ignorant.

I note that the redeployment schedule is merely going to intensify the continuing struggle regarding service troops. To meet the demands made upon us, our needs in repair and construction companies and many other units of that type will be greater than ever. At the same time they will want identical units in the Pacific to prepare for the later arrival of combat divisions. It is going to be a tough one to coordinate properly. Among other things I shall have to prepare a large assembly center where the processing of reassignment and retraining can be carried out. The area will have to house as much as four or five divisions in order to have present units in sufficient number to accomplish transfers without having men scattered all over Europe. This job will take lots of service units. However, I have a bunch of very fine men working on the problem and we will solve it. *Sincerely*

[1] General Alphonse Pierre Juin was De Gaulle's Chief of Staff for National Defense.

Dear General: Yesterday I sent you a long telegram, volunteering to get Hodges and his staff on the way to the Far East as quickly as you give the word. I am in a strong position to do this, and with the increasing signs that our whole center will soon solidly be joined to the Russian armies, I can easily spare an Army Headquarters.

With respect to Bradley, I voiced my very frank opinions. In a way I hated to send you such a message because I was fearful it might look as if I was joining the ranks of the "prima donnas", which I am not! I do not intimate that one war is tougher than another; reduced to the terms of the Private, any time that a man has to get out into the bullet-swept zone and pit his skill, his strength, and his fire power against the enemy, it is tough —regardless of geography. But it is certain that the mass feeling of the 3,000,000 American soldiers here is that they have done a remarkable job. The men remember the situation existing when we started shipping this Army to France three years ago, and recall the respect, if not awe, in which we then held the German fighting prowess. They regard their accomplishments with great pride. This mass feeling is shared by officers as well as men. For a tremendous number of them, names such as Bradley, Spaatz, and Patton have become symbols. In the reputations of those men the mass sees its own deeds appreciated, even glorified. It was some such feeling as this that I was gropingly attempting to express to you in my telegram about Bradley. I realize that a commander of his outstanding ability should scarcely be kept out of the battleline as long as there is fighting to do and except for the importance of the intangibles I have attempted to describe, I would readjust my own contemplated organization here so as to let him go. But I believe it best he should stay.

It appears that we at last have some assurance that our contacts with the Russians along our common front will be amicably handled and with some degree of understanding on both sides.

The Prime Minister is finally waking up to one danger that I have been warning him about for some weeks, namely the possibility that the Russians can reach Lubeck and the neck of the Danish Peninsula ahead of us. I have done everything humanly possible to support Montgomery and to urge him to an early attack across the Elbe to Lubeck. Originally I informed him that when we had once split the Western enemy by a drive to the Leipzig region, he could count on the Ninth Army to help him in its thrust to the North. As the certainty of success began to appear in the center I put the specific question up to him, through Bradley, to find out exactly what he wanted. He announced himself completely capable of carrying out his missions provided only that Simpson would extend his flank a little bit to the North. To this Bradley promptly agreed, and did it. The answer did not satisfy me, however, and I went back up to see Montgomery in person and found that he had found out he would require an additional corps and, moreover, needed some of the capacity of the railway bridge the United States Engineers built at Wesel. Originally he had stated that he needed no rail communications at all, even to go all the way to Berlin. I have now had this corps earmarked for Montgomery for over two weeks and it is concentrating in the exact spot and on the exact schedule he has requested. I am hopeful that before you can receive this he will be advancing rapidly on Lubeck. I sent him a telegram today, pointing out again the urgent need for speed.

This morning I approved a telegram to the German commander in Holland, telling him what I was going to do about dropping supplies and informing him that if he attempted to interfere I would treat every officer and man responsible for such interference as violators of the laws of war. Just as the telegram was going out we received a message from the German garrison, designating dropping grounds and agreeing to meet my representatives for arranging a more adequate scale of relief for the starving Dutch population. I am done trifling with them and while I have held my hand in the fear of intensifying the Dutch suffering, if the German doesn't play the game absolutely, I intend to punish him when I can turn my attention in that direction.

Within the past couple of days the Public Relations people have been after me to record a speech for use on the night of V-E Day.[1] It is difficult indeed for me, at this stage, to think of anything that I would want to say at such a moment or what anyone else would want to hear.

I have had quite a talk with General Henry[2] about some of our redeployment problems. I am completely in accord as to the necessity of getting many of our high-point men started home with a rush. Only yesterday I authorized Spaatz to withdraw two of our transport groups to place on one of the air links connecting us with the United States so as to assure an efficient air channel all the way back. It is like parting with life's blood to give up air lift these days because the appalling size of the relief problem in this continent will demand the utmost in the kind of transportation. Displaced persons, ex-prisoners of war, distribution of food, and emergency supply missions, will all place a tremendous load upon our C-47's. Heavy bombers could substitute for them if there were any fields in Germany capable of handling our heavy equipment. This is not the case, due to the fact that the German built all his airfields with very light surfacing. Our heavy bombers break through the surface and render the fields unfit for any type of craft. Just another of our problems.

Yesterday I saw Duke Shoop, a reporter on the Kansas City Star. He brought me lots of gossip, and says that you are looking as young as when the war started, and generally in fine health. I don't know how you do it, but I am mighty glad of it. *Sincerely*

---

[1] Victory in Europe Day.
[2] Major General Stephen Garrett Henry headed the Personnel Division (G-1) of the War Department.

Conclusion

THESE LETTERS DESCRIBE the education of a commander. In the final analysis, Eisenhower met all the challenges of wartime leadership, and his correspondence with his most steadfast supporter shows this. Eisenhower wrote Marshall about the creation and maintenance of an efficient organization and about the allocation of resources. He devoted less attention to matters of diplomacy and troop visits. Over a period of time, his increasing confidence is revealed in this relationship with the Chief of Staff of the U.S. Army.

Eisenhower always gave primary attention to command structure—that is, insuring unity of command and clear lines of communication, as well as staffing his organization. In 1942, having to build a command organization for the first time in his life, he wrote at length about it. His first critical moment occurred when a British directive to Anderson, the ground commander, limited Eisenhower's authority. Eisenhower successfully resisted this, as he resisted the CCS attempt in January, 1943, to limit his control over combat operations and planning. He had been so insistent on the need for close air support and so confident of his success in the fight over control of the air force in early 1944 that he wrote little on the subject, although he won a major victory on this issue in the spring. He described his major command change of establishing two ground commanders on September 1. Eisenhower also kept Marshall apprised of command adjustments, such as when his forces joined those of the southern France invasion, and when control of the strategic air forces was taken from him. However, he did not discuss his dispute with Montgomery over the latter's desire to be sole Allied ground commander in the autumn of 1944. He did write Marshall in February, 1945, after the scare of the German offensive at the Bulge when Eisenhower himself seemed to vacillate over having a single ground commander. This issue was settled by Marshall's absolute refusal to permit it, and Eisenhower wrote only after it had been settled. Throughout the war he had given more attention to filling out his organization as he mastered the task of selecting, relieving, and rewarding key subordinates.

Eisenhower's role increased most distinctly in the planning and carrying out of strategy. In 1942 he had been Marshall's staff man drawing up plans for a cross-Channel invasion which he felt was premature. He did not participate in the strategic decisions of 1943, only in their implementation. But he was the key figure in the great debate of early 1944 over whether or not to invade southern France simultaneously with OVERLORD. In the European campaign the broad strategy was entirely his, and he refused to consider various British ideas to go into the Balkans and elsewhere.

In 1942 the heads of government had decided the precise areas in North Africa he was to invade. Disagreement among subordinate commanders over where to stage a Sicilian landing in July, 1943, helped him to exert decisive control. After some early mistakes in Tunisia, he had become a cautious campaign planner. Salerno made him even more conservative. He launched a concentrated assault on the southeastern coast of Sicily and rejected Marshall's *ad hoc* plan for a narrow assault. In all of these operations he believed that close air support had saved the day.

His role in the allocation of resources also grew. Because of his experiences in the Mediterranean, he insisted that OVERLORD be strengthened by a widened assault and the use of the air force. In the European campaign he neatly balanced veiled implications to the British of pushing on to Berlin with pursuance of the tactics he intended to follow—the double envelopment of Germany through broad assault. By maintaining control over the allocation of resources—shifting men and supplies from one commander's area to another as the battle situation changed—he realized the desired effect. When he finally decided on the location of the final attack, he did not let Montgomery go to Berlin, but placed the greater weight in Bradley's sector. His confidence was such that he communicated these plans to the Russians without prior approval of the CCS and was annoyed when the CCS objected.

In contrast to comments on organization and strategy, Eisenhower's references to diplomatic matters were relatively scarce. Throughout the war he mentioned Churchill with varying frequency. He wrote about early diplomatic developments in North Africa but ceased to do so after Marshall advised him that he should leave such matters to his subordinates. The storm of criticism heaped upon him because of the arrangements with the Vichy officials resulted in his asking for permission before accepting a surrender offer from the Italian Fascist government. Because of this, each step in the negotiations was spelled out by the CCS and delivered to the Italians by Bedell Smith. Eisenhower therefore did not discuss the surrender until negotiations had been nearly completed. This pattern held throughout the war. Although his problems with the French were continuing and vexatious, he seldom mentioned them. He did offer some suggestions on postwar planning, but the limitations on his freedom to act in diplomatic matters were dramatically underlined by the intense reaction of the CCS to his forwarding of plans to the Russians.

Eisenhower wrote little about his contacts with the troops. Although he mentioned trips to the front, he stressed his visits with the commanders rather than with the men. Near the end of the war, he spoke more about the morale and excellence of the soldiers than he ever had previously.

Eisenhower had learned that unity of command was rarely accepted in actual practice and that, as a consequence, it was essential to select loyal subordinates. The encounters with Anderson's directive, Giraud's temperament, Casablanca's changes in Eisenhower's command authority, the continuing struggle over the air forces, and Montgomery's intractability, all impressed upon him the difficulty involved. These disagreements reinforced his belief in the necessity of one man's having the authority to decide quickly and have his decisions executed. Eisenhower realized that a *de facto* arrangement with clear lines of authority could overcome the limitations of a formal directive. He had been able to exert his authority over the commanders in the Mediterranean by this means. In the case of Montgomery, however, he knew that an informal delineation of command structure would not suffice. Concerning ultimate objectives, therefore, he was as flexible and vague with Montgomery as he could be.

His great tactical lesson had been caution. He had lost the race for Tunis, leaving the improperly dispersed front open to counterattack. He also came to appreciate the subtle interference of political considerations with military ones, as when he became aware that American opinion demanded a role in the Tunisian campaign for the U.S. II Corps. The awareness of the threat posed by Anglo-American nationalist differences influenced him later to let Montgomery believe he was going to Berlin.

After his experiences in the Mediterranean, Eisenhower was convinced of the necessity of close air support. Its range and magnitude became a crucial consideration in all his planning thereafter. He also learned that the first and most vital task of an amphibious invasion was to get ashore and to stay there. This induced him to initiate a concentrated assault on Sicily and later to strengthen the forces for Normandy. All that had gone before seemed to confirm the wisdom of a broad front strategy in the European campaign, seeking victory but also guarding against defeat.

When Eisenhower was named to a high staff position by Marshall in 1941, his education as a Supreme Commander began. Then, in 1942 he found himself in command of the first American offensive of the war. He had to build a unified coalition command of which the British were skeptical in an operation to which Marshall was opposed. In these circumstances Eisenhower's letters to his Chief reflected his uncertainty. He rescinded his plan for the landings in North Africa and was a less than enthusiastic supporter of the operation. He accepted a key TORCH commander whom he did not know. He was fulsomely and awkwardly loyal to Marshall and very concerned over relations with Washington.

Eisenhower faced combat for the first time late in 1942. He was more likely to write to Marshall when he felt the press of circumstances, as when operations were faring badly. But paralleling his enhanced stature in command and strategic responsibilities, was his more mature relationship with Marshall. He felt confident enough to relieve the man whom Marshall had urged upon him to command the U.S. II Corps. He turned down Marshall's idea for an *ad hoc* invasion of Sicily. He didn't hesitate to send off a barrage of complaints or to elaborate his newly learned lessons in combat. But even in this more balanced association with Marshall, he remained fiercely loyal by cheerfully accepting the relegation of his theater to a secondary position.

Eisenhower's 1944 stay in London found him participating in strategic discussions with much more authority. He differed with Marshall on the great debate over whether or not to land in southern France and rejected Marshall's plan for a strategic airborne operation.

During the final campaign in Europe he informed Marshall in detail of his general tactical plans from late August, 1944, onward. This period marked the beginning of the debate over broad versus narrow front that would endure to the end of the war. Personal references in his letters started to increase around this same time. He wrote very little about command difficulties with Montgomery in September and October, but he did ask Marshall to make a visit so that they could discuss Eisenhower's problems. He had always recognized he would have more difficulty with Montgomery than Alexander, and his request to Marshall was a clear call for help. Marshall did come, but by then the initial crisis had eased only to erupt again after the German counterattack at the Bulge. The questioning of Eisenhower's strategy had continued all the while and for the moment he appeared especially vulnerable. In a visit while enroute to the conference at Malta Marshall reassured him. During this period Eisenhower's personal references were for the most part brief and not nearly so plentiful as in 1942. In the closing day of the campaign, with victory clearly in sight, Eisenhower remarked with great satisfaction that he wished Marshall could come to Europe and see the great army that the latter had built.

Eisenhower's expressions of personal satisfaction and gratitude to Marshall were especially appropriate. Marshall had indeed built the army and had trained its commander. Supporting Eisenhower to the utmost, he had educated, encouraged, defended, shielded, shared, provided for him.

In Eisenhower's view, he had even sacrificed the command of OVERLORD.[1] Eisenhower began his tenure in the hostile atmosphere of strained American-British relations. He had insisted that he was not a diplomat and always defined his decisions as being based on military necessity. Since antagonists rarely agreed on political matters, Eisenhower's view usually prevailed. He had built a unified command by concentrating on the essential. His greatest personal asset had been flexibility coupled with a capacity to grow. George Marshall had seen the potential for these qualities in Eisenhower and Eisenhower had not proven him wrong. Eisenhower could always assuage his doubts by turning to Marshall, for no matter how tall he grew or how confident he became, he remained in the best sense of the term—Marshall's man.

---

[1] Eisenhower, *Crusade in Europe*, p. 209.

Glossary

AA	Antiaircraft
AAF	Army Air Forces
AEAF	Allied Expeditionary Air Force
AFHQ	Allied Force Headquarters
AGENT	Code name for Churchill
ANCXF	Allied Naval Commander, Expeditionary Force
ANFA	Code name for conference of the CCS, Churchill, and Roosevelt at Casablanca, January 14–23, 1943
ANVIL	Code name for invasion of the south of France in August, 1944
AT	Antitank (gun)
AVALANCHE	Code name for amphibious assault on Salerno, Italy, in September, 1943
B–17	Flying Fortress; the backbone of the Allied bombing fleet
B–24	Liberator; a heavy long-range bomber that reached higher production than any other U.S. World War II aircraft; used mainly in the Mediterranean and the Pacific
BARRACUDA	Code name for proposed sea and airborne assault on Naples, Italy, in the fall of 1943
BAYTOWN	Code name for an invasion of the toe of Italy by the British XIII Corps in September, 1943
BCOS	British Chiefs of Staff
Blade Force	British armored unit that landed at Bône, Algeria, to operate eastward into Tunisia in November, 1942
BOLERO	Code name for the buildup of American forces in the United Kingdom
BRIMSTONE	Code name for planned capture of Sardinia in 1943
BUTTRESS	Code name for proposed British operation against the toe of Italy at Gioja in the fall of 1943
CAS	Chief of Air Staff

233

CCS	Combined Chiefs of Staff
Cent Force	Task Force 85 landing near Scoglitti, Sicily, in July, 1943
CG	Commanding general
C in C	Commander in Chief
CIGS	Chief of the Imperial General Staff
CINCMED	Commander in Chief, Mediterranean
COBRA	Code name for U.S First Army operation to penetrate the German defenses in the Cotentin Peninsula in July, 1944
Com Z	Communications Zone
CORKSCREW	Code name for the operation against Pantelleria, Italy, in mid-June, 1943
COS	Chief of Staff
COSSAC	Chief of Staff to the Supreme Allied Commander and his invasion planning staff
CP	Command post
CROSSBOW	Allied code name for German preparations for, and Allied measures against, attacks by rockets and pilotless aircraft in 1943–44
C/S	Chief of Staff
D-day	The first day of any military operation; popularly used to indicate the beginning of Operation OVERLORD on June 6, 1944
Dime Force	Task Force 81 landing near Gela, Sicily, in July, 1943
DRAGOON	New code name for ANVIL, the 1944 invasion of southern France; used after July of 1944
E-boat	Small, speedy, German surface torpedo boat
EPSOM	Code name for Montgomery's battle for Caen, France, on June 25–29, 1944
ETO	European Theater of Operations
ETOUSA	European Theater of Operations, United States Army
FCNL	French Committee of National Liberation
FFI	French Forces of the Interior
FINANCE	Code name for Eisenhower's headquarters at Malta in 1943
Flak	Antiaircraft fire
Free French	Popular name for the French Committee of National Liberation
G–1	Personnel section of divisional or higher staff
G–2	Intelligence section of divisional or higher staff
G–3	Operations and training section of divisional or higher staff
G–4	Logistics section of divisional or higher staff
G–5	Civil affairs section of divisional or higher staff

GOODWOOD	Code name for the Allied 21st Army Group offensive across the Orne River, south of Caen, France, to break out of the Normandy lodgment; coincided with U.S. Operation COBRA in July, 1944
H-hour	Invasion hour of any operation
Hq	Headquarters
HUSKY	Code name for Allied invasion of Sicily in July, 1943
KINGPIN	Code name for General Henri Giraud
JCS	Joint Chiefs of Staff
JUPITER	Code name for proposed invasion of Norway
L–4	Piper Cub; small, unarmed liaison plane
L–5	Stinson "Whizzer"; a small, slow, unarmed liaison plane adapted from a commercial airplane
LCT	Landing craft, tank
L of C	Line of communication
LST	Landing ship, tank
Mark III, IV	German medium tanks
Mark V	German medium tank with heavy armor and high-velocity gun
MARKET-GARDEN	Code name for airborne operation to establish a bridgehead across the Rhine in the Netherlands in September, 1944: Operation MARKET planned to seize bridges in the Nijmegen-Arnhem area; Operation GARDEN was to open a corridor from Eindhoven northward toward Germany
MT	Motor transport
MTO	Mediterranean Theater of Operations
MULBERRY	Code name for artificial harbor built by Allies off Normandy beachheads
NATO	North African Theater of Operations
OPD	Operations Division
OVERLORD	Code name for the invasion of northwest Europe in the spring of 1944, including the entire operations, air, sea, and ground
P–38	Lightning, a fighter plane
P–39	Airocobra, a fighter plane
PM	Prime Minister
POINTBLANK	Code name for the combined strategic bombing assault on Germany's industrial facilities, especially those producing fighter aircrafts and refined petroleum, from June, 1943, to the spring of 1944
PRO	Public relations officer
RANKIN	Initially the code name for a return to the Continent in the event of a deterioration of the German position or an internal unheaval; later used to denote any sudden

	deterioration in the general German position followed by a swift Allied advance into the country for occupation purposes
ROUNDUP	Code name for various 1941–43 plans for a cross-Channel attack on Germany
RCT	Regimental Combat Team
SCAEF	Supreme Commander, Allied Expeditionary Force
SEXTANT	Code name for the international conference at Cairo in November–December, 1943
SHAEF	Supreme Headquarters, Allied Expeditionary Force
SHINGLE	Code name for the amphibious operations against Anzio, Italy, in January, 1944
SLEDGEHAMMER	Code name for a limited-objective attack across the Channel in 1942 either to take advantage of a crack in German morale or to aid the Russians
SOS	Service of Supply
SYMBOL	Code name for the international conference at Casablanca on January 14–23, 1943
TAF	Tactical Air Force
T/O	Table or Organization
TORCH	Code name for Allied invasion of north and northwest Africa
TRIDENT	Code name for U.S.-British conference in Washington on May 12–25, 1943
U-boat	German submarine
V-weapon	German vengeance weapon; the V–1 and V–2 rocket bombs
WIDEWING	SHAEF Headquarters at Bushy Park, near London
WPD	War Plans Division

Appendix

The following letters written by Eisenhower to Marshall were not reprinted:

Date	Eisenhower Papers Document Number
July 7, 1942	368
July 17, 1942	380
August 5, 1942	408
September 1, 1942	470
October 3, 1942	534
December 11, 1942	709
January 10, 1943	765
January 27, 1943	793
April 5, 1943	927
April 24, 1943	955
May 14, 1943	993
June 9, 1943	1046
July 1, 1943	1092
July 21, 1943	1129
July 25, 1943	1136
*July 27, 1943	1137
December 16, 1943	1422
*January 19, 1944	1491
January 29, 1944	1521
March 21, 1944	1596
March 29, 1944	1612
*May 11, 1944	1683
May 16, 1944	1693
May 22, 1944	1705
May 27, 1944	1696, n. 5
July 5, 1944	1797
July 8, 1944	1811
*July 29, 1944	1868
August 15, 1944	1895

August 21, 1944	1904
September 21, 1944	1978
September 28, 1944	2005
November 18, 1944	2128
November 27, 1944	2143
*November 27, 1944	2144
December 9, 1944	2160
February 25, 1945	2293
February 26, 1945	2300

* Letters to Marshall signed but not written personally by Eisenhower.

Bibliography

Ambrose, Stephen E. *Eisenhower and Berlin, 1945.* New York, 1967.

Auphan, Paul, and Mordal, Jacques. *The French Navy in World War II.* Translated by A. C. J. Sabalot. Annapolis, 1959.

Baldwin, Hanson W. *Battles Lost and Won: Great Campaigns of World War II.* New York, 1966.

Biennial Report of the Chief of Staff of the United States Army, July 1, 1941 to June 30, 1943 to the Secretary of War. Philadelphia and New York, 1947.

Blumenson, Martin. *Breakout and Pursuit.* U.S. Army in World War II, edited by Stetson Conn. Washington, 1961.

———. "General Lucas at Anzio." In *Command Decisions,* edited by Kent Roberts Greenfield. Washington, 1960.

———. *Kasserine Pass.* Boston, 1967.

Bradley, Omar N. *A Soldier's Story.* New York, 1951.

Bryant, Sir Arthur. *Triumph in the West.* New York, 1959.

———. *Turn of the Tide: Study Based on the Diaries and Autobiographical Notes of Field Marshal the Viscount Alanbrooke.* London, 1957.

Butcher, Harry C. *My Three Years with Eisenhower: The Personal Diary of Captain Harry C. Butcher, USNR.* New York, 1946.

Butler, J. R. M. *Grand Strategy.* Vol. III, pt. 2. History of the Second World War, edited by J. R. M. Butler. London, 1964.

Chandler, Alfred D., Jr., *et al.,* eds. *The Papers of Dwight David Eisenhower.* The War Years. 5 vols. Baltimore, 1970.

Churchill, Winston S. *The Second World War.* 6 vols. Boston, 1948–53. Vol. I, *The Grand Alliance*; vol. IV, *The Hinge of Fate;* vol. V, *Closing the Ring;* vol. VI, *Triumph and Tragedy.*

Clark, Mark W. *Calculated Risk.* New York, 1950.

Cline, Ray S. *Washington Command Post: The Operations Division.* U.S. Army in World War II, edited by Kent Roberts Greenfield. Washington, 1951.

Cole, Hugh Marshall. *The Ardennes: Battle of the Bulge.* U.S. Army in World War II, edited by Stetson Conn. Washington, 1965.

———— *The Lorraine Campaign.* U.S. Army in World War II, edited by Kent Roberts Greenfield. Washington, 1950.

Coles, Harry L., and Weinberg, Albert K. *Civil Affairs: Soldiers Become Governors.* U.S. Army in World War II, edited by Stetson Conn. Washington, 1964.

Conn, Stetson; Engleman, Rose C.; and Fairchild, Byron. *Guarding the United States and Its Outposts.* U.S. Army in World War II, edited by Stetson Conn. Washington, 1964.

Conn, Stetson, and Fairchild, Byron. *The Framework of Hemisphere Defense.* U.S. Army in World War II, edited by Kent Roberts Greenfield. Washington, 1960.

Craven, Wesley Frank, and Cate, James Lea, eds. *Europe: Argument to V–E Day.* The Army Air Forces in World War II, vol. III. Chicago, 1958.

————. *Europe:* TORCH *to* POINTBLANK, *August, 1942–December, 1943.* The Army Air Forces in World War II, vol. II. Chicago, 1949.

————. *Men and Planes.* The Army Air Forces in World War II, vol. VI. Chicago, 1958.

————. *Plans and Early Operations, January, 1939–August, 1942.* The Army Air Forces in World War II, vol. I. Chicago, 1948.

Cunningham, Andrew Browne. *A Sailor's Odyssey.* New York, 1951.

Davis, Kenneth S. *Soldier of Democracy: A Biography of Dwight Eisenhower.* New York, 1945.

De Gaulle, Charles. *The War Memoirs of Charles de Gaulle.* 3 vols. New York, 1955–60. Vol. I, *The Call to Honour, 1940–42,* translated by Jonathan Griffin; vol. II, *Unity, 1942–1944* translated by Richard Howard; vol. III, *Salvation, 1944–46,* translated by Richard Howard.

De Guingand, Francis Wilfred. *Operation Victory.* London, 1947.

Donnison, F. S. V. *Civil Affairs and Military Government, Northwest Europe, 1944–1946.* History of the Second World War, edited by J. R. M. Butler. London, 1961.

Dziuban, Stanley W. *Military Relations Between the United States and Canada, 1939–1945.* U.S. Army in World War II, edited by Kent Roberts Greenfield. Washington, 1959.

Ehrman, John. *Grand Strategy.* Vols. V–VI. History of the Second World War, edited by J. R. M. Butler. London, 1956.

Eisenhower, Dwight D. *At Ease: Stories I Tell to Friends.* New York, 1967.

————. *Crusade in Europe.* New York, 1948.

Ellis, L. F. *Victory in the West.* 2 vols. Vol. I, *The Battle of Normandy;* vol. II, *The Defeat of Germany.* History of the Second World War, edited by J. R. M. Butler. London, 1962–68.

Esposito, Colonel Vincent J., ed. *The West Point Atlas of American Wars.* 2 vols. New York, 1959.

Farago, Ladislas. *Patton: Ordeal and Triumph.* New York, 1964.

Feis, Herbert. *Churchill–Roosevelt–Stalin: The War They Waged and the Peace They Sought.* Princeton, 1957.

Fergusson, Bernard. *The Watery Maze: The Story of Combined Operations.* New York, 1961.

Franklin, William M. "Zonal Boundaries and Access to Berlin." *World Politics* XVI (1963), 1–31.

Funk, Arthur L. *Charles de Gaulle: The Crucial Years, 1943–1944.* Norman, Okla., 1960.

Garland, Albert N., and Smyth, Howard M. *Sicily and the Surrender of Italy.* U.S. Army in World War II, edited by Stetson Conn. Washington, 1965.

Harrison, Gordon A. *Cross-Channel Attack.* U.S. Army in World War II, edited by Kent Roberts Greenfield. Washington, 1951.

Howe, George F. *Northwest Africa: Seizing the Initiative in the West.* U.S. Army in World War II, edited by Kent Roberts Greenfield. Washington, 1957.

Ismay, Lord Hastings L. *The Memoirs of General Lord Ismay.* New York, 1960.

King, Ernest J., and Whitehill, Walter Muir. *Fleet Admiral King, A Naval Record.* New York, 1952.

Langer, William L. *Our Vichy Gamble.* New York, 1947.

Leahy, William D. *I Was There.* New York, 1950.

Lee, Ulysses. *The Employment of Negro Troops.* U.S. Army in World War II, edited by Stetson Conn. Washington, 1966.

Leighton, Richard M., and Coakley, Robert W. *Global Logistics and Strategy, 1940–1943.* The U.S. Army in World War II, edited by Kent Roberts Greenfield. Washington, 1955.

MacArthur, Douglas. *Reminiscences.* New York, 1964.

MacDonald, Charles B. "The Decision to Launch Operation Market-Garden." In *Command Decisions,* edited by Kent Roberts Greenfield. Washington, 1960.

———. *The Siegfried Line Campaign.* U.S. Army in World War II, edited by Stetson Conn. Washington, 1963.

Macmillan, Harold. *The Blast of War, 1939–1945.* New York, 1968.

McCann, Kevin. *Man From Abilene.* New York, 1952.

Marshall, Katherine Tupper. *Together: Annals of an Army Wife.* New York, 1946.

Marshall, S. L. A. *Bastogne: The First Eight Days.* Washington, 1946.

Matloff, Maurice. *Strategic Planning for Coalition Warfare, 1943–1944.* U.S. Army in World War II, edited by Kent Roberts Greenfield. Washington, 1959.

———. "The 90-Division Gamble." In *Command Decisions,* edited by Kent Roberts Greenfield. Washington, 1960.

Matloff, Maurice, and Snell, Edwin M. *Strategic Planning for Coalition Warfare, 1941–1942.* U.S. Army in World War II, edited by Kent Roberts Greenfield. Washington, 1953.

Meyer, Leo J. "The Decision to Invade North Africa (Torch)." In *Command Decisions,* edited by Kent Roberts Greenfield. Washington, 1960.

Montgomery, Bernard L. *The Memoirs of Field-Marshal the Viscount Montgomery of Alamein, K.G.* Cleveland and New York, 1958.

Moran, Lord John. *Churchill: Taken from the Diaries of Lord Moran.* Boston, 1966.

Morgan, Frederick. *Overture to Overlord.* New York, 1950.

Morison, Samuel Eliot. *The Atlantic Battle Won, May 1943–May 1945.* History of the United States Naval Operations in World War II, vol. X. Boston, 1964.

―――. *The Battle of the Atlantic, 1939–1943.* History of the United States Naval Operations in World War II, vol. I. Boston, 1964.

―――. *The Invasion of France and Germany, 1944–1945.* History of the United States Naval Operations in World War II, vol. XI. Boston, 1964.

―――. *Operations in North African Waters, October 1942–June 1943.* History of the United States Naval Operations in World War II, vol. II. Boston, 1962.

―――. *Sicily–Salerno–Anzio, January 1943–June 1944.* History of the United States Naval Operations in World War II, vol. IX. Boston, 1964.

―――. *Strategy and Compromise.* Boston, 1958.

―――. *The Two-Ocean War: A Short History of the United States Navy in the Second World War.* Boston, 1963.

Morton, Louis. *The Fall of the Philippines.* U.S. Army in World War II, edited by Kent Roberts Greenfield. Washington, 1953.

―――. *Strategy and Command: The First Two Years.* U.S Army in World War II, edited by Kent Roberts Greenfield. Washington, 1962.

Murphy, Robert. *Diplomat Among Warriors.* New York, 1964.

Pogue, Forrest C. "The Decision to Halt at the Elbe." In *Command Decisions,* edited by Kent Roberts Greenfield. Washington, 1960.

―――. *George C. Marshall.* 2 vols. New York, 1963–66. Vol. I, *Education of a General, 1880–1939*; vol. II, *Ordeal and Hope, 1939–1942.*

―――. *The Supreme Command.* U.S. Army in World War II, edited by Kent Roberts Greenfield. Washington, 1954.

Romanus, Charles F., and Sunderland, Riley. *Stilwell's Mission to China.* U.S. Army in World War II, edited by Kent Roberts Greenfield. Washington, 1953.

Roskill, Captain S. W. *The War at Sea 1939–1945*, vol. II. History of the Second World War. London, 1956.

Ruppenthal, Roland G. *Logistical Support of the Armies*, vol. I, *May 1941–September 1944.* U.S. Army in World War II, edited by Kent Roberts Greenfield. Washington, 1953.

―――. *Logistical Support of the Armies*, vol. II, *September 1944–May 1945.* U.S. Army in World War II, edited by Kent Roberts Greenfield. Washington, 1959.

―――. "Logistics and the Broad-Front Strategy." In *Command Decisions,* edited by Kent Roberts Greenfield. Washington, 1960.

Salmon, E. Dwight, *et al.* "History of Allied Force Headquarters." Lithographed, Survey Directorate AFHQ, n.d.

Sherwood, Robert E. *Roosevelt and Hopkins: An Intimate History.* New York, 1948.

Smith, Walter Bedell. *Eisenhower's Six Great Decisions: Europe 1944–45.* New York, 1956.

Stimson, Henry L., and Bundy, McGeorge. *On Active Service in Peace and War.* New York, 1947.

Summersby, Kay. *Eisenhower Was My Boss.* New York, 1948.

Tedder, Sir Arthur William. *With Prejudice: The War Memoirs of Marshal of the Royal Air Force Lord Tedder.* London, 1966.

Truscott, L. K., Jr. *Command Missions: A Personal Story.* New York, 1954.

U.S. Department of State. *Foreign Relations: The Conferences at Cairo and Teheran, 1943.* Washington, 1961.

―――. *Foreign Relations of the United States: Diplomatic Papers, 1942.* 7 vols. Washington, 1960–63. Vol. II, *Europe.*

―――. *Foreign Relations of the United States: Diplomatic Papers, 1943.* 6 vols. Washington, 1963–65. Vol. II, *Europe.*

―――. *Foreign Relations of the United States: Diplomatic Papers, 1944.* 7 vols. Washington, 1963–65. Vol. III, *The British Commonwealth and Europe.*

―――. *Foreign Relations of the United States: Diplomatic Papers, 1945.* 7 vols. Washington, 1963–67. Vol. I, *General.*

Vigneras, Marcel. *Rearming the French.* U.S. Army in World War II, edited by Kent Roberts Greenfield. Washington, 1957.

Viorst, Milton. *Hostile Allies: FDR and Charles de Gaulle.* New York, 1965.

Warlow, Charles. *The Transportation Corps: Responsibilities, Organization, and Operations.* U.S. Army in World War II, edited by Kent Roberts Greenfield. Washington, 1951.

Wedemeyer, Albert C. *Wedemeyer Reports!* New York, 1958.

Wilmot, Chester. *The Struggle for Europe.* London, 1967.

Index